THE UNIVERSITY OF NORTH CAROLINA
SESQUICENTENNIAL PUBLICATIONS

LIBRARY RESOURCES

THE UNIVERSITY OF NORTH CAROLINA SESQUICENTENNIAL PUBLICATIONS

Louis R. Wilson, DIRECTOR

CHRONICLES OF THE SESQUICENTENNIAL

THE UNIVERSITY OF NORTH CAROLINA, 1789-1835
A Documentary History

THE CAMPUS OF THE FIRST STATE UNIVERSITY

THE GRADUATE SCHOOL: RESEARCH AND PUBLICATIONS

THE GRADUATE SCHOOL: DISSERTATIONS AND THESES

STUDIES IN SCIENCE

STUDIES IN LANGUAGE AND LITERATURE

A HUNDRED YEARS OF LEGAL EDUCATION

A STATE UNIVERSITY SURVEYS THE HUMANITIES

SECONDARY EDUCATION IN THE SOUTH

IN SEARCH OF THE REGIONAL BALANCE OF AMERICA

STUDIES IN HISTORY AND POLITICAL SCIENCE

LIBRARY RESOURCES OF THE UNIVERSITY OF NORTH CAROLINA

RESEARCH AND REGIONAL WELFARE

PIONEERING A PEOPLE'S THEATER

UNIVERSITY EXTENSION IN ACTION

BOOKS FROM CHAPEL HILL

Library Resources of THE UNIVERSITY OF NORTH CAROLINA

A Summary of Facilities for Study and Research

Edited with a Foreword

BY

CHARLES E. RUSH
Director of Libraries

CHAPEL HILL
THE UNIVERSITY OF NORTH CAROLINA PRESS
1945

Copyright, 1945, by the
UNIVERSITY OF NORTH CAROLINA PRESS

Van Rees Press, New York

FOREWORD

THE Library of the University of North Carolina welcomed the opportunity to share in the Sesquicentennial Celebration of the University by editing one of the several volumes relating to the various aspects of the University's life and activities. In this contribution to the series are summarized the library resources of the University and its facilities for study and research, as well as the history of the Library and the development of its more distinctive collections of material.

The chief emphasis in this publication is placed on the role of the Library in the University's promotion of culture and scholarship. Through its many facets, the Library has sought to reflect the important functions of the University, particularly those of learning and teaching, investigation and research, extension and publication. The Library has endeavored, especially during the past half century, to extend its services and to interpret its possessions as a co-worker in instruction and a co-discoverer in investigation.

When called upon to survey its resources, the Library naturally turned for help to those specialists on the Faculty and members of the Library Staff who know intimately the strength and needs of Library holdings in their special fields. Therefore, more than a score of friends on the campus have contributed their findings to this summary, accompanied by concise, descriptive statements of important resources for advanced study, with

CONTENTS

	PAGE
FOREWORD	v

I

THE LIBRARY IN SCHOLARSHIP AND RESEARCH

1. THE ROLE OF THE LIBRARY IN THE ADVANCEMENT OF SCHOLARSHIP — 3
    Louis R. Wilson, *Professor of Library Science and Administration*
2. CO-OPERATIVE FACILITIES IN RESEARCH AND SERVICE — 17
    Charles E. Rush, *Director of Libraries*

II

COLLECTIONS AND FOUNDATIONS

3. THE COLLECTION OF NORTH CAROLINIANA — 27
    Mary L. Thornton, *Librarian, The North Carolina Collection*
4. THE SOUTHERN HISTORICAL COLLECTION — 39
    J. G. de Roulhac Hamilton, *Kenan Professor of American History and Political Science and Director of the Southern Historical Collection*
5. THE HANES FOUNDATION — 47
    Olan V. Cook, *Assistant Librarian and Curator of Rare Books*

III

BIBLIOGRAPHY AND REFERENCE

6. BIBLIOGRAPHICAL APPARATUS — 55
    Georgia H. Faison, *Head, Reference Department*
7. REFERENCE RESOURCES — 68
    Georgia H. Faison

IV
BIOLOGICAL AND RELATED SCIENCES

		PAGE
8.	BOTANY	85
	Alma Holland Beers, *Research Associate in Botany*	
9.	MEDICINE	88
	W. C. George, *Professor of Histology and Embryology*	
10.	PHARMACY	91
	Henry M. Burlage, *Professor of Pharmacy*	
11.	PSYCHOLOGY	97
	John F. Dashiell, *Kenan Professor of Psychology*	
12.	ZOOLOGY	99
	C. D. Beers, *Professor of Zoology*	

V
FINE ARTS AND PHILOSOPHY

13.	ART AND ARCHITECTURE	105
	Harriet Dyer Adams, *Instructor and Acting Director of Person Hall Art Gallery*	
14.	DRAMA	112
	Samuel Selden, *Associate Professor of Dramatic Art*, and Virginia Spencer, *Editorial Assistant*	
15.	MUSIC	117
	Glen Haydon, *Professor of Music*	
16.	PHILOSOPHY	122
	Stephen A. Emery, *Professor of Philosophy*	

VI
LANGUAGE AND LITERATURE

17.	CLASSICAL LANGUAGES AND LITERATURES	129
	T. M. Simkins, Jr., *Instructor in Latin* and P. H. Epps, *Professor of Greek*	
18.	COMPARATIVE LINGUISTICS	136
	George S. Lane, *Professor of Germanic and Comparative Linguistics*	

more emphasis on strength than on needs. It is to be hoped that the result may not only serve as a record of the Library's development as an effective institution of learning, but also may become a tool for instruction and research, and an indicator of source materials for subject specialists in the region and nation. Perhaps, further benefit may be anticipated from the state and from concerned friends when the finger of need is pointed to significant desiderata. Even so, it should be clear that in many fields this is a satisfying institution in which to study and learn, to investigate and publish, to interpret and teach. Thus these library facets reveal inner warmth and strength, reflect similar qualities in the University, and cast their light on a still brighter future.

Further appreciative acknowledgment of the co-operation of each contributor is gratefully recorded, as well as the editorial assistance of Agatha B. Adams and the aid of Louis R. Wilson, who has directed the work of the entire series from inception through publication.

C.E.R.

Chapel Hill
December 1, 1944

CONTENTS

19. ENGLISH LANGUAGE AND LITERATURE
    Gregory L. Paine, *Professor of English*
20. GERMANIC LANGUAGES AND LITERATURES
    Richard Jente, *Professor of Germanic Languages and Literatures,* and George S. Lane, *Professor of Germanic and Comparative Linguistics*
21. LANGUAGES AND LITERATURES, ROMANCE   155
    William M. Dey, *Kenan Professor of Romance Languages and Literatures,* and Sturgis E. Leavitt, *Professor of Spanish*

VII

PHYSICAL SCIENCES

22. CHEMISTRY   165
    Ralph W. Bost, *Smith Professor of Chemistry*
23. GEOLOGY AND GEOGRAPHY   168
    W. F. Prouty, *Professor of Stratigraphic Geology*
24. MATHEMATICS   171
    Alfred Brauer, *Associate Professor of Mathematics*
25. PHYSICS   174
    Nathan Rosen, *Associate Professor of Physics*

VIII

SOCIAL SCIENCES

26. ANCIENT HISTORY   179
    W. E. Caldwell, *Professor of Ancient History*
27. MEDIEVAL HISTORY AND CIVILIZATION, INCLUDING THE RENAISSANCE   181
    Loren C. MacKinney, *Professor of Medieval History*
28. MODERN EUROPEAN HISTORY   184
    Mitchell B. Garrett, *Professor of Modern European History,* and James L. Godfrey, *Associate Professor of History*
29. ENGLISH HISTORY   189
    J. C. Russell, *Associate Professor of History*

30. UNITED STATES HISTORY ... 192
    A. R. Newsome, *Professor of History*
31. LATIN AMERICAN HISTORY ... 196
    W. W. Pierson, Jr., *Professor of History and Political Science and Dean of the Graduate School*
32. COMMERCE AND ECONOMICS ... 200
    Guelda E. von Beckerath, *Librarian, Commerce Library*
33. EDUCATION ... 211
    W. C. Ryan, *Kenan Professor of Education*
34. FOLKLORE ... 217
    Ralph S. Boggs, *Professor of Spanish*
35. LAW ... 220
    Lucile M. Elliott, *Librarian, Law Library*
36. LIBRARY SCIENCE ... 230
    Lucile Kelling, *Associate Professor of Library Science*
37. POLITICAL SCIENCE ... 235
    C. B. Robson, *Professor of Political Science*
38. SOCIOLOGY ... 242
    Rupert B. Vance, *Research Professor in the Institute for Research in Social Science*

IX

LIBRARY EXTENSION

39. LIBRARY EXTENSION SERVICES TO THE STATE ... 251
    Agatha Boyd Adams, *Supervisor, War Information Center*
    INDEX ... 257

I

THE LIBRARY IN SCHOLARSHIP AND RESEARCH

Chapter 1

THE ROLE OF THE LIBRARY IN THE ADVANCEMENT OF SCHOLARSHIP

Louis R. Wilson

THE Library of the University of North Carolina, established in 1795 at the beginning of the University,[1] contains 447,562 volumes and regularly receives 4,500 journals and transactions of learned societies and other scholarly organizations. Although it is small in comparison with the libraries of the privately supported universities of the Northeast and the great state universities of the Midwest, more than 400,000 volumes have been acquired since 1905 and have been selected to support the program of instruction and research of the University. It ranks first among the libraries of the Southeast in bibliographical apparatus and manuscript material relating to the region, and second in total number of volumes.

HISTORICAL BACKGROUND

The Library has a threefold origin. It is the outgrowth of the original University Library, to which certain books were given in the first session in 1795, and of the libraries of the Dialectic and Philanthropic Literary societies, which were also established in that year.

The earliest accessions of the University Library were gifts from General William Richardson Davie, Thomas Blount, Richard Bennehan, Joseph Gautier, and others. The two largest additions to the collection prior to the Civil War were 979 volumes purchased for $3,234.74 by President Joseph Caldwell, who was sent to Europe by the Trustees in 1824 to secure books and ap-

---

1. For the early history of the Library see Fisk P. Brewer (Librarian, 1869-70), *The Library of the University of North Carolina.* (Chapel Hill, 1870?), pp. 8.

paratus, and 1,897 volumes secured at a cost of $3,500 in 1858, from the library of Professor Elisha Mitchell, of the University, following his death in 1857.

The libraries of the literary societies were built up through gifts and purchases made from funds provided by members of the societies. When, in 1886, they were placed in Smith Hall, occupied by the University Library, they contained, including many duplicates, approximately 7,000 volumes each. The University collection contained about 8,500 volumes. The collection of the Philanthropic Society was placed on shelves on the north side of the building, that of the Dialectic Society on the south side, the books in the University Library being distributed throughout the building.

The transfer of the collections by the societies to the University was made in three stages. The collections were placed in Smith Hall in the summer of 1886. They could be removed, however, at the pleasure of the societies. Each society agreed to provide $150 annually for the purchase of books and periodicals. The University agreed to provide $200 annually, to maintain the building, and to keep the Library open two hours daily from Monday through Friday and five hours Saturday. In 1895, the University assumed complete responsibility for the administration of the Library, employed a professional librarian, and began to collect a library fee from all students, the fee for society members not to exceed two dollars annually. The income from this source was to be devoted to the purchase of books and periodicals. The societies retained the right, upon a two-thirds vote of their members, to withdraw their collections. In 1906, the societies agreed to convey outright to the University the title to their collections, the agreement to become effective in 1906-1907 upon the raising of an endowment fund ($55,000) to match the cost of the Carnegie Library Building opened in September, 1907. In all three agreements it was understood that the societies were in effect endowing the Library to the extent of the number of volumes transferred, and the official title of the Library, after 1886, was the Library of the University of North Carolina Endowed by the Dialectic and Philanthropic Societies.

The principal quarters of the University Library have been Old East Building, South Building, Smith Hall, the Carnegie Building (1907–29), and the present University Library Building (1929–), which is capable of continued extension and should serve the University for an indefinite time. The departmental libraries of the University have been variously located as they have developed with departments and schools throughout the years. The society libraries were housed in the early years in the rooms of student librarians. Later they occupied quarters in Old East and Old West, New East and New West, and South buildings, until they were transferred to Smith Hall in 1886 and shelved with the University collection.

The librarians of the University Library from 1795 to 1870 were members of the University Faculty or senior tutors. From 1875 to 1895, they were members of the Faculty or students. Until the merging of the collections the duties of the librarian were slight since few books were bought, the hours of opening were few, the use of the materials was largely by members of the Faculty. After the merger more funds were available for the purchase of materials; the hours of opening were increased; and, beginning in 1894–95, one hundred years after the Library was first opened, a professional librarian, working under the supervision of a member of the Faculty (known as Supervisor of the Library) and aided by student assistants appointed by the societies, was employed. In 1907, additional professional members were added to the staff, and in 1910 the librarian became responsible directly to the President of the University for the administration of the Library.

The financial support of the University Library was irregular and meager for the first full century. A Library tax or fee was charged in the early 1800's. An appropriation of $6,000 was spent by President Joseph Caldwell in 1824–25 for books and apparatus purchased by him in Europe. The amount devoted to books was $3,234.74. From 1824–25 to 1858, when the University bought the greater part of the library of Professor Elisha Mitchell, no expenditures for books are recorded,[2] although in the 1850's the enrollment of the University reached a peak of

2. *Ibid.*, p. 5.

more than 450, which was exceeded by that of no other American university except Yale. The libraries of the societies, on the other hand, were constantly added to by gift and through purchase from fees of student members.

The collections of the libraries reflected the character of their financial support. The materials bought for the University Library were primarily for the use of the instructors. There were also gifts of governmental publications from the state and federal governments and from abroad. Professor Mitchell, in commenting on the collection of the University Library in 1836 after having visited Yale and Amherst, the Episcopal College at Hartford, and Wesleyan University at Middletown, observed that the one particular in which the University's inferiority was most glaring and palpable was the want of "material of science and literature—Books, Philosophical Apparatus, Cabinets of Minerals, Rocks and Shells." In 1850, after the completion of Smith Hall, the chairman of a Select Committee of the Trustees stated that during the last quarter of a century not a single book had been bought by the Trustees. The collections of the Society libraries were selected by the students and were chosen with relation to the work and interest of the societies. They contained many attractively bound, expensively printed volumes and they largely duplicated each other. As a result of this duplication, several thousand volumes were sold in 1891–92; and in 1895, one hundred years after the Library had been established and the three collections had been merged and duplicates had been removed, it contained approximately 22,500 volumes.

EARLY CONCENTRATIONS OF MATERIALS

During the first century of its existence the University Library possessed few materials essential to the support of instruction and research. Four movements were begun in the period which influenced the Library in its later development and contributed to the beginning of investigation and publication of university character.

The first was that of the organization of the Historical Society of the University of North Carolina which became active at the University in 1844. This organization, for which President Swain was largely responsible, assembled many materials dealing with the history of North Carolina and provided for addresses relating to the history of the state. Many historical articles and records which appeared in the *University Magazine* from its founding in 1844 to the closing of the University in 1871 were written by members of this organization or were drawn from the material accumulated by the Historical Society. Although much of this material was lost to the University after President Swain's death, some of it came to the Library and to the North Carolina Historical Commission and has been available to students of the state's history. In 1875 the General Assembly chartered the Historical Society of North Carolina which undertook to collect materials as a statewide organization. In 1887 President K. P. Battle, one of the incorporators, reorganized this society on a local basis at Chapel Hill and used it and its materials in the training of students in North Carolina history. He led a movement in 1890 to secure endowment for an alumni chair of history at the University, to which he was appointed as professor upon his retirement from the presidency in 1891, and in 1900 he began the publication of *The James Sprunt Historical Monographs.*

The second movement was the establishment of the Elisha Mitchell Scientific Society in the autumn of 1883. This organization, formed by members of the Faculty engaged in teaching the various sciences, not only began to carry out original investigations and to publish the results in the Society's *Journal,* but it established exchange relations with several hundred scientific and learned societies in other countries which brought to the University a steady stream of transactions, proceedings, and scientific periodicals which, housed separately at first, today constitute one of the Library's richest sources of scholarly materials. It is notable that this organization was formed seven years after the founding of Johns Hopkins University and that it immediately began a publication which has been maintained uninterruptedly for sixty years.

The third movement was the founding of the Shakespeare

and Philological clubs in 1885 and 1893. The former organization, discontinued in 1907, was directed by Dr. Thomas Hume, Professor of English, and was devoted to the study of Shakespeare and the collection of materials concerning the development of early English drama. The Philological Club brought together the members of the Faculty and advanced students in the departments of language and literature and laid the foundation for the publication of *Studies in Philology*, which was begun in 1906. Additions made to the Library in this period reflected the interest of these groups of scholars and three of the special endowment funds secured for the Library from 1900 to 1907 were for the support of library materials in these fields.

The fourth movement was the physical consolidation of the three libraries in 1886. Although the final transfer of the title to the collections was not made by the literary societies until 1906, the University was conscious of the necessity of increasing its library resources and it accepted the provision that the collections transferred to the Library should be considered in the nature of an endowment. It applied income from this source to the purchase of books and periodicals. This provision, safeguarding the funds given the Library for books and other library materials rather than for administration or maintenance, assured the Library of a dependable book fund by means of which the book collection could be steadily built up for scholarly purposes. In fact, to this provision may be attributed much of the steady growth of the Library and the development of the University into one of the leading centers for graduate study in the South in the past four decades.

THE DEVELOPMENT OF RESOURCES FOR GRADUATE STUDY AND RESEARCH

From 1886 to 1901 the additions to the collections were largely for the support of undergraduate teaching. From 1901 to 1910, however, policies were formulated by the University and by the Library that emphasized the collection of materials for graduate study and research. Several aspects of these policies may be noted.

The major plans of the University affecting the development of the Library were the establishment of the Graduate School (1904), the completion of a campaign to secure a new library building from Andrew Carnegie and to raise an endowment fund to equal the cost of the building (1905–1906), the establishment of *Studies in Philology* (1906), and the opening of the Carnegie Library Building (1907).

The Library, in carrying out its part in the formulation of policies, inaugurated, under W. S. Bernard, Librarian (1900–1901), a modern classification and cataloguing scheme to make its materials more easily available. Under Louis R. Wilson, Librarian (1901–32), the transfer of the title to the literary society libraries was made complete (1906). Plans were formulated for spending the income from the endowment for the building up of materials in English language, French and German languages and literatures, American poetry, chemistry, history, North Caroliniana, law, international conciliation, art and architecture, physics and electrical engineering, and materials relating to the South's participation in the Civil War. A considerable part of the income of the general fund of the Library was also earmarked for the acquisition of important reference sets and files of newspapers and periodicals. Professional assistants were added to the Library staff, the exchanges of the Mitchell Society were arranged and made easily accessible for use, and exchanges for *Studies in Philology* were secured. Close co-operation between the Library and the Faculty was perfected in a program of book acquisition, which, with increasing funds from student fees, state appropriations, and gifts resulted in the steady upbuilding of materials for scholarly use. Special quarters for the collection of North Caroliniana were provided and seminar rooms for the classics, English and German, the Romance languages, and history were equipped for graduate study. The plans formulated in the first decade of the 1900's, in fact, have served as a foundation upon which the programs of acquisition, classification and cataloguing, financial support, and use for the succeeding decades have been built. The total financial support from all sources for books, periodicals, and other library materials, amounted in 1900–1901 to $1,541.32 and in the peak year, 1928–29, to $57,336.52. The opening of the present library building in 1929 was accompanied by the announcement of gifts of more than $145,000 of which $100,000 was for the establishment of the School of Library Science. But these larger developments were the logical extension of the policies formulated in earlier years.

The nature of the additions made to the Library, while fully revealed in subsequent sections of this volume, may be briefly indicated here by selections from acquisitions at different intervals in three important fields. They illustrate the kind of growth which has occurred since the early 1900's.

In language and literature the following important materials, among others, were added in 1909–10: Balzac, *Oeuvres*, 39 vols.; Chaucer Society, *Publications*, 44 vols.; Godefroy, *Dictionnaire de l'ancienne langue française*, 9 vols.; Goethe, *Werke*, 27 vols.; Gower, *Works*, 4 vols.; Herder, *Sämtliche Werke*, 32 vols.; *Jahresbericht über die Fortschritte der klassischen Altertumswissenschaft*, 66 vols.; Kayser, *Bücher-Lexicon*, 25 vols.; Lorenz, *Catalogue général de la librairie française*, 20 vols.; *Rheinisches Museum*, 62 vols.; Sainte-Beuve, *Nouveaux Lundis*, 13 vols.; Sainte-Beuve, *Portraits contemporains*, 5 vols.; Shakespeare, *Works*, 40 vols.; Schanz, *Beiträge zu historischen Syntax der griechischen Sprache*, 4 vols.; Schlegel, *Sämtliche Werke*, 6 vols.; Schmidt, *Synonymik der griechischen Sprache*, 4 vols. New subscriptions were placed for the following journals: *Die Woche, Euphorion, Glotta, Jahresberichte für neuere deutsche Literaturgeschichte, Jahresbericht über die Fortschritte der klassischen Altertumswissenschaft, Mnemosyne, Revue des deux mondes, Zeitschrift für deutsche Philologie*.

In 1921–22 the following long runs of publications were added through the aid of members of the Faculty who were abroad: *Quellen und Forschungen zur Sprach und Culturgeschichte der germanischen Völker*, 120 vols.; *Les Grands écrivains français*, 58 vols.; *Société des anciens textes français*, 67 vols.; *Histoire littéraire de la France*, 34 vols.; *Biblioteca de autores españoles*, 71 vols.; and *Catalogue générale des livres imprimés*

THE LIBRARY IN THE ADVANCEMENT OF SCHOLARSHIP 11

de la Bibliothèque Nationale, 74 vols. The English department added largely to its collection in the fields of Elizabethan drama and the literature of Spenser. It purchased Oxford Historical Society, *Publications,* 51 vols.; Camden Society, *Publications,* 100 vols.; *Tudor Facsimile Texts,* 138 vols.; Spenser Society, *Publications,* 50 vols.

In chemistry the accessions for 1917–18 included the following journals secured through gift or purchase: *Annales de chemie et de physique,* 352 vols.; *Archiv der Pharmacie,* 28 vols.; *Berichte der deutschen chemischen Gesellschaft,* 82 vols.; *Chemical Abstracts,* 30 vols.; *Chemische Zeitschrift,* 7 vols.; *Comptes rendus,* 158 vols.; *Gazetta chimica italiana,* 70 vols.; *Journal of the American Chemical Society,* 32 vols.; *Journal of Industrial Chemistry,* 8 vols.; *Journal of the Chemical Society, Abstracts,* 38 vols.; *Journal of the Chemical Society, Transactions,* 41 vols.; *Kolloid-chemische Beihefte,* 7 vols.; *Monatshefte für Chemie,* 32 vols.; *Moniteur scientifique du chemiste,* 57 vols.; *Recueil des travaux chemiques,* 34 vols.; *Technisch-chemisches Jahrbuch,* 16 vols.; *Zeitschrift für anorganische Chemie,* 54 vols.; *Zeitschrift für Chemie und Industrie der Kolloide,* 16 vols.; *Zeitschrift für den physickalischen und chemischen Unterricht,* 26 vols.

In law, 11,688 volumes were added, 1926–29, through gift, exchange, purchase, and special appropriations. The accessions included, among others, the following: 2,064 volumes of early *State Reports to National Reporter System;* 2,100 volumes, most important of which were Mews' *English Digest, English and Empire Digests, English Statutes at Large;* 1,395 volumes of *English Collateral Reports, Canadian Reports,* Canadian and English periodicals; and numerous reporters, state statutes, codes, treatises, and other legal publications.

SPECIAL COLLECTIONS

In addition to the development of fundamental collections in the subject fields included in the University's program of instruction and research, the Library has built up a number of notable special collections, some of which are described later and have added to scholarly work in the fields to which they relate. These include the Hill Collection of North Caroliniana, numbering 19,649 volumes and 49,677 pamphlets; the Southern Historical Collection of more than two million pieces of manuscripts and many diaries, plantation records, and other manuscript and printed materials relating to the South; the Henderson Collection of American Drama; the Hanes Foundation for the Study of the Origin and Development of the Book, containing specimens of clay tablets, papyri, early manuscripts, incunabula, and books from many notable presses; the Hunter Collection of twelfth- to eighteenth-century manuscripts and fifteenth-century books; the Jacocks Collection of books pertaining to the Sinhalese language and Oriental literatures; the William Richardson Davie Collection of Early American Travel; the Sir Walter Raleigh Collection; and the collection of Latin American materials secured through co-operation with the Rockefeller Foundation and the libraries of Duke and Tulane universities. These collections contain much of the Library's rarest materials and have been developed through the constant co-operation of donors, members of the Faculty, and the Library.

BIBLIOGRAPHICAL APPARATUS AND CO-OPERATIVE RELATIONSHIPS WITH OTHER LIBRARIES

Two of the most important contributions which the Library has made to the facilitation of the scholarly work of the University have been through the development of bibliographical apparatus and co-operation with other libraries, notably those of Duke and Tulane universities.

The foundation for the bibliographical apparatus was laid in 1925–26 when a depository set of the cards issued by the Library of Congress was secured. This was added to in 1932 through a grant of $30,000 from the General Education Board by means of which many cards from the John Crerar Library and the libraries of the University of Chicago and Harvard University were secured, as well as major printed catalogues such as those of the British Museum, the Bibliothèque Nationale, the Prussian State Library, and the John Rylands Library. Many other less extensive printed catalogues were secured, as well as bibliographies of subject fields. This collection was further extended by the addition of a set of the author cards of the Library of Duke University and cards from other libraries in North Carolina. The collection also includes the major trade bibliographies of the United States and the greater European and Latin American countries, as well as union lists of manuscripts, serials, newspapers, and other indispensable bibliographical tools. The collection was the first to be established in the Southeast, and inasmuch as it is supplemented by the bibliographical resources of the Southern Historical Collection, it has proven of great value in all aspects of research and publication carried on in the region. The co-operative arrangements entered into through R. B. Downs, Librarian (1932–38), with the Library of Duke University in 1934, through Carl M. White, Librarian (1938–40), and, more recently, with the Library of Tulane University in a limited field, have challenged the attention of libraries and scholars throughout the nation and have proven of the greatest advantage to the institutions concerned. Other institutions have gained as well by increasing the number of important titles the acquisition of which has been made possible for all the libraries by the elimination of expensive duplication and by agreements reached concerning the division of certain fields.

The program of co-operation with the Library of Duke University, begun under Downs, is varied. Through an inter-campus loan service it provides for the easy use of the libraries by the faculties and graduate students of both universities. Each library, through a grant from the General Education Board in 1934, provided the other with a copy of its main author cards and supplies cards for its current accessions. In 1935, through a second grant from the same source, $25,000 was given to each library for the purchase of materials for research, care being taken that none of the materials should be duplicated. In 1940, under White, a grant of $25,000 was made by the Rockefeller Foundation to these libraries and to the Library of Tulane University for the acquisition, under similar conditions, of Latin

American materials. As a result of the close proximity of the Library of Duke University, and the operation of these various co-operative enterprises by the libraries, the resources of each library have been greatly supplemented by those of the other. In 1941, under Charles E. Rush, Librarian (1941–), the resources of both institutions were further extended by a grant from the Carnegie Corporation which has enabled the libraries to acquire and lend books not in their collections to residents of the region pursuing special studies.

Co-operation upon a different basis with a considerable number of institutions has likewise increased the service of the Library to its patrons. In 1935–36 the Library joined other libraries in the region in the compilation of a union list of serials received by them and in the description of the resources for research possessed by them. These compilations were published under the editorship of Mrs. M. L. Skaggs and R. B. Downs, both of the University of North Carolina Library in 1936 and 1938 respectively. In 1944, Charles E. Rush and O. V. Cook, Assistant Librarian (1940–), with the dean of the Graduate School and the co-ordinator of the Latin American materials program, met with representatives from other Southern libraries and institutions to consider the development of more extensive methods of co-operation for increasing the acquisition and the use of research materials within the entire Southern region.

DOCUMENTS AND MICROFILMS

The designation of the Library as a document center and the provision of apparatus for the production and reading of microfilms in the 1930's have likewise contributed to the promotion of graduate study and research. The division of the document field with the Library of Duke University for state documents and with the libraries of Duke and Tulane for Latin American documents, has also resulted in a more extensive coverage of different states and countries than would have been possible if undertaken by any one of the libraries alone. Rare materials, particularly rare state documents and early laws of the states, have been extensively filmed, and the files of the Library have been correspondingly extended and completed.

FACILITIES AND SERVICES

The facilitation of the work of the scholar, however, has not depended solely upon the presence of materials in the Library or the co-operative arrangements with other libraries. The provision of reference and bibliographical quarters, seminar rooms, stack carrels, and other physical facilities and the inclusion in the library staff of expert reference librarians, bibliographers, and other specialists, have contributed to the same end. Assistance given by the Library staff (now comprising forty-four members) to graduate students and Faculty members in the preparation of theses, manuscripts, and bibliographies, and to editors of University journals and the Director of the University of North Carolina Press concerning the distribution of the publications of the University through exchange has promoted not only these specific undertakings but has contributed to the building up of a spirit of scholarship and learning in the University.

The means which a library may employ in making itself indispensable to a community of scholars are in no sense limited to the acquisition and servicing of materials, to the provision of suitable physical facilities, and to the assistance which may be given through specialists and experts on the library staff. These are important, but their importance may be equaled by the means which the library may employ in aiding the university in shaping its administrative and educational policies. This has been especially true of the University of North Carolina Library in the last half century. Since the merging of the three libraries 1886–1906, three members of the Faculty who served as librarians—George T. Winston (1885–86), E. A. Alderman (1893–95), and E. K. Graham (1899–1900)—later became presidents of the University. Their experience in directing the Library helped them to visualize the University as a whole—a visualization that is fundamentally essential to the proper development of a university. Under Winston the first step in merging the libraries of the literary societies and the University was taken. Alderman took the second step. The third was taken by Louis R. Wilson in close co-operation with a committee consisting of President F. P. Venable, Eben Alexander, Supervisor of the Library and Dean of the University, C. Alphonso Smith, first dean of the Graduate School, which aided the Librarian in the preparation of the plans for the Carnegie Building, and with Eugene Armfield and George Stephens of the alumni, secured the endowment for library materials in 1905–1906. In varying degrees, all were involved in shaping the policy of the Library which emphasizes the integration of the library program with that of teaching and research in the University.

Later, under Wilson, and more recently under Librarians Downs, White, and Rush, the Library has aided in the development of the Division of Extension of the University and of the University of North Carolina Press; in building up the Southern Historical Collection and the collection of bibliographical apparatus; in the establishment of the School of Library Science; in the organization of the Friends of the Library to facilitate the development of special resources for scholarly purposes; in the cultivation of co-operative relations with other universities and libraries in describing and making available library resources in the Southeast; and in mobilizing the resources of the Library in relation to the War. The conception of these men and the members of the Library staff of what constitutes the role of a modern library in a great university and their ability to secure its acceptance by the state and the region may well be the greatest contribution which the Library, in its first hundred and fifty years, has made to the scholarly work of the University, the region, and the nation, and the surest forecast of what will be the nature of its service in the future.

Chapter 2

CO-OPERATIVE FACILITIES IN RESEARCH AND SERVICE

Charles E. Rush

UNIVERSITY and other research libraries in North Carolina during the past decade have not been unmindful of the benefits to be gained through co-operative effort and integration of activities. In fact, they have taken a leading part among their sister institutions throughout the country in demonstrating the possibilities of mutual aid, which among most librarians is still a matter of much discussion and little practice. Attitudes and customs of the past generally have produced independent and self-centered institutions, whose prejudices and traditions have led them into stubborn isolation, unconcern for their neighbors and often rivalry, which entailed mutual injury and loss. All admit that such practice is neither democratic nor efficient, and yet, practical procedures for relief have been followed in only a few localities in America.

However, the recent and tremendous increase in print, the development of new kinds of research and their recognition as essential resources for the nation, the growth of advanced study, and the increasing dependence of the graduate schools on effectively organized and enlarging bodies of basic materials of knowledge are slowly but surely developing a greater freedom from the barriers of indifference so long nursed by most libraries.

It was not only the inadequacy of the research libraries in North Carolina that induced them to be mutually helpful, since much of both the credit and the blame must be laid to the devastating effect of the depression in the early 1930's, which resulted in sadly reduced book and personnel budgets in all institutions within the area. Several of these libraries realized that co-ordination, organization, preservation, and use of research materials was not only wise but was also necessary. They admitted much unnecessary overlapping in special fields, too much duplication of expensive holdings, and even competition in the collection of many materials, single copies of which would serve adequately the entire region. They discovered that release from such unnecessary acquisition would enable them to concentrate their funds not only on assigned fields of strength but also on those fields previously and necessarily neglected, because of meager financial incomes. Furthermore, they proceeded to do something about it and to set up practical procedures for the integration of resources and services.

It was only natural that Duke University and the University of North Carolina, having many common interests and being only nine miles apart, should proceed to demonstrate many possibilities. Accordingly, these two Universities in 1933 appointed a Joint Committee on Intellectual Co-operation, whose membership included the librarian of each library. In March, 1935, the Committee's report appeared in print and recorded a number of examples of informal co-operation then under way, including generous interlibrary loans, mutual library privileges for the two faculties and exchanges of duplicate volumes. The report outlined a number of suggested opportunities for further co-operation relating to research materials and activities, including specialization in selected fields, the elimination of considerable duplication in purchases, the joint assembling of government publications, the extension of library privileges to graduate and special students, and the strengthening of collections and services in which both institutions were particularly interested.

Meanwhile, in 1934, through a grant from the General Education Board, the two libraries were enabled to duplicate and to exchange author cards, thus recording in each library the holdings of the neighboring institution. In 1935, regular delivery service by truck was inaugurated, with expense shared jointly and operated on a daily schedule, until conditions of war necessitated reduction in frequency.

In December of 1935, the two libraries received a two-year grant from the General Education Board to strengthen research collections in the biological, physical, and social sciences, and in English literature, on the agreement that there should be no duplication in purchase and that each acquisition should be a definite addition to the basic resources of both institutions. In 1935-36, through the aid of the North Carolina Division of Cooperation in Education and Race Relations, a program was agreed upon for the annual acquisition of material relating to the Negro, avoiding duplication, save in recent books in demand on both campuses.

An agreement in January, 1937, provided for a division of fields in the collecting of public documents, primarily on a geographical basis for state publications. In the acquisition of catalogues and reports of schools and colleges, Duke emphasizes the preservation of those from privately endowed and denominational schools, and Carolina those from public and state supported institutions. Carolina does not attempt to duplicate or to supplement Duke's collection of American newspapers before 1900, of twentieth-century non-Southern newspapers, or of foreign newspapers. When both libraries possess broken files of a serial, periodical or newspaper, of which only one file is necessary between the two, efforts are made to complete the longer file of the two by an exchange of volumes.

Naturally, each library expects to build up its own collection of ordinary reference and instructional material independently of the other. However, in the case of specialized research material and of expensive items not in constant use, duplication is avoided whenever possible, either by consultation and checking with the other library before ordering, or by the definition and assignment of specific fields of interest to each library. By allocation, such recognition has been given to separate concentration on nearly two score of special subject fields.

The program of co-operative acquisition of Latin American materials was implemented in 1940 by a grant from the Rockefeller Foundation to each institution, and also to Tulane University, to be expended over a period of five years. Division of interest and effort was made on a geographical basis, in which Argentina, Chile, Paraguay, Uruguay, and Venezuela were assigned to this Library for specialization, except in the fields of bibliography and folklore, in which North Carolina is unrestricted. This program calls for co-operation in Latin American studies, as well as in library acquisitions.

A regional library program was provided in 1941 by a grant from the Carnegie Corporation of New York for the purchase of material which properly belongs in one of the two libraries but for which the need arises in the other institution, or in colleges of the region. Purchases are made by either library upon recommendation from the other library, or from college libraries of North and South Carolina, and southern Virginia.

While each library recognizes its primary responsibility to serve its own institution, in general the facilities and privileges of each are offered to faculty members and students of both Universities on equal terms. The above concise statement relative to joint privileges, lending services, exchanges of cards to maintain duplicate catalogues, and agreements on the acquisition of material, does not include several co-operative activities and projects, which were temporary in nature and therefore have been completed or discontinued.

The Joint Committee on Intellectual Cooperation issued in 1937 a further report on co-ordinated enterprises between the two Universities, suggesting many examples of activities which could be promoted jointly by faculty members and administrators, including (in addition to library co-operation) combined action in bringing learned society meetings to the two campuses, joint seminars or classes for advanced students, the sharing of visiting professorships, and joint sponsorship of distinguished visiting lecturers, participation in doctoral examinations, publication of books and articles, and a score of other possibilities. The success of these latter ventures may not have been as extensive or as concrete as those in the library field, but the mere fact that they were considered and attempted indicates a general appreciation of the needs and possibilities, and a willingness to experiment with them, thus removing the first real barrier to much helpful integration between two or more institutions.

For several years, the University Library has enjoyed co-operative arrangements with several other North Carolina libraries, in addition to the constant and generous lending and borrowing privileges in which all libraries within the state and region participate. Through mutual assistance, the North Carolina State Library emphasizes its holdings of genealogy and local newspapers, while the University Library strengthens its collections of state documents by sharing in the distribution and exchange of official printed publications of North Carolina. Likewise, the State Department of Archives and History concentrates on the collection and preservation of official materials which are archival in nature, while the University specializes in the acquisition and use of manuscripts and records of individuals. Helpful exchange relationships, particularly in the development of special collections, exist between the Woman's College in Greensboro and State College in Raleigh. When the present war is ended, further programs of mutual aid will be promoted between these three sister institutions in the Consolidated University. Other libraries in this area, notably those of Davidson College and Guilford College, the Charlotte Public Library, and the Wachovia Historical Society, exchange resource materials to the advantage of all in the region. These are only indicative examples of many similar activities, which are definitely encouraged by an exceptionally efficient State Library Commission in Raleigh.

Joint efforts in centrally recording the special holdings of libraries within a region materially strengthen the research resources of the area. At Chapel Hill there is a growing state regional catalogue, which records not only the facilities in print at Duke and Carolina, but also the special holdings of several other libraries in the state. At intervals, the Library receives cards from North Carolina State College, the Woman's College at Greensboro, Wake Forest College Library, Guilford College Library, Charlotte Public Library, and the Sondley Memorial Library in Asheville. Files of cards listing books by and about the Negro have come from several Negro libraries in North Carolina. A still wider record is maintained in the card catalogue files representing the Library of Congress, the John Crerar Library, and the Folger Shakespeare Library, to which are added partial sets of cards from Harvard, Princeton, Chicago, and Wesleyan. These indexes, which so greatly facilitate interlibrary loans and encourage the use of microfilming processes, serve to bring close to the scholar's desk much of the world's recorded wisdom.

The Library of the University has been instrumental through print in the general effort to measure and to strengthen regional resources. Two publications, edited by members of the Library staff, definitely contributed to the awakening of widespread interest, and both are still useful as bibliographical guides. *Resources of Southern Libraries,* a descriptive survey of facilities for research, was edited by Robert B. Downs (Librarian) and published by the American Library Association in 1938. Two years earlier, *Serials Currently Received in Southern Libraries,* a union list, was edited by Alma S. Skaggs (Head, Periodicals Department) under the supervision of the A.L.A. Committee on Resources of Southern Libraries and the chairmanship of Mr. Downs.

Throughout the South, there is an increasing determination on the part of both librarians and university administrators, evidenced by recent conferences of official representatives of research centers in the region, to pool their services and materials in united effort to increase the strength and develop the specialization of their resources, particularly those on the higher research level. This is in line with recently proposed nationwide undertakings, designed not only to make known the location of reservoirs of knowledge but also to plan their further development through concerted action. These desired consummations rest more pointedly on the responsibilities of the administrative officials and professorial convictions of the institutions than upon the continuing work of their librarians. The wealth of printed resources and the cultural holdings in manuscript and other rare forms must not only be preserved but must be used effectively for the benefit of those most concerned, nationally as well as locally. Buildings become outmoded in a few years, but these intellectual resources become capital investments of increasing value, producing larger and larger dividends far into the dim future.

In the eyes of the public, current books stand foremost, but scholarship, research, professional training, invention, creative writing, and other activities advancing the frontiers of knowledge must depend upon the publications of early centuries, those of foreign academies and universities, and of societies and governments; the great journal files of science and literature, the important sets of monographs and serials, and the essential tools of bibliography and reference. These are the imperatively needed foundation works, together with other more obscure publications and primary source materials, which are essential to a basic knowledge of a general field and a thorough study of a specific branch of a subject. They must be available in any institution, or its near-by center, which even pretends to offer advanced and graduate study. Otherwise, opportunity claims are but a tinkling cymbal.

The University of North Carolina Library has inherited and otherwise acquired much from private collections, much by gift and bequest, and considerable by purchase. It possesses substantial collections in several specific fields which justify satisfaction, but no one should be unmindful that great gaps and distressing needs exist, and that ways and means to fill and to meet them are of grave concern and serious importance, not only to the University but to all citizens in North Carolina. All must remember that the needy may be helped, if they have the foresight and the fortitude to help themselves.

II

COLLECTIONS AND FOUNDATIONS

Chapter 3

COLLECTION OF NORTH CAROLINIANA

Mary L. Thornton

A HUNDRED YEARS AGO the University became a center for the collection of material dealing with the state when the Historical Society of the University of North Carolina held its first meeting at Chapel Hill under the leadership of President David Lowry Swain. The Society had as one of its main objects the collection of local publications, "as nearly as might be possible, one or more copies of every book, pamphlet, and newspaper published in this State."[1] By June, 1845, when the first report of the Society was published, a good beginning had been made, thirty-two publications and eleven collections of manuscripts relating to North Carolina being catalogued in this report.[2] Identical copies of two of the books mentioned survive as treasured possessions of the North Carolina Collection.[3] Others may also be here, though it may be impossible to identify them because of the loss of inscriptions by rebinding. President Swain followed an interest in the collection of historical material during the remainder of his administration. His leadership in this field was recognized in his appointment as agent of the state to procure material in England and America.[4]

No later catalogue of North Carolina material gathered at the University by the Historical Society seems to have been

---

1. Historical Society of the University of North Carolina, *First Report, June 4, 1845*, p. 3.
2. *Ibid.*, pp. 4-7.
3. They are *A Complete Revisal of All the Acts of Assembly of the Province of North Carolina* (Newbern, James Davis, 1773) presented to the Society by Thomas D. Benehan, and *The North Carolina Chronicle, or Fayetteville Gazette*, September 13, 1790–March 7, 1791, presented by Dr. James Webb.
4. Stephen Beauregard Weeks, "Historical Review of the Colonial and State Records of North Carolina," *State Records of North Carolina*, XXX, 47-48.

published, but collecting went on. In 1869, Fisk P. Brewer, in his report as Librarian, stated that the Library had a good collection illustrative of University history, including laws, catalogues, programs, circulars, commencement addresses and sermons, works by members of the Faculty, and local periodicals. He also mentioned a collection of 218 volumes of state laws, legislative records, and law reports.[5] Brewer wrote letters to the newspapers stressing the need for the preservation of every book and pamphlet printed in North Carolina or connected with her history.[6]

Another society, The North Carolina Historical Society, chartered after the reopening of the University in 1875, specified the collection of material as one of the objects of its creation, "especially books, manuscripts, papers and memorials ... relating to history of the State."[7] Among its incorporators was Kemp Plummer Battle, President of the University from 1876, to whom the activities of the Society were to be a consuming interest for the remainder of a long life. President Battle's contributions to history were numerous. He published books and historical monographs. In 1890, he led a campaign for the collection of subscriptions to establish a professorship of history, and, on his retirement as President, was chosen to head the new department. Not least among his contributions was the molding of students who came under his influence as members of the society. Speaking of this, President Alderman said:

"The historical instinct [as fostered by President Battle], the love and aptitude for historical research, the power to collect, arrange, deduce, and vivify historical data are entering into the equipment of University students. ... In the days to come, the commonwealth shall not lack for those able to tell the story of its spirit, its genius, and its progress."[8]

5. Fisk Parsons Brewer, *The Library of the University of North Carolina* (Chapel Hill? 1870?).
6. W. F. Brewer, Sketch of Fisk Parsons Brewer (Manuscript in North Carolina Collection), p. 4.
7. Laws of the State of North Carolina, 1874–75, pp. 648-49.
8. Quoted in Collier Cobb, "Kemp Plummer Battle," in *Biographical History of North Carolina* (Samuel A. Ashe, ed.), VI, 30.

As an illustration of the prophetic truth of this tribute, some of the students who were members of the Historical Society are listed: Stephen B. Weeks, John Sprunt Hill, William J. Andrews, Holland M. Thompson, Henry M. Wagstaff, Robert D. W. Connor, Archibald Henderson, J. G. de Roulhac Hamilton.

As a nucleus for its collection, the Society received from Mrs. Swain "50 to 60 books of great historical value" which had been in the possession of President Swain as the property of the earlier Society.[9] In 1880, an appeal for donations of material was issued in the form of a circular letter, remarkable for its evaluation of historical sources in their modern conception. Among the twenty-five classes of local material listed as desirable for preservation at the University were newspapers and periodicals; statutes; geological, topographical, educational, scientific, medical, sanitary, religious reports and statistics; works, speeches, sermons, literature by North Carolinians or pertaining to North Carolina. The circular closed with a rousing appeal to state pride.[10]

Organization of North Carolina material in a special department in the Library followed the appointment of Louis R. Wilson as Librarian. In almost every report after his appointment in 1901, Wilson recommended the collection and special treatment of state material. In 1905, he called attention to the need for an endowment of North Carolina literature.[11] A response came from John Sprunt Hill, Class of 1889, who in 1906 contributed the sum of $5,000 as a part of the Library endowment raised to meet the Carnegie gift for a new building.[12] Mr. Hill's interest in North Carolina history had been demonstrated previously through the gift of a history prize of books

---

9. "The Historical Society," *The University of North Carolina Magazine* (October, 1878), p. 86.

10. North Carolina Historical Society, *An Appeal to Its Friends* (Chapel Hill, 1880), signed, "K. P. Battle, Pres't., J. F. Heitman, Rec. Sec., George T. Winston."

11. *The University of North Carolina Record*, No. 40 (December, 1905), p. 38.

12. North Carolina University, Trustees, Minutes, January 25, 1907, p. 125 (Manuscript in University of North Carolina Library).

relating to North Carolina for the best thesis on some subject of state history.[13] In 1903 he established a fellowship in history,[14] and during the following twenty-five years he often contributed generously to the support of the Collection. In 1929, on the occasion of the dedication of the present library building, he and Mrs. Hill transferred property valued at $6,000 as an addition to his earlier endowment.[15] In 1945, Mr. Hill has stated his intention to increase the endowment of the North Carolina Collection to insure its expansion and future growth.

Meanwhile, because of the early endowment, there was a steady development in acquisitions, creating a need for a special room to house the Collection in the Carnegie Library building erected in 1907. A large corner room on the second floor was assigned to North Carolina books and pamphlets, numbering then about three thousand bound volumes and pamphlets. The new building also had a vault equipped with metal filing cases and shelving designed to accommodate fifty thousand sheets of manuscript and one thousand rare volumes.[16] Much of this material came from the collections of the two historical societies. A system of classification for printed material was adopted, as well as a special book plate. Growth of the Collection over a period of years called for a special librarian to collect, catalogue, and administer it. In 1917, the position of Librarian in charge of the North Carolina Collection was established through the generosity of John Sprunt Hill. Mary L. Thornton, a graduate of the Carnegie Library Training School of Atlanta, was appointed to this position.

An important milestone in the history of the Collection was the purchase of the Stephen B. Weeks Collection of Caroliniana in 1918. By action of the Executive Committee of the Board of

13. North Carolina University, *Catalog*, 1891–92, p. 33.
14. John Sprunt Hill, *Address Before the Alumni Association of the University of North Carolina* (No place, 1903), p. 24.
15. *The University of North Carolina Record* (December, 1929), no. 264, p. 91.
16. Louis R. Wilson, "Library of the University of North Carolina," *Library Journal*, XXXIV (December, 1909), 550–51. Manuscripts stored in this vault later became the nucleus of the Southern Historical Collection.

Trustees in a special meeting on June 4, a committee consisting of President Edward Kidder Graham, Louis R. Wilson, J. G. de Roulhac Hamilton, Robert D. W. Connor, and John Sprunt Hill was authorized to contract for its purchase.[17] The Weeks Collection, comprising ten thousand books, pamphlets, newspapers, and maps, was recognized as the most complete body of printed material relating to the state at that time.[18] In recommending its purchase to the Trustees, Wilson described the collection as "essential to the proper study of the State's life, government, history, literature and institutions." Among reasons cited for its acquisition, Wilson said:

> Dr. Weeks has not confined his interest solely to the activities of North Carolina within the borders of the State, but has been aware of North Carolina's part in the development of the states immediately south and west. In 1897 he became one of the founders and editors of the Southern Historical Association Publications (1897–1907), and in that capacity followed with keen interest the influence of North Carolina settlers in other states. Consequently, his collection contains many publications which relate to these extra-North Carolina events. The collection is well developed in this important particular, and by combining it with the Kidder collection of Southern Newspapers covering the Civil War period, the Kenan Collection of Confederate States Publications, and the University collection of the leading periodicals of the ante and post bellum South, all now in the possession of the Library, the resultant collection will furnish much of the source material from which the story and literature of the Southeast as a whole may be written. When it is kept in mind that the first English settlement in America was made upon the coast of the State, that the fortunes of the Virginia and North Carolina colonists were inseparable, that the two Carolinas were united under the same charter, that Tennessee is the daughter of North Carolina, and that through the explorations and migrations of Boone and countless other North Carolinians the Westward and Southward expansion of the Nation was begun, the full significance of the collection becomes apparent. By securing

17. North Carolina University, Trustees, Minutes, June 4, 1918 (Manuscript in University of North Carolina Library).

18. The Collection is described by Weeks in his *The Weeks Collection of Caroliniana* (Raleigh, 1907).

it, the University will not only make it available to North Carolina but for the South and the Nation as well! [19]

Its presence made the University a center of regional as well as state research, and laid a foundation for the Southern Historical Collection.

The Weeks Collection had other values. It became a model for the future collecting of North Carolina and Southern material, which followed its emphasis on sources, pamphlets, bulletins, catalogues, periodicals, as well as books; it served as a magnet to other collections, attracted by its excellence. In the years following its purchase, a number of collections came by gift. Among them were the Kemp Plummer Battle Collection, thirteen hundred titles, notable for Confederate, University, and political material; the Alexander Boyd Andrews Collection, seven hundred titles, including complete files of early railroad reports, invaluable source for the history of transportation; the James Sprunt Collection of Wilmington newspapers, complete files of dailies and weeklies for the period when that port attained great importance as the last refuge of Confederate blockade runners; the Pettigrew Collection of rare books and pamphlets; the Rowan Historical Society files of Salisbury newspapers; the William Richardson Davie Collection of rare books illustrative of the early history of the Carolinas, the gift of Preston Davie; and others, too numerous to mention here. Valuable collections were added by purchase. Among them were the John McDowell Collection of railroad, educational, and agricultural pamphlets, mainly of the period from 1840 to 1860; the William Lenoir Collection, rich in political pamphlets and broadsides of the eighteenth and early nineteenth centuries; the Nathan Wilson Walker Collection, one of the finest North Caroliniana libraries, particularly strong in literature by North Carolinians.

To these valuable collections of the past, and the many out-of-print books and pamphlets acquired one by one from dealers and private libraries, there was added year by year a flood of

19. North Carolina University, Trustees, Minutes, June 4, 1918 (Manuscript in University of North Carolina Library).

contemporary publications. Collecting received a great impetus after 1930, when the Southern Historical Collection was established under the direction of J. B. de Roulhac Hamilton, whose tireless effort as director brought much rare North Caroliniana to the Library.

Some idea of the growth of the body of material in the North Carolina Collection in a physical sense may be gathered from a comparison of its size expressed in shelf space covered by books and pamphlets. In 1917, when its administration under a special librarian was inaugurated, catalogued material filled about twenty shelves; while uncatalogued material, mainly state documents and pamphlets, required about thirty shelves, or a total of about 150 feet of shelf space. The Collection, now shelved in the North Carolina Room and the adjoining level of the stack, covers 2,013 shelves, measuring 6,039 feet. In number of items, counting books, periodicals, newspapers, pamphlets, maps, pictures, and mounted clippings, it numbers about ninety-five thousand, with an annual increase of about five thousand items.

A walk among the shelves will disclose the variety of material that has been collected. Church history, possibly more intimately connected with the individual than any other form of history, may be followed in files of minutes, periodicals, and reports of the various denominations and individual churches. Sociology, containing political, economic, legal, educational, and other social material, forms one of the largest classes. It embraces most of the public documents issued by the various state departments, the most complete body of that type of material in existence. Here are unbroken files of the session *Laws of the State of North Carolina* from the first issue in 1777, an almost complete file of the *Journal of the General Assembly* from its first session as a state body, the *Public Documents of North Carolina* from 1829 to 1919, when that series was discontinued. Files of reports of the various state departments are usually complete. There are minutes of state chapters of national societies, such as the Freemasons, and files of educational periodicals, among them Calvin H. Wiley's *The North Carolina Journal of Education*, 1858–64, a pioneer among public school journals of the United States. There is an interesting collection of textbooks used in North Carolina schools, many of them Confederate imprints; files of catalogues, bulletins, and periodicals of private schools and colleges; a complete collection of University of North Carolina publications. There are complete files of the *Report of the Superintendent of Common Schools* and the *Report of the Superintendent of Public Instruction*, which carry in their statistical tables the source for history of local public education. The history of the long struggle for better transportation facilities on water and land is recorded in reports of early navigation companies, plank road companies, early railroads, and finally in the reports of the great railway systems operating in the state and in the United States Engineers' *Report upon the Improvement of Rivers and Harbors*. A later development, probably more productive in opening the "lost provinces," may be followed in the story of the building of a system of hard-surfaced highways told in the *Report of the State Highway Commission*.

Scientific presentation of natural resources may be followed in files of journals, such as *The Elisha Mitchell Scientific Society Journal*, and in many articles reprinted or clipped from periodicals published out of the state. There are complete files of the several geological surveys financed by the state, including the Olmsted-Mitchell survey, 1824–29, the earliest state survey in the United States; the Emmons survey, 1852–63, and the Kerr survey, 1866–87. Later geological publications include complete files of the publications of the North Carolina Geological and Economic Survey and the State Department of Conservation and Development. There is a section devoted to zoology and botany, both popular and scientific works, among them one of the most beautiful books relating to American natural history, Mark Catesby's *The Natural History of Carolina, Florida, and the Bahama Islands*. The history of medicine may be followed in a complete file of *Transactions of the Medical Society of the State of North Carolina*, 1849–1943, in files of medical journals, and in the reports and bulletins of the State Department of Health. The state's advisory and regulatory work for agriculture is recorded in reports and bulletins of the

North Carolina Department of Agriculture, the North Carolina Agricultural Experiment Station, and the Extension Service of the North Carolina State College of Agriculture and Engineering of the University. Growth of various industries, among which the state is now taking a leading place in tobacco, textile, and furniture manufactures, may be followed in periodicals, reports, directories, and statistical material.

Fine arts are represented by the excellent works on North Carolina architecture recently published by the University of North Carolina Press, such as *The Early Architecture of North Carolina,* by Frances B. Johnston and Thomas T. Waterman, and *Old Homes and Gardens of North Carolina,* sponsored by the Garden Club of North Carolina; and a growing collection of original photographs of old houses made by Bayard Wootten and Frances B. Johnston. Here are also publications of the Garden Club of North Carolina, books and pamphlets on North Carolina handicrafts, music and art programs, and collections of folk songs, for which the mountain section has furnished a fertile field of research. Literature includes poetry and a full collection of drama and fiction with North Carolina setting, numbering 652 titles.

In the sections devoted to travel and history are found works dealing with North Carolina only in part, gathered here to facilitate research. For example, travel throughout the South is included, if North Carolina is traversed in the tour. In the history class there are periodicals of Southern scope, among them, *The Southern Historical Society Papers, The Southern History Association Papers,* as well as complete files of all the North Carolina historical periodicals and serial historical monographs. Histories of the Southern states as a region are here with histories of North Carolina; also, a few rare histories of the individual neighboring states which treat the colonial and pioneer period. After the general history class come sections devoted to the various periods of history, arranged in a sequence usually followed in classifying material on any American area, which begins with books and articles on the life of the Indians in prehistoric times as deduced from relics, continues through the first written descriptions by explorers and colonists, and comes down to modern times. There is a section for county and town material, both descriptive and historical, where directories and brief Chamber of Commerce compilations of facts have been preserved, as well as the full historical works.

If study of history uses the scientific method, it must begin with consideration of its smallest component, the individual who plays a part in foundation work, building the small community and state. It is the achievement of the less known man rather than of him who achieves national recognition that the local collection must rescue from oblivion. His biography is not found in many libraries. In the North Carolina Collection it may be scattered in all the classes, periodicals, minutes, church history, town history, public documents. The general clipping file of over twenty-five thousand mounted newspaper clippings is a fruitful source of biography. There is also a special biography class, containing about two thousand titles. Racial and social factors that have entered in the making of the individual may be traced in a collection of family history which contains the printed sources for North Carolina genealogy and many histories of individual families.

The rarest books and pamphlets are isolated in a special section. North Carolina "incunabula" have been located in libraries in Douglas C. McMurtrie's *Eighteenth Century North Carolina Imprints, 1749–1800*.[20] McMurtrie discovered that only the Library of Congress exceeds the University of North Carolina in number of titles, only the British Public Record Office in titles known by single copies. A section among the rare books is devoted to a collection of association volumes, with autographs and bookplates of North Carolinians, most of whom lived in the eighteenth century. Survivals of books from private libraries of an early day may serve as indicators of reading habits of that time, as well as throw light on the tastes of the individual who owned them. Also in the rare book section is the Sir Walter Raleigh Memorial Collection, made up of books, pamphlets, pictures, and manuscripts relating to Sir Walter

20. Douglas C. McMurtrie, *Eighteenth Century North Carolina Imprints, 1749–1800* (Chapel Hill, University of North Carolina Press, 1938).

Raleigh and his Roanoke Island Colonies. This Collection, established in 1939 by endowment of the Roanoke Colony Memorial Association, is an appropriate memorial to the Englishman whose effort sent the first colony to our shores.

Newspapers, about 1,700 volumes, 288 titles, include full files of papers published in Raleigh, Tarboro, Salisbury, Wilmington, New Bern, Fayetteville, and other towns and cities. Three current dailies are preserved, *The News and Observer, The Greensboro Daily News,* and *The Charlotte Observer,* two of them in film, the most indestructible form. There is a collection of newspapers published before 1801, comprising photostatic reproductions of all issues that have been located in libraries, as well as a few original issues of this rarest of printed material.

The collection of 752 maps is important as it throws light on changing boundaries, geographical names, long discarded, and the location of early towns, forts, churches, and even plantations. Some of the older ones have great artistic beauty. Among the rarer maps in the Collection are *A New Map of Carolina* by John Thornton (London, ca. 1689) and *Carte particulière de la Carolina dressée sur les memoires le plus nouveaux* [Nicholas Sanson] (Amsterdam, 1693). The largest and most detailed of the old maps are Henry Mouzon's *An Accurate Map of North and South Carolina* (London, 1775), and Captain Collet's *A Compleat Map of North Carolina from an Actual Survey* (London, 1770). The Collection also contains modern maps of the state, its counties and towns, and maps illustrative of geology, soils, and coast and harbor water heights and hazards.

No general bibliography of the state has been published. Numbers of printed and manuscript bibliographies dealing with some special phase or period have been collected. Other bibliographies are here as parts of books, pamphlets, articles in periodicals, and theses. Students may rely on the card catalogue of the Collection as the most complete general bibliography of North Carolina. It contains over a hundred thousand entries and follows a bibliographical form, listing articles in periodicals published in and out of the state, as well as books, pamphlets, maps, periodicals, and newspapers. There is a supplementary catalogue made up of author entries of material, not in the

Collection but known to have been printed. The scholarly bibliography compiled by Stephen B. Weeks, with valuable notes on authors and on publications which appeared before 1918, is here in manuscript. Also here, in manuscript, is a bibliography of North Carolina public documents, 1749–1939, compiled by Mary L. Thornton with departmental entries for all documents in the set known as *The Public Documents of North Carolina* and for all other state documents published in series or as single publications which are located in a selected group of libraries.

Emphasis on local subjects as fields of study, an important function of a state university, is apparent in the files of theses approved by the Graduate School of the University of North Carolina. In 1940, fifty-three out of a total of 164 theses dealt with the state, mainly in the fields of history, political and social science, education, and economics, but also in creative writing, which attains most success in treatment of the familiar locale. In furnishing material for research by students, the North Carolina Collection also supplements other specialized libraries on the campus. It gives a background to research in the unique Library of Rural Social-Economics, which has been the fountainhead of *The University of North Carolina News Letter;* it supplements material in the Institute for Research in Social Science for its studies in regionalism and the South; its document files, state, county, and city, are a source for the Law Library and the Institute of Government; it furnished materials for historical monographs published in the *James Sprunt Studies in History and Political Science.* It has stimulated an increasing interest in North Carolina and in the collection of North Carolina books in public and private libraries by a published annual North Carolina bibliography.[21] Use of the Collection is not limited to Chapel Hill. Through the Library Extension Service and through interlibrary loans, its resources are available to authors, teachers, reporters, government officials, lawyers, and all others interested in the state.

21. Published by the State Department of Archives and History in *The North Carolina Historical Review*, April issue, 1933–.

Chapter 4

THE SOUTHERN HISTORICAL COLLECTION

J. G. de Roulhac Hamilton

COMPREHENSIVELY SPEAKING, the Southern Historical Collection may be said to include all the large and varied holdings of the University Library that relate in any way to the history of the Southern states and their people. But many of these holdings have their own classifications and separate identities, and the Collection, as a descriptive title in this chapter, relates specifically to the material included in what is in reality the manuscript division of the Library.

Its conception and actual operation long antedate its formal establishment by the Trustees of the University in 1930. More than a century ago, in 1833, to be exact, steps were taken for the establishment of an organization charged with the collection and preservation of historical material relating to the state, and in that year, the North Carolina Historical Society was chartered by act of the General Assembly.

Eleven years later, in 1844, an organization called the Historical Society of the University of North Carolina actually came into being, and largely in the person of David L. Swain, into active operation. In spite of interruptions of war and reconstruction, with the consequent closing of the University, the cessation of the activity of the Historical Society, and the dire poverty of many years, the process of collecting such material was continued in a small way during the years that followed, down into the middle 'twenties.

In addition the Library received endowment and established a separate division for North Caroliniana which is today one of the most notable state collections in the United States. The Library also secured endowment for the purchase of books relating to the Civil War, and began the systematic gathering of all types of printed material relating to the South. The acquisition of the Weeks Collection, the establishment of the

Rural Social Economics Library and the Institute for Research in Social Science, all contributed to form a background for a new and more unusual project.

The realization of the appalling fact of widespread and continued destruction of quantities of the manuscript sources of Southern history, particularly those of a personal nature, and the knowledge of how little, relatively speaking, was being done to check that process and to preserve such material, led to the inception of a widened undertaking by the University. This was to invite Southern people generally to co-operate with the University in the establishment here of a great gathering of historical material relating to fourteen states, namely, Maryland, Virginia, North Carolina, South Carolina, Georgia, Florida, Alabama, Mississippi, Louisiana, Texas, Arkansas, Tennessee, Kentucky, and Missouri. It was of course planned to include every kind of printed material, but the main emphasis was to be placed upon the preservation of manuscripts. Books, pamphlets, newspapers, pictures would have duplicates somewhere, but manuscripts are, as a rule, unique, and their preservation consequently of supreme importance.

As it seemed to those interested in the proposed plan, Southern people, properly informed of the scope and purpose of the undertaking, would welcome the opportunity to have their family archives, those particularly high gods among their *lares* and *penates*, preserved and properly cared for so that they might contribute in a large way to historical investigation of every aspect of the Southern past, and also be available to future generations of their families. The outcome has proved conclusively the correctness of that judgment.

For some years after the plan was fully formed, its full prosecution was delayed. Means were lacking to carry it out, the Library building then in use was not fireproof, and when once its vault was full it seemed undesirable as well as highly improper to ask for the custody of manuscript collections in large numbers until a safer repository was assured. But the work went on slowly, the plan was developed, and lists of persons owning manuscripts multiplied, and with the authorization by the General Assembly in 1927 of a new and permanent Library building, the time was ripe to announce the plan and begin the work.

In December, 1927, at a dinner of the North Carolina Society of Baltimore, a formal announcement was made of the undertaking. The idea met with favor from the outset and there was widespread comment by the press and by individuals.

A generous gift by the late A. M. Kistler, of Morganton, N. C., made possible a demonstration of the practicability of the project, and the results were so encouraging that in January, 1930, the Trustees of the University formally established the Southern Historical Collection with the writer as Director, at the same time releasing him from teaching except for one quarter. Several years later, he was released from all teaching to give his entire time to the work of the Collection.

Financial aid, making extended field work possible, came from interested friends. Burton Craige, the Institute for Research, the Alumni Loyalty Fund, the University classes of 1910, 1930, and 1932, the bequest of Dr. Foster A. Sondley, Dossey Pruden, James A. Gray, Thurmond Chatham, George Stephens, Gordon Gray, Rufus Patterson, W. D. Carmichael, John Sprunt Hill, Junius Parker, A. B. Andrews, Claiborn McD. Carr, Kemp P. Lewis, J. M. Morehead, Henry F. Shaffner, A. L. M. Wiggins, and W. A. Whitaker all contributed to keep the project going. Mrs. Graham Kenan, at a critical moment, contributed generously to an endowment fund, and the Carnegie Corporation made two lifesaving grants for support.

Through the generous interest of Southern people throughout the country the Collection has grown steadily, and continues to grow with increasing rapidity. Material has poured in until it is the largest gathering of manuscripts relating to the whole South that is in existence at any one place.

It is impossible in brief space to attempt any listing of the various groups of manuscripts found in the Collection. In the "Guide to the Manuscripts in the Southern Historical Collection," published in 1940 and covering all the material available for use on June 30, 1939, are listed 809 separate collections. Since that date 915 have been added, making a total of 1,724 thus available at this writing. A number are still in the process of being accessioned. At least half as much more material has been definitely promised and slowly but steadily comes in. In size the separate collections range in number of pieces from one to one hundred thousand.

It is equally impossible to describe completely or anywhere near adequately this great body of source material. But a brief outline of its general character and outstanding features will give some idea of the richness of its holdings and the opportunities which they offer to historical scholarship and investigation.

Naturally the great bulk of the manuscripts consists of correspondence of one sort or another. There are also thousands of documents of historical significance and more than five thousand manuscript volumes. All these combine to present a cross-section record that is of incalculable historical value. In it may be found a wealth of information not only relating to war and politics, the traditional content of history, but to economics, industry, agriculture, commerce, religion, education, family life, intellectual life, the plantation system and slavery, disease and medical practice, crime and punishment, and governmental and social customs and practices. It deals with rich and poor, the bond and free. In short it is already an excellent reflection of the life and thought of a people and contains much to contribute to the ultimate picture of a civilization. If the development of the past fifteen years is any guide to the future, its value will richly increase with the passage of the years.

Among the many phases of Southern history which the Collection touches that are of historical interest and importance, three, standing out in bold relief, loom large upon its horizon. They are: (1) the social system of the old South; (2) the Confederacy and the Civil War; and (3) the plantation system and slavery. The material relating to these, by itself, would make the Collection outstanding.

Viewed from the standpoint of periods of American history, the Collection is weakest with respect to colonial history. Scattered through the separate collections, however, are many documents of the period as well as a considerable number of letters. The diary and letter-book of William Byrd of Westover, the records of the port of Roanoke (now Edenton), the account book of 1776 of Sir William Dunbar, the papers of James Hogg, and the great mass of ledgers, journals, and invoice books of Robert and John Hogg are all important.

The period from the Revolution to the turn of the century makes a better showing, the most important groups of papers being those of John Rutledge, Eliza Lucas Pinckney, Governor Thomas Burke, General Jethro Sumner, John Steele, James Webb, William Polk, William Lenoir, and John E. Calhoun.

The greatest bulk of manuscripts for any one period is made up of those between 1800 and 1860. Notable among these are the following collections: Hubard, Mackay-Stiles, Pettigrew, Polk-Yeatman, Lenoir, Hoke, McCollam, N. R. Middleton, Mitchell King, Lowndes, Lewis Thompson, David L. Swain, Jackson-Prince, Williams-Chestnut-Manning, Frederick Nash, deRosset, Meares-deRosset, Edmund Ruffin, Thomas Ruffin, Frank G. Ruffin, William A. Graham, George W. Mordecai, Cameron, Dabney Carr, Lindsay Patterson, Thomas Jefferson Green, John A. Quitman, John F. H. Claiborne, Alexander-Hillhouse, Felix Grundy, Richard Stanford, John Bragg, Richard K. Call, Gordon, J. G. B. Bulloch, Bryan, Fisher, John Hartwell Cocke, Nicholas Trist, and Benjamin C. Yancey. A larger number of smaller collections, often of proportionately equal value, belong in this period. Together they constitute a record of the life and thought of the ante-bellum South that is unequalled.

Of the period of the Confederacy there are many notable groups of papers. There are, for example, those of Generals Edward P. Alexander, Jeremy F. Gilmer, Armistead L. Long, Edmund Kirby Smith, Samuel Cooper, Thomas M. Logan, Samuel W. Ferguson, Lafayette McLaws, William Gardner, W. W. Allen, Marcellus A. Stovall, John G. Walker, John H. Winder, James J. Pettigrew, Bryan Grimes, Richard S. Ewell, Thomas Clingman, Stephen D. Lee, Alexander R. Lawton, George E. Maney, Stephen D. Ramseur, John Bratton, Raleigh E. Colston, Edward A. O'Neal, James A. Walker, D. H. Hill, Henry A. Wise, James Chesnut, John C. Pemberton, Matt W. Ransom, Henry R. Jackson, and Wade Hampton. The Confederate cabinet is represented by C. G. Memminger, and

Stephen R. Mallory, supplemented by those of John A. Campbell. The Confederate Congress is represented by William A. Graham, James Harrison, R. C. Puryear, Clifford C. Anderson, Thomas D. McDowell, John Perkins, and William Porcher Miles, the last mentioned being in the opinion of two such authorities as Avery Craven and the late Charles W. Ramsdell, the most valuable single group of papers on the Civil War now available. Among many other distinctive groups are the papers of Governors John W. Ellis and A. G. McGrath, Bishop Henry C. Lay, Lewis Hanes, and William S. Pettigrew, Harry St. John Dixon, Henry Kyd Douglas, Maxwell T. Clarke, and John Janney. There are also, scattered through the various collections, thousands of letters written by soldiers in field and camp, and as many written in the homes of the South.

Diaries, autobiographies, and reminiscences constitute a very important part of the Collection. Notable are those of Benjamin F. Perry, Jeremy F. Gilmer, Stephen D. Lee, John Taylor Wood, S. H. Lockett, Eliza Clitherall, Taylor Beatty, James J. Pettigrew, Henry C. Warmoth, Mrs. Philip Phillips, Emma La Conte, George A. Mercer, Andrew McCollam, Ellen E. McCollam, Launcelot Blackford, James C. Harper, Clinton A. Cilley, Nicholas M. Hentz, Caroline Lee Hentz, Charles Arnold Hentz, Henry A. Chambers, Henry Kyd Douglas, Joseph M. Kern, Edward P. Alexander, David P. Hillhouse, Elizabeth Allston Pringle, Louisa C. Arnold, Henry Bacon, James Barron, Overton Bernard, Joseph Davis, Emily Morrison Bondurant, Francis A. Dickins, Calvin Jones, Grace Elmore, Robert Wellford, Katherine Polk Gale, Mrs. Leonidas Polk, William W. Gordon, Mitchell King, Henry C. Lay, Edward H. McDonald, Augustus S. Merrimon, Ellen Mordecai, Emma Mordecai, Mahala P. H. Roach, Philip Phillips, J. G. M. Ramsey, William D. Valentine, and Joseph Gales and Mrs. Gales.

Plantation diaries and other records, as well as the letters of plantation owners, throw a flood of light upon Southern agriculture and the plantation system. The Collection is rich in these. There are those of the Pettigrews of "Magnolia," "Bonarva," and "Belgrade"; the Kollocks of "Woodlands," "Ossibaw," "Coffee Bluff," and "Rosedew"; the Coupers of "Hopeton"; the

Richardsons of "Bayview"; the Hardings of "Belle Meade"; the Ruffins of "Ruthven," "Marlbourne," "Redmoor," "Beechwood," and "Evelynton"; the Lawrences and Warmoths of "Magnolia"; the Polks and Yeatmans of "Hamilton Place" and "Ashwood"; the Burgwyns of "The Elms"; the Sparkmans of "Springwood"; the Gaillards of "The Rocks"; the Palmers of "Richmond" and "Gravel Hill"; Robert Mackay of "The Grange"; the Friends of "White Hill"; the Metcalfes of "Newstead"; the Hairstons of "Coolemee" and "Saura Town"; the Carters of "Scotsboro"; the Manigaults of "Gowrie" and "Silk Hope"; the Porchers of "Ophir"; and the Heywards of "Myrtle Grove," "Rotterdam," "Copenhagen," and "Hamburgh." These are only a part of those included.

For the period since 1865 the following papers may be noted: Edward Conigland, John Randolph Tucker and Harry St. George Tucker, William L. Saunders, P. Lee Phillips and William H. Phillips, Matt W. Ransom, Jacob M. Dickinson, William W. Vass, Thomas E. Watson, Marion Butler, Claude Kitchin, W. F. Stevenson, Ralph P. Buxton, Lee S. Overman, Frank Nash, Frederick Bromberg, Braxton B. Comer, Cornelia Phillips Spencer, Enoch W. Crowder, and Frank G. Ruffin. In this period, too, belongs the great collection of papers on Southern education gathered by Charles W. Dabney and A. P. Bourland.

Important scientific collections are those of Charles W. Short and Moses Ashley Curtis, botanists; the studies of John W. Achorn and M. P. Skinner, ornithologists; and Bartlett Jones, J. Marion Sims, and Christian Miltenberger, physicians.

The Collection has many important papers bearing on naval history, both Federal and Confederate. Important groups are those of Admirals Edward Middleton, Franklin Buchanan, Victor Blue, Newton A. McCully, Adolphus Staton, Andrew F. Long, Archibald H. Scales, and Percy W. Foote; Commodore James Barron; Captains Samuel Barron, French Forrest, Lyman Cotten, Rufus Y. Johnston, William V. Tomb, James H. Tomb, Francis Thornton Chew, and John Taylor Wood.

There are a number of distinctive collections of genealogical interest; the most extensive being the Curry Collection, containing, besides many other studies, a huge mass of material concerning the widely dispersed Henckel family in all the various forms of the name. The Brodnax, de Saussure, Brenizer, Clotworthy, and Baker collections are others of importance.

There are account books and business records innumerable, mill, furnace, and factory records, muster rolls, vouchers, conscript orders, Confederate forage and tax records, fee books and dockets of eminent lawyers and judges, including those of Justice James Iredell of the Supreme Court of the United States. There are large numbers of valuable and informative scrapbooks, the most extensive being those of Thomas E. Watson and Arthur P. Gorman. There are order books of the Revolution —Washington's Headquarters book of 1777–, the war of 1812, and the Civil War.

There are many maps, both civil and military, innumerable photographs, a great many broadsides, pictures, and several notable collections of prints, the most important being the Ruth Faison Shaw Collection of Kurz and Allison Civil War lithographs, and the Margaret Dashiell Collection of fashion plates. This description, covering only a part of the Collection, makes fairly clear its nature and scope.

These important manuscripts are not assembled for the use of the University of North Carolina alone. That institution is proud and happy to be the trustee of a great Southern undertaking and to serve as the custodian of priceless records of the Southern past, but they are gathered here with the single-minded thought of playing some part in preserving these records, and at the same time serving those who will make worthy use of them in the eternal, ceaseless quest for truth.

And finally the thought expressed in the following lines of William H. Trescot is not absent:

> Love thou thy land with love far brought
> From out the storied past and used
> Within the present, but transfused
> Through future time by power of thought.

Chapter 5

THE HANES FOUNDATION

Olan V. Cook

THIS SPECIAL COLLECTION, relating to the history of the book in the Library of the University of North Carolina, had its inception in 1906. In that year Librarian Louis R. Wilson, in a circular soliciting an endowment to match a gift of $50,000 offered by Andrew Carnegie for the erection of a library building, stated: "While a portion of the endowment will be used for general purchases, a portion should be devoted to special collections." Among several recommendations, he included one on "Printing and Bookmaking." Some twenty-five years later, when again gifts and endowments were being sought as a part of another library building program, this suggestion bore fruit. On April 5, 1929, Dr. Frederic M. Hanes, in an address before the Graduate Club of the University, announced the establishment of "The Hanes Foundation for the Study of the Origin and Development of the Book." The Foundation was created in memory of John Wesley and Anna Hodgin Hanes by gift of their children, Alexander S. Hanes ('03), Frederic M. Hanes ('03), James G. Hanes ('09), John W. Hanes ('14), Ralph P. Hanes, Robert M. Hanes ('12), Mrs. Thurmond Chatham, and Mrs. Robert Lassiter. The original amount was $30,000. Out of a deep cultural heritage, both family and institutional, there was begun a special collection relating to the book which today constitutes one of the most distinctive assets of the University Library.

In 1939, Dr. Hanes wrote: "The development of printing and book making not only changed the course of civilization, but it is the basis upon which civilization rests. Into books is distilled the accumulated wisdom of the ages; they are not merely storehouses of wisdom but stimulants to further advances through research. The history of the book is the history of the development of the mind of man."[1] In this statement is reflected the purpose, as well as the scope, of the Hanes Collection. It was proposed to bring together a group of illustrative materials ranging from the earliest examples of the written record in prehistoric times, Babylonian and Sumerian clay tablets, Egyptian and Greek papyri, manuscripts of all kinds, and printed books from the beginning of printing down to the present day.

Dr. Aaron Burtis Hunter, resident of Raleigh and for many years President of St. Augustine's College, served as rector of the Episcopal Church in the American colony in Florence, Italy, from 1920 to 1926. During this period he travelled extensively in European countries, collecting books, manuscripts, and art objects. In 1928, Dr. Hunter offered to the University a collection of 260 incunabula for the sum of $20,000. The University purchased these materials and they became the basic stock for the Hanes Foundation. In 1934, the Library purchased the remainder of the Hunter Collection, comprising fifty-eight volumes of incunabula and eight hundred manuscripts, and they also became a part of the Hanes Foundation. It should be noted that the proceeds of these sales and others were used to construct the library building at St. Augustine's College. Very appropriately, the inscription on the front of the building is the one word, "Incunabula."

The Library endeavors to obtain for the Collection one or more typical examples from each fifteenth-century press, and thereby to trace the development and spread of printing throughout Europe up to the beginning of the sixteenth century. Great strides have been made in attaining this objective. It is now possible to examine a leaf of the famous Bible printed in Mainz by Gutenberg around 1450, and to compare it with the product of his successor, Peter Schöffer, and the workmanship of the R-printer of Strassburg. Similarly the books done by Ulrich Zell and Johann Koelhoff of Cologne may be studied with those from the presses of Günther Zainer, Johann Schüssler, and Johann Bämler of Augsburg. There are thirty-eight

---

1. University of North Carolina, *Alumni Review*, XXVII (May, 1939), 248.

items printed by Anton Koberger of Nuremberg before 1501, and eight volumes represent some of the accomplishments of Peter Drach of Speier.

Following the same analogy for Italy, one is able to compare the work of Conrad Sweynheym, Arnold Pannartz, and Stephan Plannck of Rome with those of Vindelinus de Spira, Nicolaus Jenson, Erhard Ratdolt, and Paganinus de Paganinis of Venice. Similar comparisons may be made with volumes printed in Switzerland, Holland, France, Belgium, Austria, and England.

At this time the Collection contains 565 incunabula items representing the work of 226 different printers in forty-one cities of eight European countries.[2] Although some of the volumes are incomplete, they illustrate clearly the type and workmanship of certain printers, and as such they will serve until other more complete specimens are obtainable. A large majority of the books are not only complete but are preserved in their original bindings, and several are unique. A few are the only copies in America, and, according to the Kommission für den Gesamtkatalog, two editions are known to exist only in the Hanes Collection. A survey made by Fremont Rider in 1939 places this Collection as ninth in size in the United States, fourth in educational institutions, and first among American state universities.[3]

From the Yale University Babylonian Collection, the Foundation purchased in 1930 a group of twenty carefully selected clay tablets representing the Old Babylonian (Period of Hammurabi) and the Neo-Babylonian (Period of Nebuchadnezzar) eras of cuneiform writing. To this collection have been added other Sumerian and Babylonian cones, tablets, and seals illustrating the different types of ancient writing upon clay. Through these brick-like records with their wedge-shaped inscriptions, it is possible to trace this form of writing from 2350 B.C. to 500 B.C. Other precursors of the printed book include prehistoric pebbles from the caves of Mas d'Azil in

2. For a complete list up to August, 1940, see Olan V. Cook, comp., *Incunabula in the Hanes Collection of the Library of the University of North Carolina* (Chapel Hill, North Carolina, 1940).
3. Fremont Rider, "Holdings of Incunabula in American University Libraries," *Library Quarterly*, IX (July, 1939), 273-84.

France, inscribed with curious characters in red; leather scrolls; Greek, Coptic, and Demotic ostraka; an ancient Peruvian quipu; papyrus rolls with red and black hieroglyphic inscriptions; Palmyrene tessera; and olas or Indian palm leaf books. Also helpful in the appreciation of these specimens are ink wells, styli, and other writing instruments used by the ancient scribes.

Where original examples of the forerunners of the printed book were not obtainable, facsimile copies have been acquired. All of these represent steps in the development of writing and of the book, many of which have been obtained because of their importance to research in classical antiquities. Among them are plaster casts of monumental inscriptions both Greek and Roman, the *Palatine Virgil, Codex Alexanderinus,* the *Rockefeller-McCormick New Testament,* the Rosetta Stone, the *Lutrell Psalter, Codex Sinaiticus, Codex Nuttall, Oxyrhynchus Papyri, Book of Kells,* and *Die Wiener Genesis.*

The collections of incunabula and the predecessors of the printed book are important units of the Hanes Foundation, but there is a third group of equal importance, which includes examples of good printing from 1500 to the present time. It contains about five hundred items of sixteenth-, seventeenth-, and eighteenth-century printing, including the work of the Estiennes, Elzevirs, Didots, Tory, Plantin, Baskerville, Bodoni, and the Aldine Press, as well as illustrative examples from ninety private presses of the nineteenth and twentieth centuries, including the designs of Updike, Goudy, Hunter, De Vinne, the Grabhorns, Rogers, Rudge, Morris, and Morison. There is also a collection of seventy-five different editions of the Bible imprinted before 1800, supplemented by later Bibles and Testaments printed in twenty-five different languages. Emphasis is placed on the acquisition of distinctive current examples of printing, type design, illustrations, and binding.

In developing a collection of materials for the study of the origin and development of the book, it is essential to supplement actual examples and facsimiles by a wide variety of textual and descriptive material. To the Hanes Collection there have been added the more important histories of writing and writing materials; a large body of literature dealing with the origin and history of printing; biographies of printers, type designers, and paper makers; bibliographies of printing; and the notable descriptive bibliographies of incunabula. Among the latter are Hain's *Repertorium bibliographicum* and the supplements by Copinger and Reichling, the *Catalogue of Books Printed in the XVth Century Now in the British Museum*, together with Robert Proctor's index to the early printed books in the British Museum and the Bodleian Library. In addition, there are the *Gesamtkatalog der Wiegendrucke*, Panzer's *Annales*, and the work of Konrad Burger, M. F. A. G. Campbell, Anatole Claudin, Edward Gordon Duff, Konrad Haebler, Marie Pellechet, M.-Louis Polain, William Ludwig Schreiber, Ernst Voulliéme, and William Henry James Weale.

Dr. Hanes has maintained a generous and continuing interest in the Collection. Since the establishment of the Foundation, he has presented many fine items from his private library, including a leaf from the Gutenberg Bible; *The Golden Legend* of Jacobus de Voragine, printed in London by Julian Notary in 1503; *Aesop's Fables* from the press of Aldus Manutius, 1505; St. Augustine's *City of God*, a remarkably fine example of typography executed by Nicolaus Jenson in 1472, and leaves from the 1460 *Catholicon* and William Caxton's *Polycronicon* of 1482. Also, he was instrumental in obtaining for the Collection through Mr. John Wise a greatly desired early Peruvian quipu.

The Foundation has attracted many other gifts. Among them are the Hunter Collection of manuscripts and materials comprising one hundred medieval manuscripts, account books, diaries, official documents, unpublished poems, and dramas; a well preserved papyrus Book of the Dead received from Matthew P. Gilmour; early Spanish manuscripts from Philip H. Cummings; a copy of the Breeches Bible from the Reverend J. T. Mangum; several volumes of incunabula, including Higden's *Polycronicon*, printed in Westminster by Wynkyn de Worde in 1495, Indian palm leaf books and fine examples of printing relating to India and Ceylon from Dr. W. P. Jacocks; and gifts of money and books from John Motley Morehead and the Reverend R. G. Shannonhouse. One of the most recent acquisitions of importance is a collection of twenty pieces of "archaeologica," including clay tablets, cylinder seals, necklaces, and figurines dating from 2250 to 400 B.C., received from Arthur L. Stearns in honor of Leslie Weil.[4]

The University is fortunate in the possession and use of this important collection on the history of the book. It provides exceptional means to stimulate appreciation of the artistic and intellectual development of mankind and the preservation and dissemination of the written and printed word. To these ends the Collection is used liberally and effectively. It is of special significance and usefulness to the departments of Ancient History, European History, Greek, Latin, German, Romance Languages, English, Art, and Archaeology; the University Press, and the School of Library Science. Selections from the Collection are frequently placed on exhibition in the Library and more frequently are used in public lectures and class instruction. The incunabula items are on constant, protected display in the Browsing Room.

During the depression years the Library was unable to expand and develop the Foundation as rapidly as planned. However, within recent years many acquisitions have been made. Plans for the future call for increased emphasis on rounding out the Collection and for its location in distinctive quarters in an enlarged library building.

4. For description, see *The Bookmark* (Chapel Hill: Friends of the Library of the University of North Carolina), no. 3 (Aug., 1944), p. 3.

III

BIBLIOGRAPHY AND REFERENCE

Chapter 6

BIBLIOGRAPHICAL APPARATUS

Georgia H. Faison

A GENEROUS GRANT in 1932 from the General Education Board provided an effective stimulus in carrying on the Library's program of building up a bibliographical collection adequate for the University's research needs. With this material assistance, gratifying progress was made. Much still remains to be done before the bibliographical holdings can be measured by the same yardstick applied nationally to university and other large research libraries. As is inevitable during periods of sporadic expansion, the growth within the various fields of interest has been uneven. It reflects faithfully, however, contemporary research interests, restrictions stipulated in grants received, and the incalculable returns in the second-hand book trade of such monumental sets as the old edition of the British Museum *Catalogue*.

Subject bibliographies as a class have been omitted from this survey of bibliographical resources. An enumeration of such titles fits more logically into the separate chapters devoted to discussions of their related fields. A few general and some specific ones not falling naturally into any of the chapter-subject-divisions are included here.

It would be impractical also to list separately the bibliographies devoted to the works of, or about, an individual. For this study it will suffice to say that there are over four hundred such titles, which run the gamut from publishers' pamphlets to two and three-volume sets, such as Rius y de Llosellers' *Bibliografía crítica de las obras de Miguel de Cervantes Saavedra;* the catalogue of *The R. B. Adam Library Relating to Dr. Samuel Johnson and His Era;* and Holmes's *Cotton Mather, a Bibliography of His Works.* Tannenbaum's series of *Elizabethan Bibliographies* is also included in this class.

UNION CATALOGUES OF PRINTED BOOKS

The Library's union card catalogue is divided physically into a general catalogue and a state regional one. The general union catalogue contains complete files of author cards for the Library of Congress, the John Crerar Library, and the Folger Shakespeare Library. There are partial files of cards from the following university libraries: Harvard, Princeton, Chicago, and Wesleyan. Since 1938 the Microfilm Abstract cards for doctoral dissertations have been added.

The state regional catalogue is an outgrowth of the North Carolina-Duke University program, inaugurated in 1934, for greater co-operation between the two universities. At this time the libraries of the two universities exchanged files of their author-entry cards, and agreed to supply each other with cards for current acquisitions. Since then, from time to time, this Library has received cards from other North Carolina libraries. Cards for current acquisitions, with a few exceptions, have been received from the North Carolina State College Library since 1937, and since October, 1944, from the Woman's College of the University of North Carolina. Cards for works by and about the Baptists have been supplied by the Wake Forest College Library and similar ones concerning the Quakers by Guilford College Library. Several Negro college libraries in the state have contributed their cards for material pertaining to the Negro. There are partial files of cards also for the Sondley Memorial Library in Asheville and the Charlotte Public Library.

The union card catalogues are supplemented by the following printed union lists of material to be found in American libraries: William Warner Bishop's *A Preliminary Checklist of American Copies of Short Title Catalog Books;* Murray Barnson Emeneau's *A Union List of Printed Indic Texts and Translations in American Libraries;* the *Union List of Microfilm;* and *International Congresses and Conferences, 1840–1937, a Union List of Their Publications.*

LIBRARY CATALOGUES AND UNION LISTS OF FOREIGN COLLECTIONS

The Library is subscribing to the four national library catalogues now in progress: the photoreproduced-book edition of the Library of Congress depository set of cards; the *Catalogue général des livres imprimés;* the edition of the British Museum *Catalogue,* begun in 1931; and the *Gesamtkatalog der preussischen Bibliotheken.*

Supplementary to the union catalogues and lists of American collections and the three major foreign catalogues in progress, the Library has many catalogues of smaller libraries, special collections, and lists of union holdings in foreign countries. Among the most useful titles in the American and English group are those for the following collections: Ashley Library; Astor Library; American Antiquarian Society; Boston Athenaeum; John Carter Brown Library; *Church Catalogue of Books Relating to North and South America; Americana Collection of Herschel V. Jones;* Wymberley Jones De Renne Library; Peabody Institute; Princeton University; Wrenn Library; Henry E. Huntington Library; the Cornell University Library check lists of its Dante, Icelandic, French Revolution, and Protestant Reformation material; Surgeon-General's Office; The Carl H. Pforzheimer Library; Wisconsin State Historical Society; British Museum *Subject Index;* Faculty of Advocates; John Rylands Library; London Library, *Bibliotheca Lindesiana; Catalogue of the Pamphlets ... Relating to the Civil War ... Collected by Thomason;* the music collections in the Library of Congress, British Museum, Boston Public, and the Philadelphia Free Library; *Catalogue* of the national history division of the British Museum; *Bibliotheca Osleriana; Harvey Cushing Collection of Books in the Yale University Library;* Royal Empire Society of London; Foreign Office; India Office; and the Royal Statistical Society of London.

The major titles in the section of foreign language catalogues and union lists are the following: *Berliner Titeldrucke; Catálogo del "Fondo Anselmo Pineda,"* National Library in Bogotá; *"Museo Mitre"; Catálogos de la Biblioteca Provincial de Léon;*

Catálogo de sus libros impresos of the Biblioteca Colombina in Seville; *Catalogue abrégé de la Bibliothèque Sainte-Geneviève; Catáloga de la Biblioteca* of the University of Valladolid; *Catalogue* of the Peace Palace; *Catalogue de l'histoire de l'Amerique* of the Bibliothèque Nationale; and the catalogues of the J. T. Medina library bequeathed to Chile and located in the National Library in Santiago de Chile.

CATALOGUES OF MANUSCRIPTS

The collection of catalogues of manuscripts contains between two and three hundred volumes. For France there are eighty-one volumes of the set, *Catalogue général des manuscrits des bibliothèques publiques de France; Catalogue des manuscrits de la Bibliothèque de la Ville de Chartres;* the Bibliothèque Nationale's *Catalogue général des manuscrits français. Ancien fonds;* and its separate catalogues for the German manuscripts, the Mexican manuscripts, and the Spanish and Portuguese manuscripts.

Among the catalogues of British collections are the old Casley and Ayscough catalogues of the manuscripts in the British Museum, followed by those of the Cottonian, Harleian, and Lansdowne collections, which are supplemented in turn by the series of catalogues listing the *Additional Manuscripts.* The three-volume *Catalogue of Romances* and the *Catalogue of the Manuscripts in the Spanish Language* are owned as well. Sixteen of the James catalogues of manuscripts in the various college libraries of Cambridge University, and his records of the collections at Eton College, at the Lambeth Palace, and in the John Rylands Library are available also. For the Bodleian Library there is Madan's *Summary Catalogue of the Western Manuscripts.* Smaller collections represented by catalogues are to be found in the India Office Library, the Public Records Office, the library of Westminster Abbey, and the chapter libraries of Worcester Cathedral and Lincoln Cathedral. The *Reports of the Historical Manuscripts Commission* are also in the collection.

Other foreign catalogues of manuscripts are for scattered

collections. The Carnegie Institution's series of check lists and catalogues of source material for American history contained in the archives of foreign countries is complete.

There are catalogues for the following Spanish collections: *Bibliotheca arabico-hispana escurialensis; Catálogo de los manuscritos existentes en la Biblioteca Universitaria de Valencia, Catálogo de los manuscritos de la Biblioteca Municipal* (Madrid); *Catálogo de los manuscritos que pertenecieron a D. Pascual de Gayangos existentes hoy en la Biblioteca Nacional;* and *Catálogo de las piezas de teatro que se conservan en... la Biblioteca Nacional.* For Italy, the Library has: *Codicum Casinensium manuscriptorum catalogus cura et studio monachorum S. Benedicti archicoenobii Montis Casini;* Pierre de Nolhac's *La Bibliothèque de Fulvio Orsini,* and *Codices Vaticani Graeci,* vol. 1.

There are also a few catalogues of special collections, such as the *Catalogue of the Greek Manuscripts in the Library of the Laura on Mount Athos,* and Diels's *Die Handschriften den antiken Aerzte... auftrage der akademischen Kommission.*

A tangible evidence of the deep interest that American libraries have manifested in collecting manuscript material since the beginning of the twentieth century is the large number of published guides and check lists that have appeared in recent years. Among those that the Library has acquired are the following: Seymour de Ricci's *Census of Medieval and Renaissance Manuscripts in the United States and Canada;* Clark's *Descriptive Catalogue of Greek New Testament Manuscripts in America;* Wilson's *Catalogue of Latin and Vernacular Alchemical Manuscripts in the United States and Canada; A Catalogue of the Medieval and Renaissance Manuscripts and Incunabula in the Boston Medical Library; Guide to the Manuscript Collections in the Duke University Library; Guide to the Manuscript Collections in the William L. Clements Library of American History; The Harkness Collection in the Library of Congress. Calendar of Spanish Manuscripts Concerning Peru, 1531–1651; Check List of Manuscripts in the Edward E. Ayer Collection* in the Newberry Library; *Guide to the Manuscript Collections in the Archives of the North Carolina Historical*

Commission; Guide to the Manuscripts in the Southern Historical Collection of the University of North Carolina; the Philadelphia Free Library's two catalogues describing the John Frederick Lewis Collections of European and Oriental Manuscripts; *Guide to the Latin American Manuscripts in the University of Texas Library; An Inventory of the Manuscript Collections of the Department of Middle American Research,* Tulane University; *Guide to the Personal Papers in the Manuscript Collections of the Minnesota Historical Society; Survey of the Manuscript Collections of the New York Historical Society;* and the State Historical Society of Wisconsin's calendars of special papers forming a part of the Draper Collection. In addition to these titles, there are many guides to special collections of personal papers and inventories of archival holdings among the publications of the Historical Records Survey.

INCUNABULA AND RARE BOOKS CATALOGUES

The Hanes Foundation for the Study of the Origin and Development of the Book, established in 1929, quickened the Library's interest in incunabula and rare books. With this impetus much attention has been given to collecting the monumental sets of incunabula catalogues and the history of individual presses, both early and modern. The holdings in this particular field form what is probably the most complete bibliographical collection in the Library.

Most of the major catalogues have been acquired, such as Hain, Copinger, Reichling, Panzer, Pellechet, Polain, *Gesamtkatalog der Wiegendrucke,* the British Museum *Catalogue of Books Printed in the 15th Century;* Stillwell's *Incunabula in American Libraries* and Peddie's *Conspectus incunabulorum.* Supplementary to these general catalogues and union lists, the Library has a number of the catalogues of special collections and those from smaller libraries. The most interesting of these are the following: *Catalogue des incunables de la Bibliothèque Mazarine; Check List of Fifteenth Century Printing in the Pierpont Morgan Library;* the Newberry Library's *Check List; Incunabula in the Huntington Library;* Kleb's *Incunabula scientifica et medica; Katalog der Inkunabeln der Kgl. Bibliothek in Stockholm; Catálogo de incunables y libros raros de la Santa Iglesia Catedral de Segovia*, and *Incunabula in the Hanes Collection of the Library of the University of North Carolina.*

GENERAL BIBLIOGRAPHIES

Practically all of the older general bibliographies of importance, such as Brunet, Ebert, Georgi, Grässe, and Quaritch, are available. The more recent titles are represented by Peddie's *Subject Index of Books Published Before 1880;* Besterman's *A World Bibliography of Bibliographies; Bibliographic Index; Index bibliographicus; Internationale Bibliographie;* and *Internationaler Jahresbericht der Bibliographie.*

NATIONAL BIBLIOGRAPHY

The most satisfactory collections of national bibliographies are for the following countries: the United States, Great Britain, France, Germany, Spain, and the Latin American nations. For other nationalities the holdings are scattered over a wide territory and are fragmentary in quantity.

United States.—The holdings for the American field include all of the major titles such as: Bradford, Evans, Harrisse, and Sabin. Sets of Roorbach, Kelly, Trübner, and the *American Catalogue,* with its run of continuations and supplements, are complete.

As a federal documents depository, the Library has received the Historical Records Survey's *American Imprints Inventory* series. In addition to these publications, a moderately large number of the books issued commercially during the past decade which list regional, state, and local American imprints have been added to the collection.

Great Britain.—From the English section the following titles are available: Lowndes; Watt; Hazlitt; the *Stationers' Company's Transcript;* the *Term Catalogues;* the *English Catalogue* with supplementary trade publications; the British Museum's *Catalogue of Books . . . Printed . . . to the year 1640;* Cambridge

University Library's *Early English Printed Books; Short-title Catalogue*, and other similar early-period bibliographies sponsored by the Bibliographical Society of London; *Britwell Handlist;* Collier's *Rarest Books in the English Language;* Corser's *Collectanea Anglo-poetica;* Brydges' *Censura literaria* and his *Restituta;* Dix's *Catalogue of Early Dublin-printed Books;* Aldis' *List of Books Printed in Scotland;* Maclean's *Typographia Scoto-Gadelica;* John Bale's *Index Brittanniae scriptorum;* Tanner's *Bibliotheca Brittanico-Hibernica;* the Lambeth Palace catalogue of early printed books; Russell's *Dictionary of Writers of Thirteenth Century England;* Hoe Catalogue of Books by English Authors; and Bloom's *English Tracts, Pamphlets, and Printed Sheets.*

For regional British imprints there are Madan's *Oxford Books;* Bowes's *Catalogue of Books... Relating to... Cambridge;* the Gloucester Public Library's *Catalogue of the Gloucestershire Collection;* and Hyett's *The Bibliographer's Manual of Gloucestershire Literature.* Dobell's and Martin's catalogues are available for the privately printed book.

France.—French national bibliography is covered by these titles: Lorenz; Quérard (both series); Vicaire; Rothschild; "Biblio"; *Librairie française;* Carteret; Le Petit; *Répertoire de bibliographie française;* and the British Museum's *Short-title Catalogue of Books Printed in France.*

Germany.—For Germany the long Heinsius-Hinrichs-Kayser-Deutsches Bücherverzeichnis series is complete with the exception of eleven (vols. 7-19) volumes of Heinsius. This series is supplemented by Georg's *Schlagwort-katalog* and the *Deutscher Literatur-katalog.*

Spain and Portugal.—The list of major titles of Spanish national bibliography is fairly long. It contains for the early period Antonio's *Bibliotheca hispana vetus* and his *Bibliotheca hispana nova;* the British Museum's *Short-title Catalogue of Books Printed in Spain and of Spanish Books Printed Elsewhere in Europe Before 1601;* Burger's *Die Drucker und Verleger in Spanien und Portugal von 1501–1536;* Haebler's *Bibliografía ibérica del siglo xv;* and the Hispanic Society of America Library's *List of Books Printed Before 1601.* For longer and more recent periods there are the following: *Bibliografía española; Bibliografía general española, 1929–;*[1] *Catálogo general de la librería española e hispanoamericana, 1901–;* Gallardo's *Ensayo de una biblioteca española de libros raros y curiosos;* Hidalgo's *Diccionario general de bibliografía española;* Heredia y Livermore's *Catalogue de la bibliothèque de M. Ricardo Heredia;* Molina's *Indice para facilitar el manejo y consulta de los catálogos de Salva y Heredia;* Palau y Dulcet's *Manual del librero hispano-americano;* and Salvá y Pérez's *Catálogo de la biblioteca de Salvá.*

There are regional bibliographies for the following localities: Valladolid, Saragossa, Seville, Guadalajara, Burgos, Cadiz, Madrid, Medina del Campo, Toledo, Cordoba, Aragon, Murcia, Valencia, Catalonia and the Balearic Islands.

As supplementary aids there are Foulché-Delbosc's *Manuel de l'hispanisant* and three catalogues of American collections: *Spain and Spanish America in the Libraries of the University of California; The Spanish Drama Collection in the Oberlin College Library,* and the Boston Public Library's *Catalogue of the Spanish and Portuguese Books Bequeathed by George Ticknor.*

In addition to the Portuguese items included in the titles listed above, the Library has the following records of Portuguese imprints: Anselmo's *Bibliografía das obras impressas em Portugal no século XVI;* Barbosa's *Summario da Bibliotheca Luzitana;* the British Museum's *Short-title Catalogues of Portuguese Books and of Spanish American Books Printed Before 1601; Livros antigos portuguezes 1489–1600, da bibliotheca de Sua Majestade Fidelissima;* and *Catalogue de la bibliothèque de M. Fernando Palha.*

Latin America.–In 1940 the University of North Carolina became one of the participants in a Rockefeller grant made to a group of three Southern universities to stimulate interest in South American studies. As a part of this program the Latin American section is receiving much attention. No attempt has been made to list here many of the bibliographies of local or regional imprints. For Latin American countries in general there are the following titles: Medina's *Biblioteca hispano-americana*

1. Dates unterminated indicate work still in progress.

(1493–1810); Beristain de Souza's *Biblioteca hispano-americana setentrional;* Vindel's *Manual gráfico-descriptivo del bibliófilo hispano-americano* (1475–1850); and Luquiens' *Spanish American Literature in the Yale University Library* in addition to a number of serial publications which include the *Bibliographies of Hispano-American Literature,* published by the Harvard Council on Hispano-American Literature; the *Handbook of Latin American Studies,* 1935–; the *Pan American Bookshelf,* 1938–; and *Inter-American Bibliographical Review,* 1941–.

Some of the titles for separate countries are given below.

Argentine Republic.—Comisión Nacional de Cultura's *Obras y autores presentados en los distintos concursos;* Pinto's *Panorama de la literatura argentina contemporánea;* and *Boletín bibliográfico argentino.*

Brazil.—Alves do Sacramento Blake's *Diccionario bibliographico brazileiro;* Simões dos Reis's *Bibliografía das bibliografías brasileiras;* Velho Sobrimho's *Dicionário bio-bibliográfico brasileiro;* and *Bibliografía brasileira,* 1938–.

Chile.—Medina's *Biblioteca hispano-chilena* (1523–1817); Medina's *La literatura feminina en Chile;* Medina's *La imprenta en Lima (1584–1824);* and Briseño's *Estadística bibliográfica de la literatura chilena.*

Colombia.—Laverde Amaya's *Bibliografía columbiana,* vol. 1; Medina's *La imprenta en Bogotá* (1739–1821); and Posada's *Bibliografía bogotana.*

Costa Rica.—Dobles Segreda's *Indice bibliográfico de Costa Rica.*

Cuba.—Incomplete set of Trelles y Govín's sixteen-volume series of Cuban bibliography; Medina's *La imprenta en la Habana (1707–1810)* and *Anuario bibliográfico cubano,* 1937–.

Guatemala.—Medina's *La imprenta en Guatemala (1660–1821).*

Mexico.—Medina's *La imprenta en Mexico (1539–1821); Guía del Archivo Histórico de Hacienda, 1940–; Catalogue of Mexican Pamphlets in the Sutro Collection (1623–1888)* of the California State Library; Leon's *Bibliografía mexicana del siglo xviii; Anuario bibliográfico mexicano, 1888–* (incomplete file); *Monografías bibliográficas mexicanas* (23 titles).

Peru.—Medina's *La imprenta en Lima* (1584–1824), Schwab's *Bibliografía de libros y folletos peruanos;* and *Biblioteca peruana.*

Puerto Rico.—Pedreira's *Bibliografía puertorriqueña* (1493–1930).

MISCELLANEOUS FOREIGN NATIONAL BIBLIOGRAPHY

In addition to the national bibliographies enumerated in the preceding sections, the collection contains a miscellaneous group of broad terrritorial range, but limited in the coverage of any particular country. The most important of these titles are given below by country:

Arabia.—Chauvin's *Bibliographie des ouvrages arabes ou relatifs aux arabes.*

Australia.—Foxcroft's *The Australian Catalogue* and *Miller's Australian Literature from its Beginning to 1935.*

Belgium and Holland.—*Bibliotheca Belgica; Bibliotheca Hulthemiana;* Campbell's *Annales de la typographie néerlandaise* (vol. 1); Nijhoff's and Kronenberg's *Nederlandsche Bibliographie;* Brinkmann's *Catalogus van Boeken;* and Brinkmann's *Titel-catalogus.*

Canada.—*Bulletin bibliographique de la Société des Ecrivains Canadiens, 1941–; The Canadian Catalogue of Books Published in Canada, 1921/22–; Catalogue of Pamphlets in the Public Archives of Canada;* Dionne's *Inventaire chronologique;* Haight's *Canadian Catalogue of Books;* and Morgan's *Bibliotheca Canadensis.*

Czechoslovakia.—*Bibliografický katalog Československé Republiky.*

Italy.—Haym's *Biblioteca italiana; Bibliothèque Joseph Martini;* Pagliaini's *Catalogo generale della libreria italiana; Catalogo dei cataloghi del libro italiano;* and *La scheda cumulativa italiana.*

The Scandinavian countries.—Bruun's *Bibliotheca Danica;* Pattersen's *Bibliotheca Norvegica; Sveriges bibliografi intill år 1600,* vol. 1; and Wegener's *Bibliotheca Wegeneriana.*

LIBRARY RESOURCES

DICTIONARIES OF ANONYMS AND PSEUDONYMS

The Library lists the following titles in its collection of dictionaries of anonyms and pseudonyms: Franklin's *Dictionnaire des noms, surnoms et pseudonymes latins de l'histoire littéraire du moyen âge;* Weller's *Lexicon pseudonymorum;* Cushing's *Initials and Pseudonyms;* Halket and Laing's *Dictionary of Anonymous and Pseudonymous English Literature;* Stonehill's *Anonyma and Pseudonyma;* Thomas' *Handbook of Fictitious Names;* Barbier's *Dictionnaire des ouvrages anonymes;* Brunet's *Dictionnaire des ouvrages anonymes;* Quérard's *Les Supercheries littéraires dévoilées;* Holzmann's *Deutsches Anonymenlexikon;* Figarola-Caneda's *Diccionario de seudónimos;* Hartzenbusch é Hiriart's *Unos cuantos seudónimos de escritores españoles;* Medina's *Diccionario de anónimos y seudónimos hispanoamericanos;* and Victorica's *Errores y omisiones de diccionario de anónimos y pseudónimos hispanoamericanos de ... Medina.*

MAPS

The following bibliographical guides are available for work with maps: the several check lists of the collections in the Library of Congress, prepared by Philip Lee Phillips; *Bibliotheca geographica; Catalogue of the Printed Maps, Plans, and Charts in the British Museum;* Claussen's and Friis's *Descriptive Catalog of Maps Published by Congress, 1817–1843;* Thiele's *Official Map Publication; Atlases in Libraries of Chicago; a Bibliography and Union Checklist;* American Geographical Society of New York's *A Description of Early Maps, Originals and Facsimiles (1452–1611); Catalogo ragionato della mostra geografica retrospettiva della Biblioteca Nazionale (Braidense) di Milano, manoscritti e stampe dei secoli XV-XIX;* Winsor's *The Kohl Collection ... of Maps Relating to America; British Headquarters Maps and Sketches Used by Sir Henry Clinton While in Command of the British Forces ... in North America During ... 1775–1782; A Descriptive List of the Original Manuscripts ... now Preserved in the William L. Clements Library *at the University of Michigan;* Wilgus' *Maps Relating to Latin America in Books and Periodicals;* and the American Geographical Society of New York's *Catalogue of Maps of Hispanic America.*

DISSERTATIONS AND RECORDS OF WORK IN PROGRESS

Bibliographical guides for work in progress and accepted dissertations are fairly complete for American institutions. For foreign dissertations the coverage is limited. The American guides include the Library of Congress lists; *Doctoral Dissertations Accepted by American Universities;* and a large collection of individual lists issued by American universities.

For foreign dissertations there are these lists: Fock's *Bibliographischer Monatsbericht über neu erschienene Schul- und Universitätsschriften;* Mundt's *Bio-bibliographisches Verzeichnis;* the *Thesis Supplement* of the Institute of Historical Research; the list published by the University of Vienna; and an incomplete file of *Catalogue des thèses et écrits académiques* of the French Ministry of Public Instruction. The Library has a collection of approximately ten thousand uncatalogued German dissertations, for which an author check list has been prepared.

The following four publications listing work in progress are received: *List of Doctoral Dissertations in History now in Progress; Progress of Medieval and Renaissance Studies in the United States and Canada; The United States, 1865–1900, a Survey of Current Literature;* and *Work in Progress...in the Modern Humanities.*

Chapter 7

REFERENCE RESOURCES

Georgia H. Faison

APPARENTLY there is no accepted criterion for measuring the scope or determining the character of what is nominally called the "general reference collection" of a university library system in institutions in which only a limited amount of duplication is feasible. The line of demarcation separating the commonly considered general reference guides from the more specialized and detailed types is influenced by the Library's departmentalization policies, the institution's teaching program, and the physical facilities for housing and administering various types of materials. In this particular instance, the attempt not to stray too far into subject fields receiving special attention in other chapters of this survey enforces additional limitations upon this inventory of the Library's reference resources. At best it can be only suggestive.

GENERAL MATERIALS

Approximately two thousand titles exclusive of bibliographical works are shelved within the main reading room. This collection consists for the most part of the representative basic reference sets, such as the *Encyclopaedia Brittanica*, *Dictionary of American Biography*, Hastings' *Encyclopedia of Religion and Ethics*, the 1940 Census Reports, the *New English Dictionary*, the Cambridge histories of American and English literature, and the Cambridge series of ancient, medieval, and modern histories in addition to the usual accumulation of handbooks to meet the "quick-reference" requests. This fundamental collection, adequate for ordinary reference purposes, is supplemented by a number of the older, more scholarly and more detailed reference sets.

Encyclopedias.—Among the older general encyclopedias and

the more comprehensive foreign language titles are several editions of Bayle's *Dictionnaire historique et critique;* Diderot's *Encyclopédie,* 1751–65, with supplementary volumes; the third and ninth editions of the *Encyclopaedia Britannica;* Ripley and Dana's *The New American Cyclopedia; Enciclopedia universal ilustrada europeo-americana; Enciclopedia italiana de scienze, lettere ed arti; La Grande encyclopédie,* the Larousse series; and *Encyclopédie française,* 1935–.[1]

Dictionaries.—In addition to the standard American and English dictionaries, there are the following titles: *Dictionary of American English on Historical Principles; Dictionary of the Older Scottish Tongue,* 1931–; *Scottish National Dictionary,* 1931–; Farmer's *Slang and Its Analogues Past and Present;* Thornton's *An American Glossary;* and Wright's *Dictionary of Obsolete and Provincial English.* Among older titles are: Samuel Johnson's *Dictionary of the English Language,* 1755; *Minshaei emendatio,* 1627; and Dyche's *A New General English Dictionary,* 1794.

The list of foreign language dictionaries includes, besides such languages as French, German, Greek, Italian, Latin, and Spanish, the following other languages: Arabic, Bohemian, Chinese, Danish, Dutch, Egyptian, Hebrew, Icelandic, Indo-European, Irish, Lettish, Lithuanian, Norwegian, Pali, Polish, Russian, Roumanian, Sanskrit, Swedish, Turkish, and Welsh. The most comprehensive titles in this group are the following: *Dictionnaire de l'Academie Française* (8 éd.); Littré's *Dictionnaire de la langue française;* Huguet's *Dictionnaire de la langue française du seizième siècle,* 1925–; Godefroy's *Dictionnaire de l'ancienne langue française;* Sainte-Palaye's *Dictionnaire historique de l'ancien langage français; Tobler-Lommatzsch altfranzösisches Wörterbuch,* 1925–; *Grimm's Deutsches Wörterbuch,* 1854–; *Thesaurus linguae Latinae,* 1900–; *Diccionario de la lengua española* of the Academia Española; *Slovaŕ russkago iazyka sostavlemnnii Vtorym otdieleniyem Imperatorkoi Akademii nauk,* 1895–; *Tolkovyi slovar zhivogo velikorusskago yazyka Vladimira Dalya;* Du Cange's *Glossarium mediae et infimae latinitatis;* Alcover Sureda's *Diccionari català-valen-*

cià-balear, 1930–; Raynouard's *Lexique roman;* "*Diccionari Aguiló*"; Mistral's *Lou trésor dóu Felibrige; ou, Dictionnaire provençal-français;* the Royal Irish Academy's *Dictionary of the Irish Language;* and *Hessens irisches Lexikon.*

Biographical dictionaries.—The Library owns the standard national biographical dictionaries for America, Great Britain, and Germany; and for Austria, the *Neue österreichische Biographie, 1815–1918.* It is subscribing to *Dictionnaire biographie française,* 1933–; and the *Biographie nationale* of the Royal Academy of Belgium. For several other nationalities, particularly the South American countries, there are either smaller sets or one-volume editions. With the exception of the long runs of *Who's Who* and *Who's Who in America,* the collection is weak in the field of current national biography. Among the older general titles are Michaud's *Biographie universelle;* Chalmer's *The General Biographical Dictionary;* and Rose's *A New General Biographical Dictionary.* A list of the more specialized titles include these: Clinton's *Fasti Hellenici* and his *Fasti Romani;* Le Neve's *Fasti ecclesiae Anglicanae;* Wood's *Athenae Oxonienses;* Cooper's *Athenae Cantabrigienses;* Dexter's *Biographical Sketches of the Graduates of Yale College;* Sibley's *Biographical Sketches of Graduates of Harvard University;* Haag's *La France protestante;* Musgrave's *Obituary prior to 1800;* Fetis' *Biographie universelle des musiciens;* Chevalier's *Répertoire des sources historiques du moyen âge;* Poggendorff's *biographisch-literarisches Handwörterbuch;* Russell's *Dictionary of Writers of Thirteenth Century England;* Wickersheimer's *Dictionnaire biographique des médecins en France au moyen âge;* and Talvart and Place's *Bibliographie des auteurs modernes de langue française (1801–1927).*

SUBJECT-FIELD HANDBOOKS, MANUALS, AND COMPREHENSIVE HISTORIES

For broad subject fields, there is the usual collection of familiar reference guides, supplemented in turn by a limited inclusion of the more specialized and detailed type.

Philosophy and religion.—Among the titles in this field are the following: Eisler's *Wörterbuch der philosophischen Begriffe;* Friedrich Ueberweg's *Grundriss der Geschichte der Philosophie;* Cabrol's *Dictionnaire d'archéologie chrétienne et de liturgie; Sacred Books of the East,* edited by Max Müller; *Encyclopaedia of Islam;* Roscher's *Ausführliches Lexikon der griechischen und römischen Mythologie;* Schaff's *Bibliotheca symbolica ecclesiae universalis;* Rodkinson's edition of the *Talmud in English;* Ginzberg's *Legends of the Jews;* and Winter and Wünsche's *Geschichte der jüdisch-hellenistischen und Talmudischen Litteratur.*

Social sciences.—The collection of annuals, handbooks, state manuals, and small subject encyclopedias and dictionaries is sufficiently ample to cover the social science subjects in a general way. For more detailed work there are the *Encyclopaedia of the Social Sciences; Grundriss der Sozialökonomik;* Palgrave's *Dictionary of Political Economy; Handwörterbuch der Staatswissenschaften;* Andrée's *Geographie des Welthandel; Annual Register;* Toynbee's *Survey of International Affairs; United States in World Affairs; Inter-American Affairs; A Political Handbook of the World;* Rogers' *History of Agriculture and Prices in England ... 1259 ... to ... 1793; Handwörterbuch des deutschen Aberglaubens;* Lean's *Collectanea;* Dähnhardt's *Natursagen;* and Thompson's *Motif-index of Folk-literature.*

Sciences and fine arts.—In the fields of science and the fine arts, the main collection contains little material other than the better known general encyclopedias, dictionaries, handbooks, and brief outline-subject histories. Among the exceptions to these more popular titles are Viollet-Le Duc's *Dictionnaire raisonné de l'architecture française;* Sarton's *Introduction to the History of Science;* and *Cambridge Natural History.*

Literature.—The Library offers such guides for universal literature as the British Museum's *Catalogue of Romances in the Department of Manuscripts;* Klein's *Geschichte des Dramas;* Creizenach's *Geschichte der neuren Dramas;* Bartels' *Einführung in die Weltliteratur;* Royer's *Histoire universelle du théâtre;* Mantzius' *History of Theatrical Art in Ancient and Modern Times;* Brandes' *Main Currents in 19th Century Literature;* and *Bibliothèque de la revue de littérature comparée.*

The holdings of handbooks and indexes for individual authors in general are only fair. The collection of concordances offers titles for the following: Beda Venerabilis, Beowulf, Boethius, Browning, Caesar, Catullus, Chaucer, Cicero, Clemens, Coleridge, Collins, Cowper, Dante, Donne, Emerson, Goethe, Goldsmith, Gray, Herrick, Housman, Horace, Keats, Kyd, Lanier, Lucan, Lucretius Carus, Marlowe (incomplete), Milton, Ovid, Petrarch, Poe, Propertius, Prudentius Clemens, Shakespeare, Shelley, Spenser, Suetonius, Tacitus, Tennyson, Terence, Vergil, Wordsworth, and Wyatt.

The fields of American and English literature are well supplied with the fundamental guides in English. The collection of quotation encyclopedias, allusion books, indexes (to plays, poetry, short stories, etc.), manuals, and other similar handbooks is especially strong, since it has been developed not only to meet the ordinary needs of the Library, but to serve also as a working collection for the University's School of Library Science.

Listed among the more specialized guides, inclusive histories, and complementary material are *Notes and Queries*, 1850–; Nichols' *Illustrations* and *Literary Anecdotes of the Eighteenth Century;* Courthope's *History of English Poetry;* Baker's *History of the English Novel;* Chambers' *The Medieval Stage* and *The Elizabethan Stage;* Bentley's *The Jacobean and Caroline Stage;* Allardyce Nicoll's series of books dealing with eighteenth- and nineteenth-century English drama; and the series *Materialien zur Kunde des älteren englischen Dramas* with its continuation. Among the older titles of dramatic records are Fleay, Genest, Henslowe, and Ward. For American drama there are such titles as the Arthur Hobson Quinn series of histories, Odell's *Annals of the New York Stage;* and the *New York Theatre Critics' Reviews.*

Selected titles from the reference resources available for work with foreign literatures are Paul's *Grundriss der germanischen Philologie;* Kosch's *Deutsches Literatur-lexikon;* Merker and Stammler's *Reallexikon der deutschen Literaturgeschichte;* Goedeke's *Grundriss zur Geschichte der deutschen Dichtung aus den Quellen;* Gröber's *Grundriss der romanischen Philologie;*

Histoire littéraire de la France; Petit de Julleville's *Histoire de la langue et de la littérature française; Dictionnaire des lettres françaises,* 1939–; Joannidès' *La Comèdie-Française de 1680 à 1900; Bibliothèque dramatique de Monsieur de Soleinne;* Saintsbury's *History of the French Novel;* Gautier's *Les Epopées françaises;* Lancaster's *History of French Dramatic Literature in the Seventeenth Century; Storia letteraria d'Italia;* Scott's *Elizabethan Translations from the Italian;* Scartazzini's *Enciclopedia dantesca;* Cejador y Frauca's *Historia de la lengua y literatura castellana;* Fitzmaurice-Kelly's *A New History of Spanish Literature;* Salcedo y Ruiz's *La literatura española; The Ocean of Story* of Somadeva Bhatta; and Waxman's *History of Jewish Literature.*

Historical guides.—For the general reference needs the Library has the universally held historical guides such as Ploetz, Larned, Brand's *Popular Antiquities,* and the Cambridge history series. For the more serious needs there are such titles as these: Ebert's *Reallexikon der Vorgeschichte;* Hoops's *Reallexikon der germanischen Altertumskunde;* Schrader's *Reallexikon der indogermanischen Altertumskunde;* Daremberg and Saglio's *Dictionnaire des antiquités grecques et romaines;* Pauly's *Realencyclopädie;* Lavisse's *Histoire générale du ive siècle à nos jours;* Ivan Müller's *Handbuch der klassischen Altertumswissenschaft;* Lewis' *Topographical Dictionary of England;* Grässe's *Orbis Latinus;* Vivien de Saint-Martin's *Nouveau dictionnaire de géographie universelle; Atlas historique,* 1936–; *Great Soviet World Atlas;* Stieler's *Atlas of Modern Geography;* Madoz' *Diccionario geográfico-estadístico-historico de España y sus posesiones;* Giry's *Manuel de diplomatique;* and De Mas-Latrie's *Trésor de chronologie d'histoire et de géographie.*

For regional and national historical purposes the following titles are available: Adams' *Dictionary of American History; Australian Encyclopaedia;* Lavisse's *Histoire de France illustrée; Cambridge History of the British Empire; Political History of England,* edited by Hunt and Poole; and *Dictionnaire historique et biographique de la Suisse.*

LIBRARY RESOURCES

PERIODICAL AND NEWSPAPER REFERENCE MATERIALS

The collection of American general periodical indexes is practically complete. Most of the subject-interest ones published in this country and pertinent to the work of the University are available also. In addition to these, there are complete files of the *Subject Index to Periodicals; Review of Reviews, Index to Periodicals 1890–1902;* and the three sections of the *Internationale Bibliographie der Zeitschriftenliteratur.* The foreign subject indexes and guides to the publications of learned societies are represented by these titles: *International Catalogue of Scientific Papers, 1800–1900;* the Royal Society of London's *Catalogue of Scientific Papers, 1800–1900;* Gomme's *Index of Archaeological Papers, 1665–1890; Classified Index to the Publications of the American Philosophical Society;* Deniker's *Bibliographie des travaux scientifiques;* and Lasteyrie du Saillant's *Bibliographie générale des travaux historiques et archéologiques.* Newspaper indexes are represented by the *New York Times Index* and Palmer's *Index to the Times Newspaper.* Both of these files are complete.

The *Union List of Serials in Libraries of the United States and Canada* is supplemented for American library holdings by a rapidly expanding collection of regional, state, and local lists of periodicals published or received within or by the institutions designated. The Library's holdings of titles of this category are too numerous to list. The most important supplementary titles for foreign periodicals are the *World List of Scientific Periodicals; Gesamt-zeitschriften-verzeichnis; Gesamt-verzeichnis der ausländischen Zeitschriften* (GAZ); *Union Catalogue of the Periodical Publications in the University Libraries of the British Isles; Catalogue of the Periodical Publications in the Library of the Royal Society of London; Catálogo de todos los periódicos* of the Biblioteca Nacional in Bogotá; *Inventaire des périodiques scientifiques des bibliothèques de Paris;* René-Moreno's *Ensayo de una bibliografía general de los periódicos de Bolivia, 1825–1905;* Hatin's *Bibliographie historique et critique de la presse périodique française;* Chaves y Rey's *Historia y bibliografía de la prensa sevillana;* Diesch's

Bibliographie der germanischen Zeitschriften; and Hartzenbusch é Hiriart's *Apuntes para un catálogo de periódicos madrileños . . . 1661 al 1870.*

For bibliographical work with newspapers, the collection contains, in addition to the pertinent titles cited above, *American Newspapers, 1821–1936; a Union List,* supplemented by catalogues and check lists of collections in the Library of Congress, the New York Public Library, and in the libraries of Duke University, Yale University, and the Wisconsin State Historical Society. Many lists of state newspapers appear in the Historical Records Survey publications. The Times's *Tercentenary Handlist of English and Welsh Newspapers* and Crane and Kaye's *Census of British Newspapers and Periodicals* are the most important titles for English newspapers.

The formal indexes and biographical guides are supplemented for brief historical data by such titles as these: Bourne's *English Newspapers;* Graham's *English Literary Periodicals;* Mott's *American Journalism* and *A History of American Magazines;* North's *History and Present Condition of the Newspaper and Periodical Press of the United States;* Richardson's *History of Early American Magazines, 1741–1789;* Shaaber's *Some Forerunners of the Newspaper in England, 1476–1622;* Thomas' *The History of Printing in America;* and Caroline Ulrich's periodical directories.

GOVERNMENT PUBLICATIONS

United States federal publications.—The Library became a federal depository in 1884 and has received regularly the government's reference guides to its publications. In addition to these official catalogues, bibliographies, indexes, and collections of treaties, laws, census reports, and government manuals, there are several non-official guides, such as Hasse's *Index to United States Documents Relating to Foreign Affairs;* the Hasse series of indexes to economic material in the federal documents pertaining to several states; the various guides compiled by Jerome K. Wilcox; and the Institute for Government Research's *Service Monographs of the United States Government.*

State publications.—The separately published guides to state publications are limited. They consist of the *Manual on the Use of State Publications,* edited by Wilcox; Bowker's *State Publications;* and the National Association of State Libraries' check list of state statutes, session laws, and legislative journals, compiled by Grace E. Macdonald, with the *Supplement Check List* compiled by William S. Jenkins of the Department of Political Science. The last title was published while Professor Jenkins was serving as director of the Legislative Journal Microfilm Project undertaken jointly by the Library of Congress and the University of North Carolina. As a co-sponsor of this undertaking, the University of North Carolina acquired a complete run of the microfilm copy of state journals not previously owned by the Library of Congress. For this collection of microfilm journals there is a loose-leaf photo-print check list. A loose-leaf manuscript check list to collected state documents is available also. There are manuals for approximately one half of the states.

Publications of smaller civil divisions.—Hodgson's *The Official Publications of American Counties; a Union List;* and the non-official listing by Mr. Petersen in his *Bibliography of County Histories of the 3050 Counties in the 48 States* represent the guides for smaller civil divisions.

Publications of foreign governments.—The Library has been slow in turning its attention to collecting the official publications of foreign governments. The collection of reference aids is correspondingly poor. For Great Britain alone is there a working collection. It contains: *Members of Parliament,* published by the House of Parliament; Wedgwood's *History of Parliament, 1439–1509; A General Index to the Reports from Committees of the House of Commons, 1715–1901;* a complete set of the *General Indexes to the Accounts, Papers . . . of the House of Commons* from 1801 to 1929; the companion volumes for the reports, etc., of the House of Lords from 1801 to 1885; and a file of the *Consolidated List of Government Publications,* 1922–. These official indexes are supplemented by the *Catalogue of Parliamentary Papers, 1801–1900* with its supplements published by P. S. King; the Royal Colonial Institute's series of *Overseas Official Publications,* 1927–32; and Cole's *A Finding-list of Royal Commission Reports in the British Dominions.*

The following miscellaneous titles are somewhat indicative of the scattered holdings of the documents of other countries: *List of the Serial Publications of Foreign Governments, 1815–1931;* the Library of Congress' *Official Publications of Present-day Germany,* compiled by Otto Neuburger in 1942; *Key to League of Nations Documents;* Ker's *Mexican Government Publications . . . ;* and Child's *The Memorias of the Republics of Central America and of the Antilles.*

GENERAL PERIODICALS AND SOCIETY PUBLICATIONS

The Library's serial collection contains around eighty-six thousand volumes. Approximately twelve per cent of it is general in scope. The holdings in general periodicals and society publications are modest and inadequate to support the University's expanding research program. However, the foundations of a sound working collection have been laid.

The strength of the general periodical collection is in its long runs of English and American journals established during the nineteenth century. The files for the following are complete: *Quarterly Review,* 1809–; *Blackwood's Magazine* (Edinburgh), 1817–; *Living Age,* 1844–; *The Cornhill Magazine,* 1860–1939; *Nineteenth Century and After,* 1877–; *North American Review,* 1815–1940; *Harper's Magazine,* 1850–; *Harper's Weekly,* 1857–1916; *Atlantic Monthly,* 1857–; *Nation,* 1865–; *Century,* 1870–1930; *Forum and Century,* 1886–1940; *Scribner's Magazine,* 1887–1939; *Review of Reviews* (New York), 1890–1937; and *The Bookman; a Review of Books and Life,* 1895–1933.

Other English and American general periodicals of this period with files sufficiently long or unbroken to offer reasonably satisfactory service are: *Edinburgh Review,* 1802–1929 (vol. 153 lacking); *Westminster Review,* 1824–1914 (159 vols.); *Fraser's Magazine,* 1830–82 (62 vols.); *Chambers's Journal,* 1832– (85 vols.); *Dublin University Magazine,* 1833–80 (74 vols.); *Dublin Review,* 1836–1936 (87 vols.); *Illustrated London News,* 1842– (36 vols. lacking); *Eclectic Magazine of Foreign Literature,* 1844–1907 (146 vols.); *North British Review,* 1844–71 (49 vols.); *Independent,* 1848–1928 (vols. 50–

121); *Catholic World,* 1865– (vol. 56 lacking); *Fortnightly Review,* 1865– (vol. 117 lacking); *Contemporary Review,* 1866– (vols. 19-); *Dial* (Chicago; New York), 1880–1929 (80 vols.); *Current Opinion,* 1888–1925 (71 vols.); and *Review of Reviews* (London), 1890–1936 (vols. 1-52).

For work in the eighteenth century, the collection offers the first 103 volumes of the *Gentleman's Magazine,* 1731–1907; fifty-nine volumes of the first series of the *Monthly Review,* 1749–1789; and a complete file of the *Monthly Mirror,* 1795–1811. Of the short-period publications there are: *The Adventurer,* 1752–54; *The American Magazine,* Dec. 1787–Nov. 1788; *The British Apollo,* Feb. 13, 1708–May 11, 1711; *The Lounger,* 1785–87 (first ed. except nos. 1-4); *Mercurius Britannicus,* Jan.-Dec. 1718; and *The Student,* 1750–51. Supplementary to these titles, the Library owns a small microfilm collection of the following essay journals: *Athenian News; or, Dunton's Oracle,* nos. 1-27, 1710; *Champion; or, British Mercury,* Nov. 15, 1739–June 19, 1740 (1741 reprint); *Examiner; or Remarks upon Papers and Occurrences,* Aug. 3, 1710–July 26, 1714; *Freeholder; or, Political Essays,* Dec. 23, 1715–June 29, 1716; *Freethinker,* March 24, 1718–July 28, 1721; *Hermit; or, A View of the World,* nos. 1-30, Aug. 4, 1711–Feb. 23, 1712; *Jacobite Journal,* nos. 1-40, 42-49, 1747–48; *London Terrae Filius; or, The Satyrical Reformer,* nos. 1-6, 1707–1708; and *Monitor,* nos. 1-36, April 22–July 12, 1714.

For particular subject, period, or regional interest, the collection contains some material such as incomplete files of three Dickens publications: *All the Year Round, Bentley's Miscellany,* and *Household Words;* the 1841–44 edition of the *Dial;* a complete file of the *Yellow Book,* 1894–97; and many miscellaneous Southern periodicals, including complete runs of *Southern Review* (Charleston, S. C.), 1828–32, and *Southern Literary Messenger,* 1834–64, and incomplete ones for the *De Bow's Review,* 1846–80, and *Watson's Magazine* (Atlanta, Ga.), 1907–11.

Foreign language periodicals.—The collection of foreign-language general periodicals is meagre and scattered. For the following European titles there are complete files: *La Critica; rivista di letteratura, storia e filosofia,* 1903–; *Die Literatur;*

Monatsschrift für Literaturfreunde, 1898–; *Revue de France*, 1921–39; and *Revue des deux mondes*, 1831–. For *Revue bleue, politique et littéraire*, 1863–1939, there are fifty-six volumes. Latin-American publications are receiving special attention, and the collection is growing in usefulness. Files for the following are complete: *Revista del Rio de la Plata*, 1871–77; *Revista iberoamericana*, 1939–; *Revista nacional; literatura-arte-ciencia*, (Montevideo), 1938–; and *Sur; revista mensual*, 1931–. Among the other titles, for which the holdings are fairly complete, are: *Atenea; revista mensual, de ciencias, letras y bellas artes*, 1924–; *Nosotros; revista mensual de letras, arte, historia, filosofía y ciencias sociales*, 1907–; *Revista católica* (Santiago de Chile), 1901–; *Revista chilena*, 1875–80; *Revista chilena*, 1817–1930; *Revista de artes y letras* (Santiago de Chile), 1884–90; and *Revista de las Indias* (Bogotá), 1936–.

Society publications.—The Library has extensive holdings in the publications of learned societies. In some cases, however, the publication owned by the Library is not representative of the society's most worthwhile contribution; in others, the portions available are not sufficiently numerous or unbroken in sequence to offer the amount of material necessary for research purposes. This record, therefore, is not an exhaustive listing of titles held, but it will give some indication of the extent and character of this collection.

The holdings in the publications of national, regional, and state historical societies are reasonably strong. Some of the more significant titles are the American Antiquarian Society's *Proceedings;* the *Transactions* of the Huguenot Society of South Carolina; the *Collections* of the Massachusetts Historical Society; the *Filson Club Publications;* and the *Publications* of the Prince Society.

These additional titles of society publications, dealing with the humanities, are also available: the *Publications, Illustrated Monographs*, and *Transactions* of the Bibliographical Society of London; *Papers* of the Bibliographical Society of America; *Proceedings & Papers* of the Oxford Bibliographical Society; *Proceedings* of the British Academy; *Proceedings* of the Leeds Philosophical and Literary Society (Literary and Historical

Section); *Journal* of the Warburg and Courtauld Institutes; *Jahrbücher,* n.f., vols. 31-, of the Akademie Gemeinnütziger Wissenschaften zu Erfurt; the *Atti e memorie* of the Accademia Virgiliana di Scienze, Lettere ed Arti di Mantova, 1913–29; *Anales,* 1927–, of the Academia Nacional de Artes y Letras (Havana); *Historisk-filologiske Meddelelser* of the K. Danske Videnskabernes Selskab (Copenhagen); the *Proceedings,* n.s. vols. 22– of the Aristotelian Society; *Publications* of the Henry Bradshaw Society and of the Parker Society; the *Journal* and the *Memoirs* of the American Folk-lore Society; Finska Vetenskaps-Societeten's *Commentationes humanarum litterarum;* *Memoires* of the Société de Linguistique de Paris; the publications of the Société des Anciens Textes Français, of the Camden Society, the Chaucer Society, the Early English Text Society, the Scottish Text Society, the Irish Texts Society, the Spenser Society, and the English Dialect Society respectively; *Zeitschrift* of the Deutsche Morgenländische Gesellschaft; reprints of the Malone Society; *Cuadernos de cultura teatral* of the Instituto Nacional de Estudios de Teatro of the Argentine Republic; *Publications* of the Dunlap Society; *Annales* of the Société Jean-Jacques Rousseau; the *Boletín* and the *Memorias* of the Academia Española (Madrid); *Transactions* of the Royal Historical Society of London; *Memoirs* of the American Academy in Rome; *Papers* of the British School at Rome; *Mitteilungen* (Athenische Abteilung) of the Archäologisches Institut des Deutschen Reichs; the English Place-name Society's *Survey of English Place-names; Boletín* of the Academia Nacional de la Historia (Buenos Aires); and the *Publications* of the Canterbury and York, Selden, and Surtees societies.

In the scientific group, the Library owns either complete files or long runs of the publications of many of the older American general scientific societies. Among these sets are the *Annals of the Lyceum of Natural History of New York* of the New York Academy of Science and its superseding *Annals;* the *Bulletin* of the Torrey Botanical Club of New York; the *Memoirs* and the *Proceedings* of the Boston Society of Natural History; *Journal* of the Franklin Institute of Philadelphia; the *Proceedings* of the Academy of Natural Sciences of Philadelphia and of the

American Philosophical Society of Philadelphia; and the *Transactions* of the Connecticut Academy of Arts and Sciences and of the American Microscopical Society.

Supplementary scientific sets of sufficient length to be considered here include such titles as *Archives neérlandaises des sciences exactes et naturelles* of the Société Hollandaise des Sciences à Harlem; *Comptes rendus hebdomadaires des séances* of the Académie des Sciences (Paris); the Finska Vetenskapssocieteten's *Bidrag till kännedom af Finlands natur och folk; Bulletin* of the Académie Royal de Médecine de Belgique; *Boletim* (new series) of the Academia das Sciencias de Lisboa; *Bulletins* of the Académie Royale des Sciences, des Lettres et des Beaux-arts de Belgique; *Bulletino delle sedute* of the Accademia Gioenia di Scienze Naturali (Catania); the *Bulletin* and the *Doklady... Comptes rendus* of the Akademiia Nauk S.S.S.R. (Leningrad); *Öfversigt af Finska vetenskaps-societetens förhandlingar; Sitzungsberichte* of the Gesellschaft Naturforschender Freunde (Berlin); *Meddelelser* of the mathematics and physics division of the K. Danske Videnskabernes Selskab (Copenhagen); *Proceedings* of the Royal Society of London; *Berichte* of the Deutsche Botanische Gesellschaft (Berlin); *Proceedings of the Scientific Section* of the K. Akademie van Wetenschappen (Amsterdam); *Memoirs and Proceedings* of the Manchester Literary and Philosophical Society; the *Verhandlungen* of the Naturforschende Gesellschaft (Basel); the *Abhandlungen* of the Naturwissenschaftlicher Verein zu Bremen; *Vierteljahrsschrift* of the Naturforschende Gesellschaft (Zurich); *Schriften* of the Physikalisch-ökonomische Gesellschaft (Königsberg); *Proceedings* of the Royal Society of Edinburgh; *Natur und Volk; Senckenbergische Naturforschende Gesellschaft; Acta* of the Societas pro Fauna et Flora Fennica (Helsingfors); *Bulletin* of the Sociéte Impériale des Naturalistes de Moscou; *Rendiconti* of the Circolo Matematico (Palermo); *Proceedings* of the London Mathematical Society; *Bulletin* of the Chemical Society of Japan; *The Quarterly Journal* of the Geological Society of London; *Année biologique. Comptes rendus annuels des travaux de biologie générale* (Fédération des Sociétés de Sciences Naturelles); *Journal* of the

Royal Microscopical Society (London); the *Bulletin* of the Société Botanique de France (Paris) and of the Société Royale de Botanique de Belgique; *Verhandlungen* of the Deutsche Zoologische Gesellschaft; *Annales* of the Société Royale Zoologique de Belgique; *Verhandlungen* of the Zoologisch-Botanische Gesellschaft (Vienna); *Anatomischer Anzeiger; Centralblatt für die wissenschaftliche Anatomie. Amtliches Organ der anatomischen Gesellschaft; Medico-chirurgical Transactions* of the Royal Medical and Chirurgical Society of London; and *Jahresbericht* of the zoological section of Westfälischer Provinzial-verein für Wissenschaft und Kunst (Münster).

IV

BIOLOGICAL AND RELATED SCIENCES

Chapter 8

BOTANY

Alma Holland Beers

THE GREATER PART of the research in the Department of Botany has been done in the field of mycology. For this reason an especially strong collection of works on fungi has been built up, including some of the earliest books on this subject as well as most of the fundamental classics and the more important modern works. Among these are: Sterbeeck's *Theatrum fungorum,* 1675, said to be the first work devoted exclusively to the fungi; all the principal works of Micheli, Schaeffer, Bulliard, and Persoon and also of Schweinitz, who was the founder of systematic mycology in America; Vittadini, including his rare *Monographia tuberacearum;* Elias Fries, whose *Systema mycologicum* was accepted by the International Botanical Congress of 1910 as the starting point for the nomenclature of the gill fungi; Boudier, and such sets of books as Rabenhorst's *Kryptogamen-Flora von Deutschland.*

Another very valuable collection consists of old books of the herbal type. Some of the most interesting are: Fuchs's *New Kreüterbuch,* 1543; Dodonaeus' *Stirpium historiae pemptades,* 1583; Gerard's *Herball,* the most famous of all the English herbals; Clusius' *Rariorum plantarum historia,* 1601, and *Exoticorum libri decem,* 1605; and Parkinson's *Theatrum botanicum,* 1640. In addition to many original old herbals, there are two very interesting modern printings of ancient manuscript herbals. These are *The Herbal of Pseudo-Apuleius,* from the ninth-century manuscript in the Abbey of Monte Cassino, and the Badianus manuscript, from the Vatican, an Aztec herbal of 1552.

In addition to the more strictly herbal type of book, the Library is rich in the classical old works which have been landmarks in the development of the science of botany. A few of them are: Bauhin's *Pinax theatri botanici,* 1671; Ray's *His-*

toria plantarum; Grew's *Anatomy of Plants;* Hales's *Vegetable Staticks;* and all the principal works of Conrad Gesner, Linnaeus, Tournefort, De Candolle, Hofmeister, Darwin, Strasburger, De Bary, and others.

Many systematic works on the plants of America, including some of the very earliest ones, have been accumulated. Among them are: Monardes' *History of Medicinal Plants from the New World,* 1605; Banister's *List of Plants of Virginia* (published in Volume II of Ray's *Historia*); Plumier's *Description des plantes de l'Amérique,* 1693; Sloane's rare *Catalogue of the Plants of Jamaica,* 1696; Catesby's *Natural History;* Clayton's *Flora Virginica,* published by Gronovius in 1762; Walter's *Flora Caroliniana,* 1788; as well as the main works of Muhlenburg, Michaux, both father and son, Pursh, Nuttall, Stephen Elliott, M. A. Curtis, Chapman, Torrey, Asa Gray, C. S. Sargent, and the set of *North American Flora,* as far as published.

There are in the Botany Library a number of important sets of books of wide interest. Some are beautifully illustrated works on foreign floras, others are of a morphological nature. These include Engler and Prantl's *Die natürlichen Pflanzenfamilien;* Engler's *Das Pflanzenreich;* Banks's *Illustrations of Australian Plants Collected in 1770;* Ames's *Orchidaceae;* and Thomé's *Flora von Deutschland.*

All of the principal standard manuals are in the collection. Of primarily horticultural interest are such sets as Curtis' *Botanical Magazine,* of which there are ninety-two volumes; Maund's *Botanic Garden; Sertum botanicum;* and the various works of L. H. Bailey and Alfred Rehder.

The Library contains a large collection of books on the history of the sciences, mainly botany. Among these are: Sprat's *History of the Royal Society,* 1667; Weld's *History of the Royal Society;* Ornstein's *Role of Scientific Societies in the Seventeenth Century;* and various histories by Meyer, Sachs, Green, Oliver, Locy, Harvey-Gibson, Gunther, and Nordenskiold.

In the section devoted to periodicals, most of the important American Journals and many foreign ones are available. Among them are *Addisonia; American Journal of Botany; Annales du jardin botanique de Buitenzorg; Annales mycologici; Annals of*

Botany; Arkiv för Botanik; Botanical Gazette; Botanisches Archiv; Botanische Zeitung; Bulletin of the Societé Botanique de France; *Bulletin* of the Societé Mycologique de France; *Ecology; Flora; Jahrbücher für Wissenschaftliche botanik; Journal of Mycology; Mycologia; Revue algologique; Transactions* of the British Mycological Society.

The collection of bibliographical aids is quite extensive, including *Index Kewensis; Index Londonensis; International Catalogue of Scientific Literature* (botanical part); Pritzel's *Thesaurus;* Saccardo's *Sylloge fungorum;* Lindau and Sydow's *Thesaurus;* van Wijk's *Dictionary of Plant Names;* Meisel's *Bibliography of American Natural History;* and Lemée's *Dictionnaire des genres des plantes.*

Finally, the Botany Library includes a collection of carefully arranged and catalogued reprints of articles numbering about twenty-five thousand. These have been collected over a period of forty years by Dr. W. C. Coker, and more recently by Dr. J. N. Couch and others, with additions from the libraries of the Reverend M. A. Curtis and the late Mr. W. W. Ashe. They have come from many parts of the world and cover a wide range of subject matter, and are of great value to the research student in botany.

Chapter 9

MEDICINE

W. C. George

THE MEDICAL SCHOOL LIBRARY contains about ten thousand volumes, consisting in the main of books and journals devoted to the preclinical sciences, but containing in addition a number of volumes dealing with the major aspects of clinical medicine. The collection has been assembled gradually through purchase and gifts during the fifty-odd years of existence of the Medical School.

A number of gift collections should be noted, including especially the libraries of H. T. Bahnson, Peter Evans Hines, G. E. Newby, F. W. Potter, Nathaniel Shober Siewers, James S. Smith, Thomas F. Wood, and Charles S. Mangum. In these collections there are a number of old and rare volumes concerning the various fields of medical art and science during the eighteenth and nineteenth centuries, and a few older books, such as Sir Thomas Willis' *De anima brutorum quae hominis vitalis ac sensitiva est, exercitationes duae*, Oxford, 1672.

The Library receives currently about 150 periodicals, including the more important American and foreign journals in the field of preclinical medical science and many clinical journals. Among the journals dealing primarily with the preclinical sciences, of which there are complete series or long runs, are the following: the *Journal of Anatomy; American Journal of Anatomy; Anatomical Record; Journal of Comparative Neurology; Journal of Morphology; Arquivo de anatomía e anthropología;* the *Journal of Physiology; Journal of General Physiology; American Journal of Physiology; Pflüger's Archiv für die gesammte Physiologie; Archives neérlandaises de physiologie de l'homme et des animaux; Journal de physiologie et de pathologie générale; Quarterly Journal of Experimental Physiology*.

MEDICINE

In pathology and bacteriology the Library has the *American Journal of Pathology; Archives of Pathology; British Journal of Experimental Pathology; Centralblatt für allgemeine Pathologie und pathologische Anatomie; American Journal of Clinical Pathology; Journal of Pathology and Bacteriology; Journal of Bacteriology; Journal of Infectious Diseases; Journal of Immunology.*

In biochemistry and pharmacology there are, among others, the *Journal of Biological Chemistry; Biochemical Journal; Biochemische Zeitschrift;* Hoppe-Seyler's *Zeitschrift für physiologische Chemie; Archiv für experimentelle Pathologie und Pharmakologie; Journal of Pharmacology;* and *Experimental Therapeutics.*

Clinical journals, in complete series or long runs, include the following important representative journals: *American Journal of the Medical Sciences; Archives of Internal Medicine; Annals of Internal Medicine; Annales de médecine; Bulletin de l'academie royale de médecine de Belgique; Archives of Surgery; Annals of Surgery, American Journal of Surgery; American Journal of Diseases of Children; American Journal of Obstetrics and Diseases of Women and Children; American Journal of Obstetrics and Gynecology; Archives of Neurology and Psychiatry; Archives of Ophthalmology; American Journal of Ophthalmology; American Review of Tuberculosis; Heart; American Heart Journal; American Journal of Cancer; Radiology; American Journal of Roentgenology and Radium Therapy; American Journal of Syphilis; American Journal of Tropical Medicine; Journal of Urology; American Journal of Digestive Diseases.*

Miscellaneous: *Journal of Experimental Medicine; Journal of Medical Research; Journal of Nutrition; Yale Journal of Biology and Medicine; American Journal of Medical Sciences; Japanese Journal of Medical Sciences; Medical Record; Revista Sud-Americana de endrocrinología, immunología y quimioterapía;* and others.

Throughout the course of the years it has been the desire of those in charge of the Library to accumulate adequate bibliographic material to enable investigators to find the known data on any subject in the medical field. In addition to minor items, the Library has the *Index Medicus; Index-Catalogue of the Library of the Surgeon-General's Office; Biological Abstracts; International Catalogue of Scientific Literature* (O, Q, R); *Wistar Institute Bibliographic Service; Abstracts of Bacteriology; Abstracts of Physiology; International Abstracts of Surgery; Public Health Engineering Abstracts.*

The serial publications and books in the Medical School Library are supplemented by those of the main Library and of the Department of Zoology. These libraries contain many important books and periodicals fundamental to medical science, especially in the fields of anatomy and physiology.

The School of Public Health, established in 1936, is the youngest of the professional schools of the University. Consequently, its library has not been extensively developed. Housed in the Library of the Medical School, the collection contains, in addition to general medical books and serials with public health significance, the various state and federal public health reports and a number of books and serials of a specialized nature. In the general field of public health the Library receives such journals as *The American Journal of Public Health; Canadian Public Health Journal; American Journal of Hygiene; Journal of Social Hygiene; Journal of School Health; Journal of Public Health and Tropical Medicine of Puerto Rico; Collected Papers* of the School of Hygiene and Public Health of Johns Hopkins University; *Transactions* of the National Association for the Study and Prevention of Tuberculosis; *Boletín de la oficina sanataria Panamericana; Journal of Industrial Hygiene and Toxicology; Journal of Milk Technology;* League of Nations *Quarterly Bulletin of Health Organizations; Quarterly Bulletin* of the Milbank Memorial Fund; *American Journal of Nursing* and *Public Health Nurse*. In the field of sanitary engineering the Library has *The American City; Transactions* of the American Society of Civil Engineers; *Engineering Record; Heating, Piping and Air Conditioning; Journal* of the American Water Works Association; *Journal* of the New England Water Works Association; and others.

The regular exchange service that the Library maintains with the Duke University Library enables each library to extend its usefulness to the other institution.

Chapter 10

PHARMACY

Henry M. Burlage

IN ORDER TO HAVE a clear conception of the value and importance of a modern library to pharmacy, one should be aware of the objectives of the curriculum in pharmacy and the demands made upon the practicing pharmacist by the laity, the physician, the dentist, the veterinarian, and other workers in the public health professions, as well as the hospitals and the manufacturers of medicaments. The main objectives are to train students to become registered pharmacists in the retail outlets, and professional and hospital pharmacists; to prepare students for graduate work and for teaching in the schools of pharmacy; to train them as laboratory and research workers in industry and in the government and public health agencies. To aid the prospective pharmacist in following these lines of endeavor, the School of Pharmacy maintains a library of about five thousand volumes grouped under the following broad headings:

Biographies and histories of pharmacy.—The Library contains practically all of the important histories dealing specifically with the profession and some dealing with the allied professions. These include such works as Phillippe's *Histoire des apothicaires,* 1853, the first work devoted specifically to the history of pharmacy; Peter's *Aus pharmazeutischer Vorzeit,* 1886 (also Netter's translation of the first volume of this work); Thompson's *Mystery and Romance of Alchemy and Pharmacy,* 1897; Andre-Pontier's *Histoire de la pharmacie,* 1900; Schelenz's *Geschichte der Pharmazie,* 1904; Wootton's *Chronicles of Pharmacy,* 1910 (2 vols.); and all the more recently issued works. Of special importance are Poiret's *Histoire des plantes de l'Europe,* 1825 (8 vols.); Sprengel's *Geschichte der Arzneikunde,* 1921 (8 vols.); Baudot's *L'Etude historique sur la pharmacie en Bourgogne avant 1803,* 1905; and Lloyd's *Origin and History of Vegetable Drugs, Chemicals, and Preparations.*

LIBRARY RESOURCES

Legal and nonofficial standards and commentaries.—Copies of all the Pharmacopoeias issued in this country, with the exception of the *Pharmacopoeia of the New York Hospital*, are available. The collection includes a number of those issued in foreign countries but lacks many of those of the city and district type. Among the more important items in this group are the *Pharmacopoeia of the Massachusetts Medical Society*, 1808, and a facsimile of the Lititz *Pharmacopoeia*, 1778. The file of national formularies of this country is complete, but many foreign ones of a similar character are lacking.

Dispensatories and similar works of foreign origin.—Holdings in this important field include *Pharmacopoeia Augustana*, 1564 (a facsimile); *Das Dispensatorium des Valerius Cordus*, 1546 (a reprint); Quincy's *English Dispensatory*, 1761; Lewis' *New Dispensatory*, 1782; *Edinburgh New Dispensatory*, 1794, 1801, 1804, 1818; Coxe's *American Dispensatory*, 1810, 1814, 1818; Thatcher's *New Dispensatory*, 1814; Thomsen's *Vereinigte Pharmacopoeen*, 1827; Jahr's *Nouvelle pharmacopée et posologie homopathie*, 1841; Mayne's *Dispensatory and Formulary*, 1848; Martindale's *Extra Pharmacopoeia*; and all editions of the *American Dispensatory* and *The United States Dispensatory*.

Formularies and other books of formulas.—In the field of formularies, the Library has a greater collection of those of the nineteenth than of the twentieth century. These include Donaldson's *Formulae selectae*, 1818; Ellis' *Medical Formulary*, 1834, 1854; Griffith's *Universal Formulary*, 1856, 1874; *Formulaire pharmaceutique* (French Military Hospital), 1857, 1870; *British Pharmacopoeial Codex*; McEwan's *Pharmaceutical Formulas*; Prinz's *Dental Formulary*; Lucas and Stevens' *Book of Recipes*; and others.

Because of the rapid development of synthetics used in many formulas of a pharmaceutical, medical, cosmetic, dermatologic, or technical nature, it is highly important that the Library maintain a complete file of those works that have appeared in the last twenty-five years and are appearing from day to day. Of the recent ones the Library has *The Recipe Book* of the American Pharmaceutical Association and Bennet's *Chemical*

Formulary. Its holdings of hospital formularies should be brought up to date and maintained.

Dictionaries, encyclopedias, herbals, treatises, and similar specialized works.—Available in the Pharmacy Library are Webel's *A German-English Technical and Scientific Dictionary,* 1930; Dorland's *American Illustrated Dictionary,* latest edition; Gould's *Illustrated Dictionary of Medicine,* 1915; Watt's *Dictionary of Chemistry* (old); Couch's *Dictionary of Chemical Terms* (not the latest edition).

Rare old editions in the files are Lemery's *Dictionnaire universel des drogues simples,* 1733; Quincy's *Lexicon Physicomedicum,* 1734; Motherby's *A New Medical Dictionary,* 1791; De Gregoric's *Diccionario elemental de farmacia,* 1803; Coxe's *Philadelphia Medical Dictionary,* 1808 (4 vols.); *American Medical Lexikon,* 1811; Ewell's *The Medical Companion,* 1816; Hooper's *Lexicon-Medicum,* 1826, 1838, 1841; Nysten's *Dictionnaire de médicine,* 1855; Dunglison's *Dictionary of Medical Science,* 1858 (3 vols.); and others. Holdings of an encyclopedic character include Moeller and Thoms's *Real Enzyklopädie der gesamten Pharmazie,* 1904–14; Hager's *Pharmazeutische-Technische Manuale,* 9th ed., and his *Handbuch pharmazeutischen Praisx für Apotheker, Artze, Drogisten und Medicinalbeamte,* 9th ed.; and Goris and Loit's *Pharmacie galenique* (2 vols.).

Many rare herbals, materia medicas and medical botanies at hand include Charas' *Histoire naturelle,* 1668; Gerard's *Flora gallo-provincialis,* 1761; Meyrick's *The New Family Herbal,* 1790; Coste and Willemet's *Indigenous Materia Medica,* 1793; De LaMarck and De Candolle's *Flore française,* 1805 (6 vols.); Adams' *Observations on Morbid Poisons,* 1807; Barton's *Collection for an Essay Towards Materia Medica,* 1810; Cullen's *Treatise of Materia Medica,* 1812; Thornton's *British Flora,* 1812 (2 vols.); Murray's *System of Materia Medica,* 1815 (2 vols.); Chaumerton's *Flore médicale,* 1814–20; Bigelow's *Medical Botany,* 1817 (3 vols.); Barton's *Medical Botany,* 1817 (Vol. I); Michaux's *The North American Sylva,* 1818 (3 vols.); Hanin's *Cours de matière médicale,* 1819 (2 vols.); Rafinesque's *Medical Flora,* 1828–30 (2 vols.); Carpenter's *Essay of Materia*

Medica, 1831; Colla's *Herbarium pedemontanum,* 1833 (7 vols.); Frost's *Syllabus in Materia Medica,* 1834; Bigelow's *New Remedies,* 1839; Griffith and Taylor's *Poisons,* 1848, 1859; Flückiger's *Pharmacographia,* 1879; Kohler's *Medicinal-Pflanzen,* 1887–92 (5 vols.); Sawer's *Odorographia,* 1892–94; Meyer and Schumann's *Atlas der Officinellen Pflanzen,* 1891 (4 vols.); and Tschirch's *Handbuch der Pharmacognosie* (Vols. I and III).

The Library has several works dealing with drug and plant analysis and toxicology, including a complete file of the several editions of the *Methods of the Association of Official Agricultural Chemists;* seven volumes on *Pharmaceutical Analysis* by C. A. Rojahn and his co-workers; Fuller's *Qualitative Analysis of Medicinal Preparations;* Nelson's *Introduction to the Analysis of Drugs;* Allen's *Commercial Organic Analysis* (4th and 5th eds.); Dragendorff's *Plant Analysis,* English Translation, 1921, and his *Heilpflazen,* 1898; and Weisner's *Die Rohstoffe des Pflanzenreiches,* 1927 (2 vols.). Several works are available dealing with fixed and volatile oils, and perfumes and cosmetics.

Handbooks and tables of constants.—The Library was presented with a complete set of Beilstein's *Handbuch der organische Chemie* by the Executive Committee of the North Carolina State Pharmaceutical Association and it possesses a complete set of *Organic Syntheses* and the first edition and Volume I of the second edition of Mulliken's *Identification of Pure Organic Compounds.*

Tables of solubilities, which are of extreme importance to the dispensing pharmacist, include the third edition of Seidell's *Solubilities of Inorganic and Organic Compounds,* and a number of the smaller works.

Monographs, surveys, symposia, annual reports, proceedings, and reviews.—Monographs of the American Pharmaceutical Association and files of the *Proceedings* of the National Association of Boards of Pharmacy, the American Association of Colleges of Pharmacy, American Drug Manufacturers Association, and the North Carolina State Pharmaceutical Association are complete, as are the *Annual Review of Biochemistry,* the

Applied Chemical Reports, and the *Digest of Comments of the Pharmacopoeia of the United States.* Volumes VII-XX of the *Annual Reports of the Chemical Laboratory of the American Medical Association* are available.

Scientific and abstract journals, including cumulative indexes.—Library holdings in this important group of publications include the *Proceedings* (complete), the *Bulletin* (complete), and the *Yearbook* (complete) of the American Pharmaceutical Association; the *American Journal of Pharmacy* (complete with cumulative indexes); *Journal of the American Chemical Society* (vols. 2, 7, 8, 19, to date); *Industrial and Engineering Chemistry* (complete); *Chemical Abstracts* (complete with cumulative indexes); *Industrial and Engineering Chemistry, Analytical Edition* (complete); *Bulletin of the National Formulary Committee* (vol. 6 to date); *Journal of the American Medical Association* (vols. 42, 44, 46-61, 67-123); *Journal of Chemical Education* (complete); *Contributions of the Boyce Thompson Institute* (complete); *Pharmaceutical Archives* (to date); *Pharmazeutische Rundschau; Pharmaceutical Review; Squibb Abstract Bulletin* (vol. 3-11); and *American Journal on Pharmaceutical Education* (complete).

The collection includes an unusual file of American journals, particularly medical, which are no longer being issued. The value of this file is somewhat marred by missing volumes and issues. The file includes *The Medical Repository,* 1800–12; *American Journal of Medical Sciences* (vols. 21-29, 31-94); *Medical Examiner,* 1841–56; *Philadelphia Museum* (vols. 1-17). The English journals are represented by the *Pharmaceutical Journal* (vols. 1-104, 128 to date) and the *Yearbook of Pharmacy* (complete with one cumulative index). Other foreign journals include *Journal de médecine chirurgie et pharmacie,* 1754–93 (complete with the exception of vols. 76-78, 95, probably the oldest journal with the word pharmacy in its title); Trommsdorf's *Journal der Pharmacie,* 1793–1812 (vols. 1-21); Buchner's *Reportorium für die Pharmacie* (vols. 1-72 with collective indexes but lacking 13, 15, 41, 57, 67); *Jahrbuch für Pharmacie Landau* 1854–73 (vols. 1-40); *Pharmazeutische Zentralhalle* (vols. 1-57, 74-81); *Pharmazeutische Monatshefte* (vols. 13-19); *Pharmazeutische Post; L'union pharmaceutique; Vierteljahresschrift für praktische Pharmazie,* 1905–20; *Archiv der Pharmazie* (vols. 205-58, 265-76); and *Journal de pharmacie* (3rd series, vols. 1-46 complete; 4th series, 1-30 complete; 5th series, 1-30 complete with index 1880–94; 6th series, 1-30, 1943).

In summarizing the immediate needs of the Library of this School, emphasis should be placed on completion of a number of sets of journals already catalogued, a more adequate subscription list of the current pharmaceutical journals, a complete file of foreign pharmacopoeias and official compendia, and duplicate copies of standard textbooks for reference by the students.

Chapter 11

PSYCHOLOGY

John F. Dashiell

LIBRARY RESOURCES in the field of psychology are adequate for most investigative work. The book collections are shelved in the main Library and are as available to the campus public as those in other related fields. The journals, bound and current, are lodged in a departmental library housed in the psychology building, and thus are made of ready access for research workers, seminar members, and others whose interests are more in the journal type of research studies than in the usual book type of systematic expositions and of semi-popular presentations. While the list of journals is not complete, nearly all of those in the English language and a few in French and German are on file.

Among the periodicals, the following should be recorded here: *American Journal of Psychiatry; American Journal of Psychology; Archiv für die gesamte Psychologie; Archives of Psychology; Brain; British Journal of Psychology; British Journal of Psychology Monographs; Character and Personality; Child Development; Comparative Psychology Monographs; Educational and Psychological Measurement; Genetic Psychology Monographs; International Journal of Psychoanalysis; Journal de Psychologie; Journal of Abnormal and Social Psychology; Journal of Applied Psychology; Journal of Comparative Psychology; Journal of Consulting Psychology; Journal of Educational Psychology; Journal of Experimental Psychology; Journal of General Psychology; Journal of Genetic Psychology; Journal of Nervous and Mental Diseases; Journal of Psychology; Journal of Social Psychology; Mental Hygiene; Occupational Psychology; Personnel Journal; Psychoanalytic Quarterly; Psychoanalytic Review; Psychological Abstracts; Psychological Bulletin; Psychological Monographs; Psychological Record; Psychological Review; Psychometrika; The Nervous Child;*

Training School Bulletin; Zeitschrift für pädagogische Psychologie.

From private collections within the department, these additional titles are also often available to qualified research students: *Journal of Criminal Law and Criminology; Journal of Educational Research; Journal of Mental Science; Journal of Neurophysiology.* One of these journals, the *Psychological Monographs*, is edited by a member of the department.

The general collection of psychology books in the University Library is fairly adequate, not being heavily loaded in any specific division of the psychological field, but rather well balanced on the whole. Clinical, experimental, statistical, and theoretical treatments of animal, child, abnormal, psychological, industrial, social, differential, personality, and other fields are all represented. One series of books, the McGraw-Hill Publications in Psychology, is edited by a department member.

Chapter 12

ZOOLOGY

C. D. Beers

BOUND VOLUMES of journals in the Library of the Department of Zoology total approximately thirty-five hundred. These have been selected with special reference to the fields of descriptive and experimental embryology, general and cellular physiology, ecology, hydrobiology, genetics and general morphology of animals. They include such standard and largely indispensable research journals as the following: *Archives de biologie; Archives de zoologie expérimentale et générale; Annales des sciences naturelles* (*zoologie*); Wilhelm Roux's *Archiv für Entwicklungsmechanik der Organismen; Archiv für mikroskopische Anatomie; Archiv für Hydrobiologie; Anatomischer Anzeiger, Zoologischer Anzeiger; Zoologische Jahrbücher; Biological Bulletin; Journal of Morphology, Journal of Experimental Zoology; Journal of Cellular and Comparative Physiology; American Midland Naturalist; Transactions of the American Microscopical Society; American Naturalist; Physiological Zoology; Papers from the Department of Marine Biology of the Carnegie Institution of Washington; Ecological Monographs; Journal of Genetics; Journal of the Royal Microscopical Society; Proceedings of the Royal Society of London* (series B); *Nature;* and *Quarterly Journal of Microscopical Science.* Three abstracting journals, *Biological Abstracts, L'Année biologique* and *Zoologischer Bericht,* as well as the *Zoological Record* and *Bibliographia zoologica,* are received regularly and constitute invaluable bibliographic aids.

Bound volumes aside from journals number approximately sixteen hundred. In the selection of these, special emphasis has been placed on monographic works, treatises, and comprehensive text-books rather than on works of a semi-popular or general nature, which are available in the main Library. Among the more notable comprehensive works may be mentioned the following: Brachet, *Traité d'embryologie des vertébrés;* Korschelt, *Regeneration und Transplantation;* Neave, *Nomenclator zoologicus;* Hertwig, *Handbuch der Entwickelungslehre der Wirbeltiere;* Bronn, *Klassen und Ordnungen des Tierreichs;* Délage et Herouard, *Traité de zoologie concrète;* Brumpt, *Précis de parasitologie;* Stephenson, *The Oligochaeta;* Kent, *Manual of the Infusoria;* Forbush, *Birds of Massachusetts and Other New England States;* Calkins and Summers, *Protozoa in Biological Research;* Dean, *A Bibliography of Fishes;* Brehm, *Tierleben;* Blatchley, *Coleoptera of Indiana;* Lankester, *A Treatise on Zoology;* Howard et al., *Mosquitoes of North and Central America;* Holbrook, *North American Herpetology,* including the very rare fourth volume.

The publications of the U. S. Government, many of which concern systematic zoology, general natural history, economic and applied zoology, fisheries, wild-life conservation, and the like, are available practically without exception, some in the main Library of the University, others in the various departmental libraries. Notable among the zoological publications of the government are certain of the *Memoirs of the National Academy of Sciences,* as well as *Bulletin of the U. S. National Museum* and the *Bulletin of the U. S. Bureau of Fisheries.*

The proceedings and journals of a considerable number of American and foreign scientific societies and research institutes are received by the University Library in exchange for the *Journal of the Elisha Mitchell Scientific Society.* Many of these contain valuable source-material in zoology, but since they deal not uncommonly with other fields of science as well, most of them are housed in the main Library. Representative of these exchanges are the following: *Proceedings* of the Academy of Natural Sciences (Philadelphia); *Memoirs* of the Boston Society of Natural History; *Proceedings* of the American Academy of Arts and Sciences; Chicago Natural History Museum, *Zoological Series;* British Museum, *Natural History, Economic Series, Zoology; Biological Reviews* (Cambridge); *Archives de l'Institut Pasteur d'Algérie; Bulletin du Muséum d'Histoire Naturelle* (Paris); *Archives du Musée Teyler* (Haarlem); *Archives néerlandaises de physiologie de l'homme et des animaux; Arkiv* for *Zoologi* (Stockholm); *Entomologisk Tidskrift* (Stockholm); *Abhandlungen herausgegeben vom Naturwissenschaftlichen Verein zu Bremen; Arbeiten über morphologische und taxonomische Entomologie aus Berlin-Dahlem; Mitteilungen aus dem Zoologischen Staatsinstitut und Zoologischen Museum in Hamburg; Mémoires de la Société Zoologique Tchécoslovaque; Mémoires de la Société Royale des Sciences de Bohême; Arbeiten des Naturforscher-Vereins zu Riga; Arbeiten der Limnologischer Station zu Kossino; Proceedings of the Indian Academy of Science* (Bangalore); *Australian Journal of Experimental Biology and Medical Science; Journal of the Royal Society of New South Wales; New Zealand Journal of Science and Technology; Boletin da Faculdade de Filosofia, Ciêncas e Letras* (Sao Paulo); *Anales del Museo Nacional de Historia Natural de Montevideo; Anales del Instituto de Biologia de la Universidad Nacional de Mexico; Proceedings and Transactions of the Royal Society of Canada.*

Library resources in zoology are further supplemented by the anatomical, biochemical, physiological, and parasitological journals in the Library of the School of Medicine.

Finally, the Zoology Library contains approximately ten thousand reprints, including the special collection of the late Professor H. V. Wilson on the taxonomy and embryology of sponges. While these are now merely arranged by subject rather than catalogued by author, they contain many titles which are not represented among the journals and constitute therefore a valuable research adjunct.

V

FINE ARTS AND PHILOSOPHY

Chapter 13

ART AND ARCHITECTURE

Harriet Dyer Adams

THE UNIVERSITY OF NORTH CAROLINA's collection of books on art was given its start in 1907 with the establishment of the Milburn Fund. The income from this fund was used for many years to acquire dictionaries, encyclopedias, periodicals, and other publications on various phases of art and architecture. Many volumes on the cathedral architecture of European countries were secured in the early years. A collection of bulletins from museums in New York, Chicago, Cleveland, Detroit, Cincinnati, Boston, and other cities was started in the early 1920's and continues to the present day on an exchange basis.

Further impetus was given the Art Collection in 1927 by a gift from the Carnegie Corporation of New York. Volumes on ancient and Renaissance art were acquired together with a number of items in other fields, including English, French, and American painting. A series of about two thousand photographs was also presented by the Carnegie Corporation at this time.

Serious study of Renaissance art has been stimulated in recent years by the loan of a collection of more than seven thousand photographs on Italian art from Mr. Herman Weil of Goldsboro. A collection of projection slides, which grew from three hundred to nine hundred plates during the Art Department's first year in 1937, now numbers 5,200 slides on ancient, medieval, Renaissance, and modern works in the fields of painting, sculpture and architecture.

In 1941 the Carnegie Corporation of New York made a substantial grant for teaching materials on modern art. Books acquired with this grant included a number of important works. This same year saw the teaching of courses in modern art further enhanced by a gift from Mr. Georges Lurcy.

LIBRARY RESOURCES

In Person Hall, books reserved for use in current courses include about three hundred volumes on ancient and Renaissance art, and some two hundred works on modern and contemporary art. Volumes on design, architecture, modern sculpture, photography, art education, technical subjects and general reference bring the total of volumes in the Art Reference Library in Person Hall to seven hundred. About fifteen hundred volumes on a wide variety of art subjects are in the stacks of the main Library. Titles included in the Art Reference Library in Person Hall may be listed in nine groups.

REFERENCE WORKS

Bibliographies.—Schlosser, *Die Kunstliteratur.*

Periodicals.—*The Studio* (London); irregular from 1906 on; *International Studio*, vols. 1-99; *Architectural Forum*, 1919–43; *Architectural Record*, 1892–1940 (with about eighty single copies); *Cahiers d'art*, 1929–40 (broken file); *Jahrbuch der Jungen Kunst*, 1921 and 1924; *Signature*, 4 vols.

Bulletins.—*Carnegie Magazine*, broken file from 1940; *Metropolitan Museum Bulletin*, 1928–43; *Museum of Modern Art Bulletin*, broken file from 1940.

Dictionaries and encyclopedias.—Harper, *Encyclopedia of Art, Architecture, Sculpture, Painting, Decorative Arts*; Fleming, *An Encyclopedia of Textiles*; Schmitz, *Encyclopedia of Furniture*; Benezit, *Dictionnaire critique et documentaire des peintres, sculpteurs*; Bryan, *Dictionary of Painters and Engravers.*

HISTORY OF ART

General.—*Handbuch der Kunstwissenschaft*; *Klassiker der Kunst*; Mâle, *L'Art religieux en France*; Michel, *Histoire de l'art*; Perrot and Chipiez, *Histoire de l'art dans l'antiquité*; *Propylaen Kunstgesichte*; several of the Warburg Institute series.

Primitive.—Basler and Brummer, *L'Art precolombien*; Kelemen, *Medieval American Art*; Lehmann, *The Art of Old Peru*; Guillaume and Munro, *Primitive Negro Sculpture.*

ART AND ARCHITECTURE

ARCHITECTURE

Bumpus, *Cathedrals and Churches of Northern Italy; Belgium; England and Wales; France; Italy;* Fletcher, *History of Architecture on the Comparative Method;* Morey, *Early Christian Art; Library of Architectural Documents* (4 vols.); Dalton, *Byzantine Art and Archaeology;* Dalton, *East Christian Art, A Survey of the Monuments;* Morey, *East Christian Art;* Baum, *Romanische Baukunst in Frankreich;* Benoit, *L'Architecture, l'Occident médiéval du romain au roman;* Mâle, *L'Art religieux du XIIe siècle en France* and *L'Art religieux de la fin du moyen âge en France;* Porter, *Medieval Architecture, Its Origins and Development;* Gall, *Die Gotische Baukunst in Frankreich und Deutschland;* Lasteyrie, *L'Architecture religieuse en France a l'epoque gothique;* Hempel, *Francesco Borromini;* Ricci, *Architecture and Decorative Sculpture of the High and Late Renaissance in Italy* and *Baroque Architecture and Sculpture in Italy;* Teufel, *Die Wallfahrtskirche Vierzehnheiligen;* Circle, *International Survey of Constructive Art,* ed. by Martin, Nicholson and Gabo; Le Corbusier, *The City of Tomorrow and its Planning,* and *Towards a New Architecture;* Jeanneret, *Le Corbusier und Pierre Jeanneret* (3 vols.); Yerbury, *Modern Dutch Buildings.*

PAINTING, EIGHTEENTH CENTURY

Flemish.—Clemen, *Belgische Kunstdenkmaler;* Destrée, *Roger de la Pasture van der Weyden;* Friedländer, *Die Altniederländische Malerei;* Valentiner, *Die Handzeichnungen Rembrandts.*

German.—Burckhard, *Matthias Gruenewald;* Deusch, *Deutsche Malerei des fünfzenten Jahrhunderts* and *Deutsche Malerei des sechzehnten Jahrhunderts;* Panofsky, *Albrecht Dürer.*

Italian.—Berenson, *Studies and Criticism of Italian Art* and *Studies in Medieval Painting;* Crowe and Cavalcaselle, *History of Painting in Northern Italy* and *A New History of Painting in Italy;* Van Marle, *The Italian Schools of Painting;* Venturi, *Italian Painting in America;* Weigeld, *Sienese Painting of the Trecento;* Tosca, *Florentine Painting of the Trecento;* Bode,

Florentiner Bildhauer der Renaissance; Troche, *Italienische Malerei des 14 und 15 Jahrhunderts;* Venturi, *North Italian Painting of the Cinquecento;* Fiocco, *Venetian Painting of the Seicento and the Settecento;* Rinaldi, *Neapolitan Painting of the Seicento;* Post, *History of Spanish Painting;* Zervos, *L'art de la Catalogne de la seconde moité du neuvième siècle à la fin du quinzième siècle.*

PAINTING, NINETEENTH AND TWENTIETH CENTURIES

Burger, *Einführung in die moderne Kunst;* Coquiot, *Les Independants;* Focillon, *La Peinture au XIXe siècle;* Gillet, *La Peinture de Poussin à David;* Gleize, *Cubism;* Janneau, *L'Art cubiste;* most publications of the Museum of Modern Art; Ozenfant and Jeanneret, *La Peinture moderne;* Raynal, *Modern French Painters;* Venturi, *Les Archives de l'impressionisme;* Wilenski, *French Painting, Modern French Painting and Modern Movement in Art;* Zervos, *Histoire de l'art contemporain;* Bonnard, *Terrasse;* Einstein, *Braque;* Zervos, *Braque;* Phaidon press, *Cezanne;* studies of Cezanne by Rewald, Barnes, Mack, Venturi, Vollard, Loran, Fry, Chappuis, and Rivière; Waldemar George, *Chirico;* Soby, *The Early Chirico;* Leger, *Courbert;* studies of Daumier by Fuchs, Ghirardelli and Rosenthal; Cantinelli, *David;* Meier-Graefe, *Degas;* Vollard, *Degas;* Escholier, *Delacroix;* Meier-Graefe, *Delacroix;* Faure, *Derain;* Berr de Tourique, *Dufy;* Morand, *Foujita;* Fontainas, *Letters of Gauguin to Vollard and Fontainas;* Gauguin, *Noa Noa* (facsimile); studies of Gauguin by Burnett, Fletcher, Guèrin, Morice, Olmos, Rewald, Pola Gauguin; Grohmann, *Kandinsky;* Klee, *Pedagogical Sketch Book;* Grohmann, *Klee;* Nierendorf, *Klee;* Westheim, *Kokoschka;* Lapauze, *Ingres;* Teriade, *Lèger;* Moreau-Nelaton, *Manet;* Tabarant, *Manet;* Schardt, *Marc;* Barnes, *Matisse;* Pfannsteil, *Modigliani;* Geffroy, *Monet;* Alexander, *Monet;* Sauerlandt, *Nolde;* Reed, *Orozco;* Osborn, *Pechstein;* studies of Picasso by Barr, Cassou, Danz, Level, MacKenzie, Stein, Zervos (3 vols.), and Raynal; Delteil, *Pissaro;* Tabarant, *Pissaro;* Desjardins, *Poussin;* studies of Renoir by Barnes, Delteil, Duret, Meier-Graefe, Vollard; Charensol, *Rouault;* Venturi,

Rouault; Basler, *Rousseau;* Jamot, *Segonzac;* Rich, *Seurat;* Rewald, *Seurat; Dessins de Seurat,* ed. by Bernheim-Jeune; Scheffler, *Slevogt;* Soby, *Tchelitchew;* studies of Toulouse-Lautrec by Coquiot, Delteil, Joyant, Lassaigne, and Mack; Tabarant, *Utrillo;* Van Gogh, *Dear Theo,* ed. by Stone; Van Gogh, *Further Letters;* Phaidon press edition of Van Gogh; De la Faille, *Catalogue raisonnée;* studies of Van Gogh by Meier-Graefe, Pach, Pfisterer, Barr, and Scherjon; Duhamel, *Vlaminck.*

SCULPTURE

Chase and Post, *History of Sculpture;* Duchamps, *French Sculpture of the Romanesque Period;* Gardner, *Medieval Sculpture in France;* Porter, *Romanesque Sculpture of the Pilgrimage Roads* (10 vols.); Vitry, *French Sculpture during the Reign of Saint Louis, 1226–1270;* Aubert, *French Sculpture at the Beginning of the Gothic Period;* Roy, *Artistes et monuments de la renaissance en France;* Braum, *Das Christliche Altargerat in seinem Sein und in seiner Entwicklung;* Von Falke, Schmidt, and Swarzenski, *The Guelph Treasure;* Panofsky, *Die deutsche Plastick des 14 Jahrhunderts;* Brinckmann, *Barockskulptur;* Feulner, *Die deutsche Plastik des sechzehnten Jahrhunderts,* and *Die deutsche Plastik des siebzehnten Jahrhunderts;* Sauerlandt, *Die deutsche Plastik des achtzehnten Jahrhunderts;* Rewald, *Maillol;* Phaidon press edition of Rodin.

MINOR ARTS

General.—Benedictus, *Nouvelles variations;* Bossert, *Geschichte des Kunstgewerbes* (6 vols.), and *Peasant Art in Europe* and *Ornament in Applied Art;* Burkhalter, *Collection des decors et couleurs;* Gladky, *Nouvelle composition decorative;* Merida, *Carnival in Mexico;* Speltz, *Color-Ornament of All Historical Styles;* Von Falke, *Kunstgeschichte der Seidenweberei;* Valmier, *Album No. 1.*

Graphic arts.—*European Drawings from the Collections of the Metropolitan Museum of Art* (Vol. I, Italian; Vol. II, Flemish, Dutch, German, Spanish, French, and British drawings);

Glasser, *Die Graphik der Neuzeit;* Hind, *A History of Engraving and Etching from the 15th Century to 1914* and *Introduction to a History of Woodcut;* Holman, *The Graphic Processes;* Kristeller, *Kupferstich und Holzschnitt in vier Jahrhunderten;* Meder, *Die Handzeichnung;* Meister, *Der Graphik* (3 vols.); Mongan and Sachs, *Drawings in the Fogg Museum of Art; The Poster* (5 vols., Alexander and MacCleay publication); Singer, *Die moderne Graphik;* Berenson, *Drawings of the Florentine Painters* (3 vols.); Teitze-Conrat, *Der französische Kupferstich der Renaissance;* Dürer, *Complete Woodcuts;* Springer, *Dürer, Kupferstiche;* Kurth, *Complete Woodcuts of Dürer;* Grosz, *Interregnum;* Roger-Marx, *French Original Engravings from Manet to the Present Time;* Delacroix-Rosenthal, *Manet;* Moreau-Nelaton, *Manet, graveur et lithographe;* Friedlaender, *The Drawings of Nicolas Poussin;* Voltaire, *La Princesse de Babilone* (illustrated by Imre Reiner); Delteil, *Le Peintre graveur illustré* (Degas, Goya, Ingres, Delacroix, Pissaro, Sisley, Renoir, Toulouse-Lautrec); Johnson, *Ambroise Vollard, editeur;* Vlaminck, *Lithographs;* Goya, *Desastres de la guerra;* Price, *Etchings and Lithographs of Davies;* Mac-Orlan, *Atget photographe de Paris;* Blum, *Origin and Early History of Engraving in France;* Murrell, *A History of American Graphic Humor;* Seidlitz, *History of Japanese Color Prints;* Laver, *History of British and American Etching, Modern Masters of Etching* (*The Studio,* Nos. 1-33).

METHOD AND MATERIAL

Getten, *Painting Materials;* Dorrance, *Materials of the Artist;* Mayer, *Artist's Handbook of Materials and Techniques;* Muybridge, *Animals in Motion* and *The Human Figure in Motion.*

AESTHETICS

Bunim, *Space in Medieval Painting and the Forerunners of Perspective;* Dvorak, *Kunstgeschichte als Geistesgeschichte;* many works by Woefflin and Worringer.

Shortages exist in nearly every classification, but the collection is growing and contains many important monographs and considerable secondary material. Careful selection of volumes obtained for art studies, together with exhaustive use of other available resources and considerable outside assistance, has enabled the Art Department to offer a steadily increasing number of courses since its establishment eight years ago.

Chapter 14

DRAMA

Samuel Selden and Virginia Spencer

THE RESOURCES in dramatic literature and the theatre now housed in the University Library include a considerable number of plays from many countries, both in the original languages and in translation, and most of the standard works of history, criticism, and technique. Altogether they represent a body of reference books generally adequate for the fundamental requirements of graduate and undergraduate study and research, but not especially distinguished, except in a very few fields, for the materials needed by the specialist.

The resources can be divided roughly into ten major groups: long plays published separately, collections of plays, history and criticism of the drama, theory of the drama, acting, the dance, technical aspects of the theatre, biographies, bibliographies, and periodicals. In all, there are approximately 7,700 volumes covering the theatre in the United States, Latin America, England, Germany, France, Spain, and four other European countries. There are also a few scattered works dealing with Oriental drama.

The group containing the largest number of volumes is that of the long plays published separately, numbering 3,503, of which 990 are American. These include the works of all the better known playwrights from the earliest to the most modern. The period in American drama best represented is the contemporary. Most of the plays of Maxwell Anderson, Eugene O'Neill, and Paul Green are in the group. British plays run a fairly close second with 869 volumes. All the principal playwrights are included from the first up to Bernard Shaw. In addition there are 259 volumes of Shakespeare's plays catalogued separately. Ranking next in number and range are those of Germany, which fill 696 volumes and are representative of the growth of German drama from its beginnings to the present time. There are 442 volumes of the singly-published French plays, covering the development of French drama through the various periods since its beginnings. The largest number, however, comprises the plays written in the latter half of the nineteenth century. Spanish plays include those by both Spanish and Latin American dramatists, available in 369 volumes. Deserving special mention is a separate collection of Spanish drama of 607 volumes containing twelve thousand plays. There is, in addition, a smaller collection of 125 plays in twenty-five volumes. The Library owns several volumes of Hungarian, Japanese, Chinese, Latin, and Italian dramas, some of which are in the original language.

The second group, collected plays, is much smaller than the first. Of the 592 anthologies in this classification, 270 contain Greek plays (in the original and in translation); 163 contain British plays, ninety-seven contain American plays; and the remaining volumes include Spanish, French, German, Italian, Japanese, and Hungarian plays, mostly translated.

The Library possesses a special collection of Greek drama and critical studies, which is catalogued separately and includes 872 volumes. A number of these plays are in the original Greek.

Books of history and criticism of the drama in the various countries are still fewer in number. Of the 511 volumes in this group, two hundred are devoted to the history and criticism of British drama, most of which are standard works written within the last fifty years. French history and criticism number 117, German, eighty. There are only twenty-four volumes devoted to the history and criticism of American drama, and these largely emphasize regional drama, the Negro theatre, and such special themes as the drama in the war. In addition, there are 158 volumes dealing with the history and criticism of the drama in general.

Some four hundred titles are concerned with the technical aspects of the theatre, such as stage settings, scenery design, lighting, sound effects, and make-up. In another group are 152 books on theatre acting, some of which include also the ballet. Classified separately are seventy-eight volumes dealing with costuming, including not only the histories of the art but also discussions of the various trends to the present day, and the technical problems of costume construction and design.

Only a few books dealing specifically with the dance have been published. The Library lists 184 in this classification. Biographies of dramatists, actors and other personalities connected with the theatre number sixty-one volumes, including most of the leading writers in this field.

Bibliographies, while not impressive in number, are adequate for general reference. There are eighteen, not including the forty-three volumes of Shakespearean bibliographies catalogued separately. Also not included in this list is the *Annual Magazine Subject Index,* containing an index to the articles and illustrations on the stage in the leading periodicals of America and England, together with a record of books on drama published during each year.

The Library preserves nineteen periodicals concerned exclusively with the theatre. Among these are *Theatre Arts Monthly,* twenty-seven volumes; *Theatre,* fifty-two volumes; *The Drama Magazine,* twenty-one volumes; *The Stage,* sixteen volumes; and *Players,* sixteen volumes.

Constituting a very important part of the reference resources in dramatic art are four special collections of theatre material. Two of these, the Archibald Henderson Collection and the Winge Collection, are housed in the Library. The famous Roland Holt Collection and the Scrapbooks of The Carolina Playmakers are in the Theatre Museum in Murphey Hall.

The Winge Collection was a gift made by John H. Winge, a German refugee, to Professor Frederick H. Koch and the University Library in December of 1940. The collection consists of two hundred books and pamphlets relating to the history of the theatre and dramatic art, most of which were written in Germany.

The Archibald Henderson Collection contains the major portion of the Library's holdings in plays by American authors; it is made up of both single plays and collections. It had its origin in a generous gift made by Dr. Archibald Henderson to the Dramatic Art Department and to the Library in 1929.

The Roland Holt Collection, presented to The Carolina Playmakers in April of 1936 by Mrs. Constance D'Arcy Holt, widow of the late Roland Holt, has been evaluated by some experts as the finest theatre collection of its kind outside of New York City. This collection, composed of a wide range of books, documents, and other materials, covers fifty years of American theatre from 1881 to 1931, and is inclusive, rather than exclusive, in nature. It was gathered by Mr. Roland Holt, who began collecting theatrical items of interest when he was a young man and followed it as a hobby throughout his life.

The fifteen thousand clippings, together with programs, pictures, special articles, photographs, and autographs, represent what was happening in the theatre from week to week throughout the fifty years the collection covers. The material is arranged chronologically in thirteen scrapbooks, supplemented by nineteen letter files of correlated material. There are approximately 250 photographs of actors and actresses, from Lotta on, which are filed in special albums. Most of the books in the collection are biographies of persons prominent on the American stage. There are, in addition, one hundred librettos of the better-known operas. American stock-company history may be traced from the early days of its development to its peak.

One of the most interesting features of the Holt Collection is the almost complete set of programs of the Madison Square Theatre and of Augustin Daly's Theatre. Also present are many programs of later groups, such as the Washington Square Players and the Provincetown Players. The theatrical careers of Mary Anderson, Edwin Booth, Barrett, Modjeska, Richard Mansfield, Julia Marlowe, Maude Adams, and many others may be studied through representative sequences of their programs and critical comment.

The Theatre Museum is preserving a complete history of The Carolina Playmakers, from the date of its founding to the present time. Here in bound scrapbook form are the playbills, press clippings, articles from magazines, and special materials which provide a detailed record of the growth and development of dramatic art at the University of North Carolina. Mirrored here are twenty-six years of activity in the field of native American drama. The Carolina Playmakers Scrapbooks now number twenty-four volumes, and others will follow. There are, in addition, other scrapbooks covering special phases of the Playmakers' work, both on and off the campus. One of the most interesting of these is the Picture Book, which contains at least one photograph of every performance of both public and experimental productions. Nine volumes cover the period from 1926 to 1944. There is also a three-volume set of scrapbooks containing the playbills of Playmaker productions. A rich part of the Scrapbook Collection is found in the three volumes of *The Christmas Carol Book,* recording Professor Koch's tours with Dickens' famous Christmas story.

Of special interest to those concerned with native and historical drama are *The Lost Colony* and *The Highland Call* books. There are three of the former, covering the five seasons of *The Lost Colony,* containing playbills, photographs, press clippings, and programs. *The Highland Call* has one volume covering its two seasons. *The Dakota Playmakers,* a three-volume set, dates back to Professor Koch's dramatic work at the University of North Dakota, where his dream of a native American drama had its beginnings.

The Scrapbook Collection contains much that gives an intimate view of what has happened in the theatre at this University and of the growth of theatrical interest generally, and particularly in the South. It affords rich reference and research material for anyone who wishes to study native trends in the theatre during the last twenty-five years.

In the Library Extension Department there are 1,343 titles of long plays published separately, as well as 452 anthologies of one-act plays and 867 short plays. Plays for special occasions should be mentioned, particularly those for Christmas, Easter, and Thanksgiving. Most of these are American, with some British, and fewer French and German in translation. Also, the Library has available for lending a number of technical books and biographies of theatre personalities. All of this material in the Extension Library will be lent by mail on request and for a modest service charge.

Chapter 15

MUSIC

Glen Haydon

MUSICOLOGY, that branch of learning which concerns the discovery and systematization of knowledge pertaining to music, is a very ancient discipline. Although it began with the early Greek philosophers and throve through the middle ages, yet its development in the American university has come within the last twenty-five years. Its growth in the modern European university extends back only a few decades before that. Nevertheless, within this period of slightly more than half a century, there has come into being a great wealth of library materials, consisting mainly of scholarly writings about music and reliable editions of the music itself. The music division of the Library now contains a substantial and representative portion of the basic musicological materials: books on music, three thousand, musical scores, four thousand, phonograph recordings, four thousand.

GENERAL REFERENCE MATERIALS

Bibliographies.—The Library has a fairly comprehensive list of bibliographical works, including the Eitner *Quellen-Lexikon;* Forkel's *Allgemeine Literatur der Musik;* Becker's *Die Tonwerke des XVI. und XVII. Jahrhunderts;* Frere's *Bibliotheca musicaliturgica;* Blom's *Musical Literature;* Squire's *... Music ... in the British Museum;* Sears's *Song Index;* Gregory and Sonneck's *Library of Congress Catalogue of Early Books on Music Literature;* the catalogues of the Brown, Fleisher, Wolffheim, and Hirsch collections; the *Verzeichnis der ... Bücher und Schriften über Musik* of the *Jahrbuch der Musikbibliothek Peters;* and *Bibliographie des Musikschrifttums* of Taut, and Karstädt.

Encyclopedias and dictionaries.—The collection of musical

encyclopedias and dictionaries contains the works of Albert, Baker, Brenet, Cobbett, Ewen, Hull, Eitner, Lavignac, Fétis, Gerber, Grove, Thompson, Moser, Mendel, Key, Pratt, Riemann, Ronald, Rousseau, Scholes, Slonimsky, and Vannes.

Histories.—All the standard general histories of music and a number of less common works are available. Authors represented include Adler, Ambros, Bekker, De la Borde, Bücken, Burney, Cambarieu, Dumesnil, Einstein, Eximeno, De la Fage, Fétis, Ferguson, Finney, Forkel, Gerbert, Gerold, Glyn, Hamilton, Hadow, Hawkins, Hogarth, Kinsky, Kretzschmar, Landormy, Láng, Lavignac, Leichtentritt, McKinney and Anderson, Martini, Merian, Moser, Naumann, Nef, Parry, Pratt, Prosniz, Prunières, Reese, Riemann, Rockstro, Schering, Scholes, Slonimsky, Storck, and Wolf.

SERIAL PUBLICATIONS

Publications of learned societies.—The collection includes most of the publications of the International Musicological Society, the society "Union Musicologique" of The Hague, Die Neue Bach Gesellschaft, The Plainsong and Medieval Music Society, and other similar organizations. Certain of these publications are referred to elsewhere in this list.

Periodicals.—Complete files of most of the musicological periodicals are in the collection. Among these may be mentioned *Acta musicologica; Archiv für Musikforschung; Archiv für Musikwissenschaft; Bulletin of the American Musicological Society; Mitteilungen der schweizerischen Musikforschenden Gesellschaft; Modern Music; Monatshefte für Musik-Geschichte; Music and Letters; The Musical Quarterly; The Musical Times; Note d'archivio per la storia musicale; La Rassegna musicale; La Revue musicale; Revista musicale italiana; Studien zur Musikwissenschaft; Vierteljahrsschrift für Musikwissenschaft; Zeitschrift der internationalen Musikgesellschaft; Zeitschrift für Musikwissenschaft.*

MUSIC

SPECIALIZED WORKS

Books.—The collection of books covers in reasonably comprehensive fashion the wide ranges of musical history and criticism; biography, theory, harmony, counterpoint, analysis, composition, orchestration and instrumentation, pedagogy, and interpretation; and the auxiliary fields of acoustics, psychology, aesthetics, and comparative musicology. It may be worth noting that in addition to the modern writings on these subjects, many of the collected reprints and facsimiles of earlier works, such as those of Meibom, Jan, Gerbert, Coussemaker, and Macran are here. Also in the collection are most of the standard biographies of the more important composers and for certain composers, such as Bach, Mozart, Beethoven, Wagner, and Brahms, there are especially extensive biographical materials. Of particular interest among the writings on musical theory are the original works of Gebbardi, Fux, Heinichen, Holder, Kircher, Kirnberger, Marpurg, Martini, Quantz, Rameau, Tartini, and Zarlino.

Music in notation.—Paralleling the literature about music is the collection of music in notation. Basic in this connection are the sets of the complete works of important composers of which the following are on the shelves: Bach (47 vols.), Beethoven (33 vols.), Berlioz (20 vols.), Brahms (26 vols.), Chopin (14 vols.), Des Prez (in progress), Lasso (21 vols., incomplete), Mendelssohn (36 vols.), Monteverdi (14 vols.), Mozart (74 vols.), Palestrina (33 vols.), Purcell (26 vols.), Schubert (40 vols.), Schumann (34 vols.), Victoria (8 vols.). Among the modern collections of older music may be mentioned: *Denkmäler deutscher Tonkunst, I. Folge* (65 vols.); *Denkmäler deutscher Tonkunst, II. Folge* (36 vols.); *The English Madrigal School* (36 vols.); *The English School of Lutenist Song Writers* (32 vols.); *Das Erbe deutscher Musik* (ca. 13 vols. to 1938); *Les maîtres musiciens de la renaissance française* (23 vols.); *Monuments de la musique française au temps de la renaissance* (10 vols.); Torchi's *L'Arte musicale in Itala* (7 vols.); *Tudor Church Music* (10 vols.). In addition, there is a representative collection of vocal and instrumental scores, including solo vocal music, operas, oratorios, masses, symphonies, chamber music, and solos for the various instruments. Files of chamber music works issued by the Society for the Publications of American Music (45 vols.), *New Music* (43 vols.), and other similar organizations in the field of contemporary music are practically complete.

Materials in auxiliary fields.—Library holdings in the auxiliary fields of acoustics, psychology, aesthetics and education, supplemented by the materials in the several departmental libraries and in the main Library, are adequate for ordinary research needs.

Folk music.—The Institute of Folk Music, a division of the Folklore Council of the University, has a small but growing collection of folk music materials in its archives, including original recordings of Spanish music from Florida, French music from Louisiana, North Carolina folk tunes, and California Indian songs. There is also a representative collection of books, periodicals, reference materials, and musical scores of the folk music of the world. These materials are supplemented by the folklore collection described elsewhere in this volume. A complete set of the albums of recordings of the folk music of the United States from the Archive of American Folk Song, issued by the Recording Laboratory of the Division of Music of the Library of Congress, and a special collection of recordings of Latin American music are in the collection.

Microfilm.—The Library owns a complete file of the *Music Microfilm Archive*, issued under the auspices of The Oberlander Trust (to date five rolls of some 2,500 frames each). Among other special materials in the Library may be mentioned such facsimile editions as Aubry's *Cent motets du xiiie siècle*, Aubry's *Les Plus anciens monuments de la musique française*, Beck's *Les Chansoniers des trouvères*, Coussemaker's *Histoire de l'harmonie au moyen âge*, Wooldridge's *Early English Harmony*, Hughes's *Worcester Mediaeval Harmony*, Frere's *Antiphonale Sarisburiense*, his *Graduale Sarisburiense*, Briggs's *The Musical Notation of the Middle Ages*, Wolf's *Schrifttafeln*, Wolf's *Veröffentlichungen der Musikbibliothek Paul Hirsch* (c. 10 vols.), Schünemann's *Musikerhandschriften von Bach bis*

Schumann, and the Beethoven Association's edition of Beethoven's "Sonata in F Minor" for pianoforte.

Theses.—The following theses by University of North Carolina students are in the Library: Kathryn L. Kennard, "The Beginnings of the Violincello Sonata in Italy" (M. A., 1938); Peter S. Hansen, "The Life and Works of Domenico Phinot" (Ph. D., 1939; has as a manuscript supplement most of the extant works of Phinot transcribed into full score); David P. Bennet, "A Study in Fiddle Tunes from Western North Carolina" (M. A., 1940); Nan Cooke Smith, "A Study of the Problem of Expressiveness as Exemplified in Certain of the Choral-Orchestral Works of Johannes Brahms" (M. A., 1941); Louise Gail Schmeisser, "A Study of the Development Section of the Sonata Form as Exemplified by Beethoven's Piano Sonatas" (M. A., 1944); Josephine Andoe, "The Clavier-suites of Kindermann, Pachelbel, Johann Krieger, Kuhnau and Franz Murschhauser; a Style-Critical Study" (M. A., 1942).

Most of these materials mentioned above have been collected within the past few years, and therefore, it is only natural that the Library should lack many important basic items which must be acquired in the near future. Nevertheless, the collection on hand is fairly representative, being carefully selected for the special study needs of the serious student in this field.

Chapter 16

PHILOSOPHY

Stephen A. Emery

HUMAN KNOWLEDGE radiates so continuously from its philosophical center into more peripheral fields that the boundaries of philosophy cannot be fixed with even rough accuracy. Most of the departmental collections within the University Library contain many books of philosophical value. The following survey, however, concerns philosophy in a fairly strict sense. In this section there are perhaps four thousand volumes.

There is very little material available in the Library on Oriental philosophy, and that deals chiefly with the Chinese. This analysis is limited almost exclusively to Occidental philosophy.

Among the general reference works available are Baldwin's bibliography, the *Journal of Philosophy*'s annual international bibliography (1933–36), the International Institute of Philosophical Collaboration's *Bibliographie de la philosophie pour l'année 1937–*, and many more special lists. Baldwin's *Dictionary of Philosophy and Psychology*, Eisler's *Wörterbuch der philosophischen Begriffe*, Hastings' *Encyclopedia of Religion and Ethics*, Matthews and Smith's *Dictionary of Religion and Ethics*, and Runes's *Dictionary of Philosophy* are in the Library.

Periodical files include twenty-three philosophical journals (490 vols.). Of these, fourteen are in English (ten sets complete, two almost), three in French (one complete), five in German (three complete), and one in Italian. The journals in English include *Mind, Philosophy, Philosophical Review, Journal of Philosophy and Ethics*. Especially valuable is a complete set (22 vols.) of the now long-terminated *Journal of Speculative Philosophy*. In French, there are available the *Revue d'histoire de la philosophie et d'histoire général de la civilisation, Revue de metaphysique et de morale, Revue philosophique de la France et de l'étranger;* in German *Jahrbuch für Philosophie und phänomenologische Forschung, Kant-Studien,* and *Logos;* in Italian, *Rivista di filosofia neo-scholastica.*

Holdings in the publications of learned societies are rather meagre. Of the *American Catholic Philosophical Association Proceedings* (1926–) the Library has only one year. It has less than half (1921–43) of the *Aristotelian Society Proceedings* and only three of the *Supplementary Volumes,* almost all of the British Academy *Proceedings,* less than half of the *University of California Publications in Philosophy,* and the *International Congress of Philosophy Proceedings* for only the Seventh Congress (Oxford, 1930) and the Ninth (Paris, 1937).

Most of the important general historical surveys, such as J. E. Erdman, Hegel, Tenneman, Ueberweg, Windelband, and Wundt, are available, as well as more recent popular ones. The collection of "systematic" surveys (most of them introductory) is far from complete.

In ancient philosophy, the collection includes the standard histories: Adamson, Benn, Burnet, Gomperz, Ritter, Robin, Windelband, Zeller, and others. The complete Loeb Classical Library covers most of the primary sources. There are a few anthologies. The Pre-Socratic period is represented by Burnet, Diels, and Zeller. On Socrates and the Sophists, the collection is rather weak. Most of the primary and secondary material on Plato is present, with the standard translations by Burnet (Latin), Jowett (English), and others. There are translations of many separate dialogues, and considerable material on Plato by leading American and European scholars. The Aristotle collection also contains most of the primary and secondary sources: the Ross translation of the complete works, many standard Greek and English editions of separate treatises, and the most important works on Aristotle. In the post-Aristotelian schools, the Library is strongest on Neo-Platonism, weakest on the Skeptics.

In medieval philosophy the Library has *Beiträge zur Geschichte der Philosophie des Mittelalters* (33 vols.), and a few standard histories, such as Gilson and de Wulf. The chief lack is the great Minge *Patrologiae cursus completus* (383 vols.). Since the whole set, however, is in the neighboring Duke University Library, it has not been necessary to incur the expense of duplication. There is considerable material on Augustine, Anselm (*Opera omnia*) and Thomas; very little on Abelard and Duns Scotus. The collection is weak in the Gnostic, Arabian, and mystical literatures.

In modern philosophy (1600–1900) most of the important histories, such as Cousin, Falckenberg, Kuno Fischer, Höffding, Merz, Ruggiero, Windelband, and others, are available. There are standard English editions of the complete works of the leading British empiricists; Bacon, Hobbes, Locke, Berkeley, Hume, J. S. Mill, and Spencer, as well as separate philosophical works, and much of the important interpretative philosophical literature, especially on Locke and J. S. Mill. The exponents of continental rationalism, Descartes, Spinoza, Leibniz, and others, are available in important editions of complete works, excepting the Gerhardt editions of Leibniz, and separate treatises in the original and in English. There is on hand an especially large collection stressing Descartes and Spinoza. The Library has standard editions of the complete works, and individual works in German and English of the chief German idealists, such as Kant, Fichte, Schelling, and Hegel. The critical literature on Kant and Hegel is largest.

The contemporary philosophy holdings are stronger in American and British authors than in French and German, and weakest in Italian. In general, the primary sources far exceed the secondary. Much expository and critical literature appears in journal articles and doctoral dissertations. Most of the articles are here, but few of the dissertations.

As for the various fields in a "systematic" survey of philosophy, logic (Aristotelian, Hegelian, and symbolic) is well represented in Prantl's *Geschichte der Logik in Abendlande,* and in treatises by Bosanquet, Bradley, Carnap, Cook, Wilson, Hegel, Husserl, Jevons, Johnson, Keynes, Lotze, Mill, Russell, Sigwart, and Whitehead, as well as in many lesser works and elementary texts. Metaphysics overlaps too many fields for much detailed mention, but most of the standard works, ancient, modern, and contemporary, are here. In ethics, the Library has virtually all of the classic and important recent works, with a large number of introductory texts and popular books; in mathematical philosophy, Hilbert, Poincare, Russell, Weyl, and Whitehead; in the philosophy of natural science, Bridgman, Carnap, Cassirer, Eddington, Planck, Reichenbach, and Russell; in the philosophy of history, Buckle, Condorcet, Croce, Flint, Hegel, Sorokin, Spengler, Toynbee, and many others; in political philosophy, histories by Coker, Dunning, Gierke, Janet, Merriam, Sabine, all the great classics, and more recent works by Barker, Bluntschli, Green, Hobhouse, Krabbe, and Laski; in aesthetics, Hammond's bibliography, histories by Bosanquet, Gilbert and Kuhn, Listowel, Lotze, the classics, and recent works by Samuel Alexander, Collingwood, Croce, Dewey, Lotze, Maritain, Santayana, and others. The fact that the University has no department of religion has tended to restrict the collection of books in the philosophy of religion, but the holdings of Duke University Divinity School are available here. The Library does possess the important works of Höffding, Hügel, James, Kierkegaard, Kroner, Reinhold Niebuhr, Rudolf Otto, Pfleiderer, Royce, Tennant, and Webb, to mention only a few.

VI

LANGUAGE AND LITERATURE

Chapter 17

CLASSICAL LANGUAGES AND LITERATURES

T. M. Simkins, Jr., and P. H. Epps

THE LIBRARY provides good facilities for advanced study in the classics, its resources being particularly strong in the central fields of classical bibliography, Latin and Greek literature, and archaeology, as well as in the adjunct fields of ancient history and civilization, papyrology, and epigraphy. Considerable material is offered also in the more highly specialized peripheral fields, paleography (especially Latin), religion and mythology, classical linguistics and numismatics. Facilities for research are augmented by regular inter-library loan service with the Duke University Library, only nine miles away.

The files of general classical periodicals are essentially complete: *American Journal of Philology,* vols. 1-64; *Transactions and Proceedings of the American Philological Association,* vols. 1-73; *Athenaeum,* vols. 3-18; *California University Publications in Classical Philology,* vols. 1-12; *Classical Journal,* vols. 2-39; *Classical Philology,* vols. 1-38; *Classical Quarterly,* vols. 1-37; *Classical Review,* vols. 1-57; *Classical Weekly,* vols. 1-37; *Cornell Studies in Classical Philology,* vols. 3-19, 21-27; *Gnomon,* vols. 1-14; *Harvard Studies in Classical Philology,* vols. 1-54; *Hermes,* vols. 1-76; *Hermes Einzelschriften,* vols. 1-7; *Mnemosyne,* vols. 1-11, 1-60, 1-8;[1] *Philological Quarterly,* vols. 1-22; *Philologische Wochenschrift,* vols. 41-59; *Philologus,* vols. 47, 67-94; *Revue de philologie,* vols. 1-2, 1-50, 1-14; *Revue des études latines,* vols. 1-17; *Rheinisches Museum für Philologie,* vols. 1-3, 1-6, 1-89; *Speculum,* vols. 1-18; and *Yale Classical Studies,* vols. 1-8. In archaeology the Library has the general

---

1. Two or more sets of volume numbers for the same periodical, each beginning with one, indicate new series of volume numbering.

periodicals: *American Journal of Archaeology,* vols, 1-11, 1-47; *Annual of the British School at Athens,* vols. 1-30; *Annals of Archaeology and Anthropology,* vols. 17-27; *Die Antike,* vols. 6-16; *Antiquity,* vols. 1-17; the *Jahrbuch,* vols. 44-54, and *Mitteilungen,* vols, 1-64, of the Archäologisches Institut des Deutschen Reichs; *Hesperia,* vols. 1-12; *Hesperia Supplements,* vols. 1-6; *Journal of Hellenic Studies,* vols. 1-61; *Journal of Roman Studies,* vols. 1-32; *Klio,* vols. 1-22, 24-33; *Klio Beihefte,* vols. 1-42; *Memoirs of the American Academy in Rome,* vols. 1-16; *Revue archéologique,* 5th ser. vols. 23-36; 6th ser. vols. 1-14; *Revue des études anciennes,* vols. 25-41; and *Syria,* vols. 11-20. The following, of special importance to the student of classical linguistics, are also in the collection: *Beiträge zur Kunde der indogermanischen Sprachen,* vols. 1-30; the *Bulletin,* vols. 39-40, and *Mémoires,* vols. 1-23, of the Société de Linguistique de Paris; *Glotta,* vols. 1-28; *Indogermanische Forschungen,* vols. 1-57; and *Zeitschrift für vergleichende Sprachforschung,* vols. 1-66.

Reference materials available in the Library include the monumental *Real-Encyklopädie der classischen Altertumswissenschaft* (Pauly-Wissowa) in twenty-four bound volumes with supplements; Daremberg and Saglio's *Dictionnaire des antiquités grecques et romaines,* 10 bound vols.; and the complete *Müllers Handbuch der klassischen Altertumswissenschaft,* 48 bound vols. There are, besides, Baumeister's *Denkmäler des klassischen Altertums;* Wilamowitz-Moellendorff's *Die griechische und lateinische Literatur und Sprache;* Sandys' *History of Classical Scholarship,* 3 vols., and *Companion to Latin Studies;* and Whibley's *Companion to Greek Studies,* together with all the important classical dictionaries, of both "literary-and-antiquities" and linguistic character.

Invaluable for classical research of any kind are the exhaustive annual bibliographies (all foreign), of which the Library possesses a full quota: Bursian's *Jahresbericht über die Fortschritte der klassischen Altertumswissenschaft,* 251 vols., and its most useful accompaniment, the *Bibliotheca philologica classica,* 64 vols.; *The Year's Work in Classical Studies,* 32 vols.;

and Marouzeau's *Dix années de bibliographie classique*, 2 vols., with its continuation, *L'Année philologique*, 12 vols.

The Greek and Latin authors are represented by full sets of the *Bibliotheca Teubneriana*, the *Oxford Classical Texts*, and the *Loeb Classical Library*. Complete for Latin is the *Collection ... de l'Association Guillaume Budé*, and all volumes of the *Corpus scriptorum Latinorum Paravianum* have been obtained. Further, the Library possesses all important individual editions, critical and annotated, of major classical authors. Minor authors and fragments appear in such works as Diels's *Fragmente der Vorsokratiker;* Halm's *Rhetores Latini minores;* Keil's *Grammatici Latini,* 7 vols. with supplement; Kock's *Comicorum Atticorum fragmenta;* Peter's *Historicorum Romanorum reliquiae;* and Postgate's *Corpus poetarum Latinorum*. Among other useful bibliographies of literature are Engelmann's *Bibliotheca scriptorum classicorum;* the Nairn *Classical Hand-List;* Masqueray's *Bibliographie pratique de la littérature grecque;* also Palmer's *List of English Editions and Translations of Greek and Latin Classics Printed before 1641;* Foster's *English Translations from the Greek: a Bibliographical Survey;* and Smith's *The Classics in Translation*. For reference purposes, almost all of the published *indices verborum*, concordances, and special dictionaries for both Greek and Latin authors are available.

In Greek literary history and criticism, in addition to standard general works by Croiset, Murray, Stanford, Wright, Sinclair, Atkins, and others, there is a full array of such special studies as Koerte's *Die hellenistische Dichtung*, Couat's *La Poésie alexandrine sous les trois premiers Ptolemées,* Pearson's *Early Ionian Historians*, Blass's *Attische Beredsamkeit*, and Bowra's *Early Greek Elegists* and *Greek Lyric Poetry from Alcman to Simonides*. The field of Greek drama is amply covered by a comprehensive collection of all the recent works and most of the older standard volumes. The same is true of Homer.

The subject of Roman literature is represented with similar completeness. The collection contains all the general works by Duff, De Labriolle, Mackail, Teuffel, D'Alton, Frank, Glover, Ribbeck, Stuart, Sellar, Summers, Norden, and others. Particularly noteworthy is the body of authoritative scholarly material devoted to the authors Cicero, Catullus, Vergil, Horace, Livy, and Tacitus.

The advanced student of classical linguistics finds in the Library the Boisacq *Dictionnaire étymologique de la langue grecque* (3rd ed., 1938) and the corresponding Ernout-Meillet volume for Latin (1939); the Forcellini *Totius Latinitatis Lexicon*, 4 vols.; the Krebs *Antibarbarus der lateinischen Sprache;* the Olcott *Thesaurus linguae Latinae epigraphical*, 2 vols. (in progress; complete to date), and the Walde-Hoffman *Lateinisches etymologisches Wörterbuch*. The Walde-Pokorny *Vergleichendes Wörterbuch der indogermanischen Sprachen* is also available. Representative of offerings in comparative grammar are the Brugmann-Delbrück *Grundriss der vergleichenden Grammatik der indogermanischen Sprachen;* Buck's *Comparative Grammar of Greek and Latin* and *Introduction to the Study of the Greek Dialects;* Conway's *Italic Dialects;* Draeger's *Historische Syntax der lateinischen Sprache;* Grandgent's *Introduction to Vulgar Latin;* Kent's *Sounds of Latin;* Meillet's *Esquisse d'une histoire de la langue latine;* the Meillet-Vendryes *Traité de grammaire comparée des langues classiques;* Sommer's *Handbuch der lateinischen Laut- und Formenlehre;* and Sturtevant's *Pronunciation of Greek and Latin.* To this representative rather than complete list of titles should be added other important works by Hirt, Meillet, Kretschmer, Kühner, Meisterhans, Juret, Stephanus, Norden, and others, as well as all the ancient texts useful in linguistic study.

Paleographical works in the Library worthy of special mention include Birt's *Das antike Buchwesen* and *Die Buchrolle in der Kunst;* Chatelain's *Paléographie des classiques latins;* Clark's *Descent of Manuscripts;* Hall's *Companion to Classical Texts;* Lowe's *Codices Latini antiquiores* (in progress; 3 vols. to date) and *Scriptura Beneventana;* Prou's *Manuel de paléographie latine et française;* the Steffens facsimiles; and Traube's *Nomina sacra* and *Vorlesungen und Abhandlungen*, 2 vols. The manuals of Thompson, Schiaparelli, Kenyon, Lindsay, Ehrle and Liebaert, Van Hoesen, and Capelli offer valuable aids to those working in this field. There are complete, large-size facsimiles of the Palatine manuscript of Vergil, the Vienna Livy, and the Ambrosian Terence. Many important late liturgical texts are available in the publications of the Henry Bradshaw Society, 80 vols. The above works are supplemented by materials in the Hanes Collection and other special collections elsewhere described. For example, there are microfilm or photostatic facsimiles of 250 treatises from about 160 Latin manuscripts, chiefly comprising classical and medieval works on medicine and alchemy but including also the manuscripts Vatic. Lat. 3429 of Tacitus' *Agricola*, Palat. Lat. 1615 and Vatic. Lat. 4929 of Plautus' *Asinaria* and *Aulularia* and the late pseudo-Plautine *Aulularia* or *Querolus*, and Munich MS. Lat. 6388 of Liutprand's *Historia Ottonis*.

Among the approximately one hundred volumes dealing with papyrology are the complete Oxyrhynchus and Tebtunis sets, the *Papiri Greci e Latini*, and the very important periodical *Archiv für Papyrusforschung* (nearly complete), along with several smaller collections, and manuals by Schubart, Goodspeed and Colwell, Kenyon, Winter, and others.

In epigraphy, besides such handbooks as those of Egbert, Sandys, Cagnat, Hicks, and Roberts and Gardner, the Library provides the entire *Corpus inscriptionum Latinarum*, 16 vols. plus many supplements, and Inscriptiones Graecae, 10 vols., together with the sets *Ephemeris epigraphica, Inscriptiones Graecae ad res Romanas pertinentes;* Dittenberger's *Sylloge inscriptionum Graecarum* and *Orientis Graeci inscriptiones selectae;* the *Supplementum epigraphicum Graecum*, and Dessau's *Inscriptiones Latinae selectae*. Other notable works are the *Prosopographia imperii Romani* (first edition, and second as far as published to date), Liebenam's *Fasti consulares*, Dow's *Prytaneis*, Rushforth's *Latin Historical Inscriptions*, Tod's *Greek Historical Inscriptions*, and the Olcott epigraphical thesaurus already mentioned. These materials are augmented by complete files of *Notizie degli scavi di antichità* and *L'Année épigraphique*. There is also, in particular, a very complete assemblage of studies pertaining to the *Res gestae* of Augustus.

There are some historical works in the Library of special value to the student of classics and which in some instances it would now be impossible to replace. Wilamowitz-Moellendorff's *Staat und Gesellschaft der Griechen und Römer*, the large work of Mommsen and Marquardt on Roman antiquities, 19 vols., Frank's *Economic Survey of Ancient Rome*, 5 vols., Clinton's *Fasti Romani*, and Gardthausen's *Augustus und seine Zeit* are in this category. *The Cambridge Ancient History* presents indispensable material, in its text and its unexcelled concise bibliographies. In the special fields of Roman law, military affairs, and provinces, there are, among many other books, Bruns's *Fontes iuris Romani*, Buckland's *Manual of Roman Law*, Cheesman's *Auxilia of the Roman Imperial Army*, Domaszewski's *Die Rangordnung des römischen Heeres*, Parker's *Roman Legions*, and Jones's *Cities of the Eastern Roman Provinces*.

Studies of ancient religion and mythology are represented by such works as Roscher's *Ausführliches Lexikon der griechischen und römischen Mythologie*, Frazer's *Golden Bough*, Cook's *Zeus*, Harrison's *Themis*, and the standard volumes of Bailey, Cumont, Fowler, Glover, Moore, Murray, Nilsson, Picard, Preller, Rouse, and Zielinski. Related works are Burnet's *Early Greek Philosophy*, Zeller's *History of Greek Philosophy*, and Gomperz' *Griechische Denker*, to name but three of the works on philosophy.

The archaeological collection comprises a very good representation of the chief works in the field. The following list will indicate the scope of the Library's offerings: *Bulletin of the American Schools of Oriental Research*, some numbers lacking; the University of Chicago Oriental Institute *Communications, Publications,* and *Studies*, total, 38 vols.; the *Yale Oriental Series Researches*, 19 vols.; Dörpfeld's *Troja und Ilion*; Rostovtzeff's *Excavations at Dura-Europos* and *Dura-Europos and Its Art*; Kraeling's *Gerasa*; the full report *Excavations at Olynthus*, 11 vols.; Griffith's *Archaeological Survey of Egypt*, 25 vols.; the *Memoirs of the Egypt Exploration Society*, 35 vols.; Winlock's *Excavations at Deir el Bahri*; the *Annual of the American School of Oriental Research in Jerusalem*, 20 vols.; the Wellcome-Marston Expedition's *Lachish*; important works on Biblical archaeology by Albright, Barton, Woolley, and

Duncan; the *Papers and Monographs* of the American Academy in Rome, 7 vols.; *Papers* of the British School at Rome, 15 vols.; Beyen's *Die pompejanische Wanddekoration;* Mau's *Pompeji;* Van Deman's *Building of the Roman Aqueducts;* Blegen's *Prosymna;* the *Tiryns* of the Archäologisches Institut des Deutschen Reichs; Evans' *Palace of Minos,* 4 vols.; and Pendlebury's *Archaeology of Crete.* The collection contains also the important books on Greek and Roman art, including some large works on Greek vases.

In the field of numismatics there are available many important treatises, notably Gardner's *History of Ancient Coinage;* Head's *Historia Numorum;* Hill's *Coins of Ancient Sicily* and *Select Greek Coins;* Milne's *Greek Coinage* and *Development of Roman Coinage;* and Seltman's *Greek Coins; The Roman Imperial Coinage,* 5 vols., by Mattingly, Sydenham, and Webb; Grueber's *Coins of the Roman Republic in the British Museum;* and Mattingly's *Coins of the Roman Empire in the British Museum.*

The classical collections here summarized have been enriched in recent months by a special fund established by Lionel Weil. Lists of needed serial files and basic sets are being held until the end of the War makes foreign purchases possible.

Chapter 18

COMPARATIVE LINGUISTICS

George S. Lane

CONSIDERABLE progress has been made in the accumulation of the necessary library resources for graduate work in Indo-European linguistics since the organization of this discipline into a separate curriculum in 1937. Complete sets, up to the present war, of the following general periodicals are now available: *American Journal of Philology; Beiträge zur Kunde der indogermanischen Sprachen; Indogermanische Forschungen; Language; Norsk Tidsskrift for Sprogvidenskap; Zeitschrift für vergleichende Sprachforschung.*

Thus far, however, only partial sets of the *Bulletin* and *Mémoires* of the Société de Linguistique de Paris have been acquired. For general bibliography, a complete set of the *Indogermanisches Jahrbuch* is in the collection.

There are available such essential sets of books and handbooks as Brugmann's *Grundriss der vergleichenden Grammatik der indogermanischen Sprachen;* Hirt's *Indogermanische Grammatik;* all that has appeared of the Brugmann-Thumb *Grundriss der indogermanischen Sprach- und Altertumskunde;* most of the grammars published in the C. Winter *Indogermanische Bibliothek;* the Vandenhoeck and Ruprecht *Göttinger Sammlung indogermanischer Grammatiken;* the volumes of the *William Dwight Whitney Linguistic Series* of Yale University; as well as many of the individual grammars and monographs from the W. de Gruyter Verlag. The French collection of grammars and linguistic studies published by the Société de Linguistique is poorly represented, however.

Aside from general Indo-European linguistics, the curriculum is responsible for the Library acquisitions in the following more special fields. (For Classical, Germanic, and Romance linguistics, see the reports of those departments.)

No attempt has yet been made to accumulate more than the

bare linguistic necessities in Indo-Iranian. For Sanskrit, a good collection of grammars, dictionaries and handbooks, including the Petersburg lexicon in both the longer and the abbreviated edition, and the *Grundriss der indoarischen Philologie*, is available. Texts and critical apparatus are for the most part on the list of desiderata. In Iranian, only the most essential handbooks have been acquired. The collection includes, however, Geldner's *Avesta* text and the *Grundriss der iranischen Philologie*.

For Oriental studies in general, fairly complete sets of the *Zeitschrift der deutschen Morgenländischen Gesellschaft*, the *Bulletin of the School of Oriental Studies* of the University of London, and the Harvard Oriental Series are present. The Duke Library, however, is depended upon for the *Journal Asiatique*, the *Arkiv Orientální*, and even for most of the *Journal of the American Oriental Society*, not to mention a long list of others of less importance.

In Lithuanian, Lettic, Old Prussian, and Church Slavic most of the essential grammars and dictionaries necessary for introductory work are available. Texts and periodicals are noticeably absent, as are also essential material for any research in modern Slavic languages or literatures.

Irish in particular is fairly well represented in handbooks, texts, and critical materials. Three essential periodicals, *Eriu*, the *Revue celtique*, and the *Zeitschrift für keltische Philologie* are complete, as is also the collection of the Irish Text Society. Holder's *Altkeltischer Sprachschatz* is also available, as well as Pedersen's *Vergleichende Grammatik*. British Celtic (Welsh and Breton) is urgently in need of essential materials.

Of the other Indo-European languages, the Library owns materials worth mentioning only in Hittite and Tocharian. In the latter the collection is rather good.

One of the greatest weaknesses of the Library, insofar as Indo-European linguistics is concerned, is the conspicuous absence of the publications of most of the foreign academies of science. It is to be hoped that a serious effort will be made immediately at war's end to acquire these, for their lack is not only felt painfully in this department but in all fields of research in the University.

Chapter 19

ENGLISH LANGUAGE AND LITERATURE

Gregory L. Paine

IN THE PROCESS of meeting the continued demand by students and professors of English for books and more books, the Library has acquired a notable collection of poetry, fiction, drama, essays, and biography, with the critical aids for their study. For freshmen and sophomores, who are required to read literature in courses, there are shelves of reference works and parallel readings in the Reserved Book Room. For juniors and seniors in required and elective courses in English and American literature, the Library supplies the standard editions of the chief British and American authors, with biographies and critical interpretations. It also continues to acquire the best books concerning a hundred or more authors from Chaucer to Thomas Wolfe which appear each year. For reference and general reading there are available current magazine weeklies and monthlies, such as the *Saturday Review of Literature* and the *Atlantic Monthly,* and quarterly journals, such as the *Sewanee Review, American Literature,* and *Studies in Philology.*

In the field of English the Library is rich in bibliographical aids, guides to libraries, treatises on literature, collections of standard works, the publications of societies, and files of learned journals. The basal books for the study of the English language and literature are here, as is revealed by a checking of items in such manuals as Kennedy's *A Concise Bibliography for Students of English* (1940), Spargo's *A Bibliographical Manual for Students of the Language and Literature of England and the United States* (2nd ed., 1941), and Cross's *Bibliographical Guide to English Studies* (8th ed., 1943).

In each of the major fields of English literature there are extensive collections, although they are sometimes inadequate for the specialist working on some limited phase. However, research students may borrow books through interlibrary loans, secure films of rare books and manuscripts, and make journeys to larger libraries not too far distant. Probably the Library's largest holdings are in the Renaissance period, but the collections are significant in Old English, Middle English, the Restoration, the Eighteenth Century, Romanticism, and the Nineteenth Century, including American literature.

OLD AND MIDDLE ENGLISH

The library has all the standard bibliographies and treatises for the study of English literature and language before 1500, including the bibliographies and library lists of incunabula. Since, as in other portions of this volume, it is impossible to give exhaustive lists of the Library's holdings, the following titles should be regarded as only suggestive of the materials available to the student of Old and Middle English: Ames and Herbert, *Typographical Antiquities;* Brown, *Register of Middle English Religious and Didactic Verse;* Brown and Robbins, *Index of Middle English Verse;* Chambers, *The Mediaeval Stage; Gesamtkatalog der Weigendrucke,* Vols. I-VIII (1940); Hammond, *Chaucer: A Bibliographical Manual,* with continuations by Griffith and Martin; Hecht and Schücking, *Die englische Literatur im Mittelalter;* Heusinkveld and Bashe, *Bibliographical Guide to Old English;* Kennedy, *Bibliography of Writings on the English Language;* Parry and Schlauch, *Bibliography of Critical Arthurian Literature;* Paul, *Grundriss der germanischen Philologie;* Peddie, *Conspectus Incunabulorum* and *Fifteenth Century Books;* Tucker and Benham, *Bibliography of Fifteenth Century Literature;* Wells, *Manual of the Writings in Middle English,* with supplements; Wülker, *Grundriss zur Geschichte der angelsächsischen Literatur;* Young, *Drama of the Medieval Church.*

For students of the English language the Library has many dictionaries, glossaries, grammars, and dialect studies. The following list includes some basal works: Bosworth and Toller, *An Anglo-Saxon Dictionary;* Halliwell, *Dictionary of Archaic and Provincial Words, etc.;* Holthausen, *Altenglisches etymolo-*

gisches Wörterbuch; Murray, *New English Dictionary on Historical Principles;* Palmer, *Folk Etymology;* Skeat, *Etymological Dictionary of the English Language;* Stratmann, *Middle-English Dictionary;* Sweet, *Student's Dictionary of Anglo-Saxon;* Wright, *Dictionary of Obsolete and Provincial English; English Dialect Dictionary;* Wyld, *Universal Dictionary of the English Language.*

The Library has extensive files of learned journals for the study of Old English and Middle English literature and language, such as the *Journal of English and Germanic Philology, Modern Philology, Modern Language Notes, Studies in Philology,* and others, which contain articles, reviews of books, and current bibliographies; there are also files of such specialized journals as *Anglia, Archiv für das Studium der neueren Sprachen, Englische Studien, Germanisch-romanische Monatsschrift, Indogermanische Forschungen, Medium Aevum, Speculum, Zeitschrift für romanische Philologie,* and *Zeitschrift für vergleichende Litteraturgeschichte.*

During the nineteenth century there arose in Great Britain and the United States a number of literary and historical societies of learned men interested in the reprinting of manuscripts and old texts and in their scholarly study. The histories of the founding of these societies with the analysis of their publications are available in such books as Thompson's *Handbook of Learned Societies and Institutions,* Steeves's *Learned Societies and English Literary Scholarship,* Williams' *Book Clubs and Printing Societies of Great Britain and Ireland,* and Griffin's *Bibliography of American Historical Societies.* The Library has most of the serial publications, of which the following are especially pertinent to Old and Middle English: *The Anglo-Saxon Poetic Records,* 4 vols.; *Bibliothek der angelsächischen Prosa in kritisch bearbeiten Texten,* 13 vols.; Bodley Head Quartos, 15 vols.; Henry Bradshaw Society, 80 vols.; Camden Society, 299 vols.; Chaucer Society, 154 vols.; Early English Text Society, 343 vols.; English Dialect Society, 80 nos. in 32 vols.; English Place-Name Society, 19 vols.; Facsimile Text Society, 56 vols.; Hunterian Club, 76 vols.; Malone Society, 88 vols.; Medieval Academy of America, *Publications,* 43 vols.,

Monographs, 13 vols.; Parker Society, 55 vols.; Percy Society, 99 nos. in 30 vols.; Scottish Text Society, 105 nos.; *Studien zur englischen Philologie,* 96 nos.; Surtees Society, 154 vols. This list might be supplemented by adding series of studies from the European universities, such as *Anglistische Forschungen* (Heidelberg), 86 nos.; *Bonner Studien zur englischen Philologie,* 34 nos.; *Beiträge zur englischen Philologie* (Leipzig), 12 of the 30 nos.; *Palaestra,* 218 nos.; *Studien zur englischen Philologie,* 89 vols.

Although there are few early manuscripts in the Library, there is an increasing quantity of facsimiles and photographic reprints. The following books are a few of those that are available for paleography: Christopher, *Paleography and Archives;* DeRicci and Wilson, *Census of Medieval and Renaissance Manuscripts in the United States and Canada;* Historical Manuscripts Commission, *A Guide to the Reports of Collections of Manuscripts;* Johnson and Jenkinson, *English Court Hand A.D. 1066–1500;* Keller, *Angelsächische Palaeographie;* Skeat, *Twelve Facsimiles of Old English Manuscripts;* Wattenbach, *Das Schriftwesen im Mittelalter.* The Library does not have the facsimiles of manuscripts published by the Paleographical Society (London, 1873–94) or the publications of the New Paleographical Society.

THE RENAISSANCE PERIOD

The Library has all of the standard bibliographies and treatises for the study of English literature from 1500 to 1660. Of especial importance are the following items: Arber, *Transcript of the Registers of the Company of Stationers of London 1554–1640,* 5 vols.; Case, *Bibliography of English Poetical Miscellanies, 1521–1750;* Corser, *Collectanea Anglo-Poetica,* 5 vols.; Craig, "Recent Literature of the Renaissance," *Studies in Philology,* 1916 to date (annual bibliography, first issued by Shirley Graves, now compiled by Professors Craig and Wells); Esdaile, *List of English Tales and Prose Romances Printed Before 1740;* Greg, *Bibliography of the English Printed Drama to the Restoration; List of English Plays Written Before 1643 and Printed Before 1700;* Greg and Boswell, *Records of the*

Court of the Stationers Company, 1576–1602; Hazlitt, *Collections and Notes in Early English Literature* (seven series); Pollard, *English Miracle Plays, Moralities, and Interludes;* Pollard and Redgrave, *Short-Title Catalogue of Books...1475–1640.*

The learned journals print many articles, reviews, and bibliographies in the field of Renaissance literature, especially on Shakespeare and Milton. In addition to the journals listed in the preceding section on Old English and Middle English language and literature, complete files of the following quarterlies are available: *English, English Studies, Litteris, Humanisme et renaissance, Philological Quarterly, Publications of the Modern Language Association,* and *Review of English Studies.*

In the series of society studies and reprints the Library has important holdings of interest to the Renaissance scholar, in addition to those listed in the section of Old English and Middle English language and literature. The following items make the Library significant: Edward Arber, ed., *British Anthologies,* 10 vols., *English Garner,* 12 vols., *English Reprints,* 30 vols.; Bibliographical Society, *Monographs,* 24 vols., *Publications,* 24 vols., *Transactions,* 15 vols., *Transactions: Supplement,* 16 vols.; British Academy, *Proceedings,* 26 vols.; English Association, *Bulletin,* 81 nos., *Essays and Studies,* 28 vols.; Royal Society of Literature of the United Kingdom, *Essays,* 36 vols.; Spenser Society, *Publications,* 53 nos.; *Tudor Facsimile Texts,* 152 vols.; *Tudor Translations,* 56 vols.

The Library has a good collection by and about Shakespeare. The Shakespeare sets, biographies, criticism, and various studies of Shakespeare are placed together in the same section of the stacks. For the bibliography of Shakespeare there are the compilations of Bartlett, Ebish and Schücking, Jaggard, Simpson, Tannenbaum, and others. There are concordances and dictionaries by W. H. D. Adams, Baker, Bartlett, Becket, Mrs. Clarke, Cunliffe, Dyce, and Schmidt. Of the editions of Shakespeare there are sets by such editors as Collier (8 vols.), Hudson (20 vols.), Porter and Clarke (12 vols.), Rolfe (40 vols.), Dyce (10 vols.), Gollancz (12 vols.), Halliwell (16 vols.), Her-ford (10 vols.), Kittredge (14 vols.), Quiller-Couch and Wilson (17 vols.), and Theobald (8 vols.); also the Yale Shakespeare (36 vols.) and the 23 published volumes of Furness' New Variorum edition.

Although the Library has none of the original quartos and folios, it has facsimile reprints of the *First Folio*, Furnivall's *Shakespere-Quarto Facsimiles* (43 nos.), the five published numbers of the *Shakespeare Quartos in Collotype Facsimile*, and the *Facsimiles* (15 vols.) of the Shakespeare Society. Of the *Publications* of the Shakespeare Society the Library has a complete run (48 nos. in 20 vols.) and of the *Publications* of the New Shakespeare Society almost the complete issue (53 vols.). It has seventy-one volumes of the *Shakespeare Jahrbuch*. It is impossible in this report to list the hundreds of books on sources, influence, language, criticism, and interpretation.

ENGLISH LITERATURE AFTER 1660

The bibliography of English literature after 1660 is rapidly enlarging with the increasing interest in the fields of the Neo-Classic, Romantic, and Victorian periods. The Library has the following bibliographical aids, of varying importance and value: Arber, *Term Catalogues, 1668–1709;* Baker, *Dramatic Bibliography;* Brussel, *Anglo-American First Editions,* 2 vols.; Crane and Kaye, *A Census of British Newspapers and Periodicals, 1620–1800;* Danielson, *Bibliographies of Modern Authors;* Draper, *Eighteenth Century English Aesthetics;* Ehrsam and Deily, *Bibliographies of Twelve Victorian Authors;* Millett, *Contemporary British Literature;* Sadleir, *Excursions in Victorian Bibliography;* Summers, *A Bibliography of the Restoration Drama;* Tobin, *Eighteenth-Century English Literature;* Williams, *Seven XVIIth Century Bibliographies.* There are also several current annual bibliographies in restricted fields, published in the spring numbers of learned journals, which are used extensively by advanced students. Among them are "English Literature, 1660–1800: A Current Bibliography," *Philological Quarterly,* V (1926)–; "Victorian Bibliography," *Modern Philology,* XXX (1933)–; "The Romantic Movement: A Selective and Critical Bibliography," *E L H, a Journal of English Literary History*, VI (1937)–.

The Library has supported the lively interest in English literature since 1660 by securing complete editions, individual bibliographies, biographies, and concordances of all the major and most of the minor writers from Dryden to Bernard Shaw. For the study of seventeenth- and eighteenth-century literature there are, in addition to the basic works of major writers, many general and special historical and critical studies; for example, Dunlop, *History of Prose Fiction*, 2 vols.; Gosse, *Seventeenth Century Studies;* Grierson, *Cross Currents in English Literature of the Seventeenth Century;* Nichols, *Literary Anecdotes of the Eighteenth Century*, 9 vols.; Nicoll, *British Drama, History of Restoration Drama, History of Early Eighteenth Century Drama, History of Late Eighteenth Century Drama*, and others; Saintsbury, *The English Novel;* Stephen, *English Thought in the Eighteenth Century*, 2 vols.; Williamson, *The Donne Tradition*. Important eighteenth-century periodicals are listed below in another connection.

For the nineteenth century the Library has the complete works of major authors and many biographical and critical studies. The following are representative: Browning, *The Complete Poetical Works* in the Riverside and Macmillan editions; Byron, *Poetical Works*, 7 vols., and *Letters and Journals*, 6 vols.; Carlyle, Centenary Edition in 31 vols. with numerous biographies and critical studies concerning him; Coleridge, *Letters*, edited by Griggs, and *Shakespearean Criticism*, edited by Raysor; De Quincey, *Collected Writings*, edited by Masson, 14 vols.; Dickens, two sets of collected works and also the volumes of *All the Year Round* (1859–87) when Dickens was editor; George Eliot, collected novels; Galsworthy, collected works; Hardy, collected works in the rare Mellstock Edition and biographies by Mrs. Hardy and Weber; Hazlitt, *Collected Works*, edited by Waller and Glover, 12 vols.; Lamb, *Works*, edited by Lucas, 7 vols., and also the edition by Macdonald, 12 vols.; Meredith, *Collected Works;* Morris, *Collected Works* in the limited edition of 1910–15; Ruskin, *Collected Works*, edited by Cook and Wedderburn; Scott, complete works and also *Letters* edited by Grierson; Shelley, *Complete Works* in the Julian Edition, 10 vols.; Wells, collected works in the Atlantic Edition; Wordsworth, complete works and also *The Early Letters of William and Dorothy Wordsworth*, edited by De Selincourt. Students of nineteenth-century literature also have access to all the general and most of the special studies of the period, including Beach, *The Conception of Nature in Nineteenth Century English Poetry*; Brandes, *Main Currents in Nineteenth Century Literature*; Collins, *The Profession of Letters*; Cunliffe, *Leaders of the Victorian Revolution*; Elton, several volumes of a survey of English literature from 1730 to 1880; Harrison, *Studies in Early Victorian Literature*; Lippincott, *Victorian Critics of Democracy*; Magnus, *English Literature in the Nineteenth Century*; Massingham, *The Great Victorians*; Saintsbury, *A History of Criticism*, 3 vols., and *A History of Nineteenth Century Literature*; Walker, *The Literature of the Victorian Age*.

For both the eighteenth and the nineteenth century the Library has notable sets of periodicals. Before 1800 three types of literary periodicals arose and flourished in England. First, before 1750, appeared the essay periodicals, such as the *Tatler* and the *Spectator*, followed by their imitators; Johnson's *Rambler* (1750–52) also had many successors. The best of these essay periodicals are listed under such authors as Steele, Addison, and Johnson. Second, the magazines, or miscellanies, appeared with Edward Cave's establishment of his *Gentleman's Magazine* in 1731. Third, the critical review, an older literary form, was revived by Ralph Griffiths in 1749 in his *Monthly Review*, with its successors continuing the popularity of this type in the first part of the nineteenth century. Of these early magazines and reviews the Library has, among others, the *Adventurer* (1752–54), complete; the *Anti-Jacobin Review* (1798–1821), 34 of the 61 vols.; the *British Apollo* (1708–11), complete; the *Gentleman's Magazine* (1731–1907), the first 103 vols.; the *London Magazine* (1732–85), first 21 vols. and 12 other scattered vols.; the *Lounger* (1785–87), complete, except nos. 1-4; the *Monthly Mirror* (1749–89), complete; the *Monthly Review* (1749–89), 59 vols. of the first series. Microfilms of the following essay periodicals have been secured: the *Athenian News* (1710), nos. 1-27; *Champion; or British Mercury* (Nov. 15, 1739–June 19, 1740); the *Examiner* (Aug. 3, 1710–July 26, 1714); the *Freeholder* (Dec. 23, 1715–June 29, 1716); the *Freethinker* (March 24, 1718–July 28, 1721); the *Hermit* (Aug. 4, 1711–Feb. 23, 1712); the *Jacobite's Journal* (1747–48); *Terrae Filius* (1707–1708); the *Monitor* (Apr. 22–July 12, 1714).

The Library contains almost complete files of the best British magazines and reviews of the nineteenth century, such as the *Athenaeum* (1828–1931), 92 of the 153 vols.; *Bentley's Miscellany* (1837–69), 42 of the 64 vols.; *Blackwood's Magazine* (1817–1905), complete; *Chambers' Edinburgh Journal* (1832–), 85 vols.; the *Contemporary Review* (1866–), all vols. except 1-18; the *Cornhill Magazine* (1860–1939), complete; the *Edinburgh Review* (1802–1929), complete; *Fraser's Magazine* (1830–82), 62 vols.; the *Living Age* (1844–), complete; the *Nineteenth Century Review* (1877–), complete; the *North British Review* (1844–71), 49 vols.; the *Quarterly Review* (1809–), complete; the *Westminster Review* (1824–1914), nearly complete.

AMERICAN LITERATURE

The Library has a very good working collection, for students and scholars, of bibliographies, literary histories, biographies, critical studies, poetry, fiction, drama, and essays for the study of American literature. The best of the general bibliographies and literary dictionaries are the following: Allibone, *Critical Dictionary of English Literature and British and American Authors;* "American Literature" section of "American Bibliography," *Publications Modern Language Association,* XXXVIII (1922)–; *Cambridge History of American Literature,* 4 vols, (Bibliographies in Vols. I, II, and IV); *Dictionary of American Biography,* 21 vols.; Duyckinck, E. A. and G. L., *Cyclopaedia of American Literature,* 2 vols.; Evans, *American Bibliography,* 12 vols.; Foley, *American Authors, 1795–1895;* Kelly, *American Catalogue,* 2 vols.; Modern Humanities Research Association, *Annual Bibliography of English Language and Literature,* 1921–38; Roorbach, *Bibliotheca Americana,* 4 vols.; Sabin, *Bibliotheca Americana,* 29 vols.; Trübner, *Bibliographical Guide to American Literature.* Of the many special bibliographies and check lists the following are significant: Blair, *Native American Humor 1800–1900;* Firkins, *Index to Short Stories;* Hill, *American Plays Printed Prior to 1860;* Merle Johnson, *American First Editions;* J. G. Johnson, *Southern Fiction Prior to 1860;* Kunitz, *Living Authors;* O'Neill, *A Description and an Analysis of the Bibliography of American Literature;* Rusk, *The Literature of the Middle Western Frontier,* 2 vols.; Stillwell, *Incunabula and Americana 1450–1800;* Wegelin, *Early American Poetry;* and Wright, *American Fiction 1744–1850.* The book bibliographies of individual authors include noteworthy compilations on Cooper, by Spiller and Blackburn; Edwards, by T. H. Johnson; Emerson, by Cooke; Irving, by Langfield, and also by Williams and Edge; Cotton Mather, by Holmes; Poe, by Heartman and Rede; Thoreau, by Allen; and Whittier, by Currier.

Among the significant or stimulating writings in literary history and criticism are such authors and books as Canby, *Classic Americans;* Foerster, *American Criticism;* Howard, *The Connecticut Wits;* Jones, *America and French Culture;* Mott, *A History of American Magazines,* 3 vols.; Mumford, *The Golden Day;* Parrington, *Main Currents in American Thought,* 3 vols.; Quinn, *A History of the American Drama,* 3 vols.; Pattee, *The Development of the American Short Story;* Rourke, *American Humor;* Tyler, *History of American Literature,* 4 vols.; and Carl Van Doren, *The American Novel 1789–1939.*

The Library acquires all of the biographies of American authors, including such detailed studies as Holloway, *Whitman;* Murdock, *Increase Mather;* A. B. Paine, *Mark Twain,* 3 vols.; Quinn, *Edgar Allan Poe;* Starke, *Sidney Lanier;* Carl Van Doren, *Benjamin Franklin;* Williams, *Washington Irving,* 2 vols.

For the study of fiction there are standard editions, separate novels, and edited works. The following editions are considered definitive: Franklin, *Writings,* edited by Smyth, 10 vols.; *Mark Twain, Works,* Stormfield Edition, 37 vols.; Hawthorne, Riverside Edition, 13 vols.; Emerson, *Complete Works,* 12 vols., *Journals,* 12 vols., and *Letters,* edited by Rusk, 6 vols.; Melville, *Works,* Constable Edition, 16 vols.; Poe, Virginia Edition, edited by Harrison, 17 vols.; Thoreau, *Works* and *Journals,* 20 vols.; Whitman, *Writings,* Camden Edition, 10 vols.

For the study of early American drama there are many volumes of old and reprinted plays, supplemented by the Archibald Henderson Collection of American Drama, which includes over two thousand plays. The history of the theatre is narrated in volumes by Dunlap, Hornblow, Moses, Quinn, Seilhamer, and the volumes of Odell's incomplete *Annals of the New York Stage.* The out-of-print publications of the Dunlap Society have been secured, and also the recent *America's Lost Plays,* 20 vols.

The Library has complete files or facsimile reprints of many of the older magazines and reviews which have ceased publication, with incomplete files of many others. Some of the periodicals in practically complete files are the *Century Magazine,* the *Democratic Review,* the *Dial* (the Rowfant Club reprint), the *Galaxy, Knickerbocker Magazine,* the *North American Review, Russell's Magazine, Scribner's Monthly,* the *Southern Literary Messenger,* and the *Southern Review* (Charleston). Among the current learned journals are *American Literature* and *New England Quarterly;* among the critical reviews are the *Saturday Review of Literature,* the *Sewanee Review,* and the *Virginia Quarterly Review.*

For the study of Southern literature the Library is rich in resources. All the works of Southern literary history and criticism are available, including Baskervill, *Southern Writers,* 2 vols.; Brevard, *Literature of the South;* Davidson, *The Living Writers of the South;* Holliday, *History of Southern Literature;* Link, *Pioneers of the South,* 2 vols.; Moses, *The Literature of the South;* Parks, *Segments of Southern Thought;* Rogers, *Four Southern Magazines;* Smith, *Southern Literary Studies;* and Wroth, *The Colonial Printer.* Of the valuable writings which are on the margin between literature and history, politics, and economics there are such books as *American Studies in Honor of William Kent Boyd;* Couch, *Culture in the South;* Eaton, *Freedom of Thought in the Old South;* Gaines, *The Southern*

Plantation; McIlwaine, *The Southern Poor-White from Lubberland to Tobacco Road;* Mims, *The Advancing South;* and Twelve Southerners, *I'll Take My Stand.* Among the sets of Southern material are *A Library of Southern Literature,* 17 vols., and *The South in the Building of the Nation,* 12 vols. There is some completeness in the bibliographies, biographies, and works of many individual authors, such as the following: Byrd, the manuscript and edited printing of a portion of the *Secret Diary,* all his writings in first editions, all the reprints; Cable, nearly all his writings; J. E. Cooke, the biography by Beaty and most of his writings; Longstreet, nearly complete; J. C. Harris, biographies, copies of the *Countryman,* large collections of writings; O. Henry, approaching completeness; Kennedy, biographies and most of his writings; Lanier, biographies and poems; Mary Murfree, biography by Parks and the fiction; W. H. Page, complete; T. N. Page, most of his writings; Poe, a large collection of bibliographies, biographies, critical studies, and writings; Simms, bibliographies, biography by Trent, volumes of poetry and fiction; Timrod, all available writings. The C. Alphonso Smith collection contains association books with Smith's penciled comments, volumes of criticism, German dissertations in American literature, and studies in folklore.

The students of American literature use many books and magazines purchased for the related fields of American history, political science, and philosophy. Recently the Library acquired a complete set of the *Collections* of the Massachusetts Historical Society, to supplement the volumes of the *Proceedings.*

UNIVERSITY PUBLICATIONS

The Library has almost complete runs of the following serial publications of universities: University of California *Publications in Modern Philology,* 23 vols.; *Publications of the University of California at Los Angeles in Languages and Literatures,* 4 nos.; Catholic University of America, *Philosophical Studies,* 56 of the 66 vols.; *Studies in American Church History,* 31 vols.; *University of Colorado Studies,* 26 vols.; *Columbia University Studies in English and Comparative Literature,* 160 vols.; *Cornell University Studies in English,* 34 vols.; *English Association Pamphlets,* 77 of the 94 nos.; *English Association Essays and Studies,* 28 vols.; *Harvard Studies in Comparative Literature,* 16 vols.; *Harvard Studies and Notes in Philology and Literature,* 20 vols.; *Harvard Studies in English,* 21 vols.; *University of Illinois Studies in Language and Literature,* 26 vols.; *Indiana University Studies,* 26 vols.; *Indiana University Publications, Humanities Series,* 8 vols.; *University of Iowa Humanistic Studies,* 5 vols.; *University of Kansas Humanistic Studies,* 6 vols.; *Leeds Studies in English and Kindred Languages,* 4 vols.; *Maine University Studies,* 61 vols.; *University of Michigan Publications: Language and Literature,* 21 vols.; *University of Minnesota Studies in Language and Literature,* 9 nos.; *University of Missouri Studies,* 17 vols.; *University of Nebraska Studies in Language, Literature, and Criticism,* 18 vols.; *Northwestern University Studies in the Humanities,* 8 vols.; *Ohio State University Contributions in Languages and Literatures,* 11 vols.; *Princeton Studies in English,* 28 vols.; *Rice Institute Pamphlets,* 29 vols.; *St. Andrews University Publications,* 16 of the 43 nos.; *Smith College Studies in Modern Languages,* 21 vols.; *Society for Pure English Tracts,* 59 nos.; *Stanford University Series: Language and Literature,* 6 vols.; *University of Texas Bulletin: Humanistic Series,* 17 nos.; *University of Texas Studies in English,* 19 nos.; *University of Toronto Studies: Philological Series,* 11 nos.; *Washington University Studies: Language and Literature,* 7 nos.; *University of Washington Publications in Language and Literature,* 10 vols.; *University of Wisconsin Philology and Literature Series,* 6 vols.; *University of Wisconsin Studies in Language and Literature,* 38 vols.; *Yale Studies in English,* 100 vols.

DISSERTATIONS AND THESES

The dissertations and theses which have been approved by the Graduate School are collected, catalogued, and shelved in the Library. In the past dozen years two copies of each Ph.D. dissertation and M.A. thesis have been received; therefore copies can be lent locally or sent out through interlibrary loan.

In the English Department many graduate studies have been written since S. B. Weeks's thesis on "The Chester Mysteries" in 1887. For convenience in teaching and examination, the English Department has divided the English graduate program into six fields, in which courses are taught by specialists competent to guide graduate study: Old English, Middle English, Renaissance (including Milton), Seventeenth and Eighteenth Centuries, Nineteenth Century, and American Literature. The following tabulation indicates the distribution and nature of the dissertations and theses in the various fields, with the exception of seventeen theses or dissertations not classifiable in one of the above categories.

Old English and Language.—Six dissertations and thirteen theses, including those in allied linguistic fields. Sample titles: "A Modern English Version of the Old English Dialogues of Gregory" and "The Language and Linguistic Interests of Sir Thomas Elyot."

Middle English.—Four dissertations and fifteen theses, with such titles as "Chaucer's Relative Constructions" and "A Study of Some Relations between Literature and History in the Third Estate of the Fourteenth Century: Chaucer, *Piers the Plowman* and the English Mystery Cycles."

Renaissance.—Twenty-five dissertations and 112 theses, with such titles as "Milton's Use of Personal Epithet," "Elements of English Medieval Romance in the Plays of Robert Greene," and "The Interest in Learning in Shakespeare's Plays."

Seventeenth and Eighteenth Centuries.—Thirteen dissertations and fifty-one theses, with such titles as "Sir Thomas Browne and Seventeenth Century Thought," "The Background of Bishop Joseph Butler's Ideas of Conscience," and "The Neo-Classic Theory of the Epic in England."

Nineteenth Century.—Eight dissertations and sixty-four theses, with such titles as "Wordsworth's Problem of Loss and Recompense" and "Scientific Fiction in English: 1817–1914."

American Literature.—Twenty-two dissertations and eighty theses, with such titles as "Henry Thoreau's Literary Theory and Criticism," "Charleston Periodicals, 1795–1860," and "A History of American Humor to 1765."

Chapter 20

GERMANIC LANGUAGES AND LITERATURES

Richard Jente and George S. Lane

THE development of the Library of the Department of German extends over but a few decades, and yet, in spite of the limited annual appropriation, it is at the present time a very creditable collection. The aim has been, first of all, to secure the leading dictionaries, reference works, and journals, as well as the best available editions of each standard author, the recognized biographies and histories of literature, together with the best critical treatments of the authors, their works, and the literary problems. The collection at large has thus a distinctly modern aspect. The classical period and the nineteenth century are fairly well represented and form a nucleus for graduate work.

The standard bibliographies are here, such as the *Jahresberichte für neuere deutsche Literaturgeschichte* and the *Jahresberichte über die wissenschaftlichen Erscheinungen auf dem Gebiete der neueren deutschen Literatur*, Goedeke's *Grundriss zur Geschichte der deutschen Dichtung*, and Fock's *Report of Dissertations*.

Besides complete files of American and British journals, the leading German serials are here, e.g., *Acta Germanica; Archiv für das Studium der neueren Sprachen und Literaturen; Beiträge zur Geschichte der deutschen Sprache und Literatur; Deutsche Rundschau* (early numbers); *Deutsche Vierteljahrsschrift; Die neue Rundschau; Die Literatur; Euphorion* and its sequel, *Dichtung und Volkstum; Germanisch-Romanische Monatsschrift; Jahrbuch des freien deutschen Hochstifts; Literatur; Literaturblatt für germanische und romanische Philologie; Wörter und Sachen; Zeitschrift für Deutschkunde;*

Zeitschrift für deutsche Philologie; Zeitschrift für deutsche Wortforschung; Zeitscrift für deutsches Altertum.

The Library has a complete file of the more popular journals, such as *Die Woche*, some early numbers of the *Gartenlaube*, and a mixed set of the *Illustrierte Zeitung*. Several necessary journals are lacking, e.g., *Literarisches Zentralblatt* and the contemporary *Das innere Reich* and *Mass und Wert*, which are available at Duke University.

The leading collective works are represented, e.g., Kürschner's *Deutsche National-Literatur; Deutsche Literatur; Deutsche Literaturdenkmale des 18. Jahrhunderts; Neudrucke deutscher Literaturwerke des 16. und 17. Jahrhunderts; Palaestra; Quellen und Forschungen; German-American Annals; America Germanica.*

Several outstanding authors are represented in greater detail, e.g., Goethe. Besides numerous popular editions, biographies, and critical works, the *Ausgabe letzter Hand*, the extensive Weimar edition, and the *Propyläen Ausgabe*, as well as the *Goethe Jahrbuch*, and the *Jahrbuch* and *Schriften der Goethegesellschaft* are in the collection. Of Schiller, the *Säkular Ausgabe* and the Goedeke edition and lesser works are here. Well represented by the best standard editions and critical works are Lessing, Kleist, Tieck, Grillparzer, and Hebbel. An important work for the study of the drama is Litzmann's *Theatergeschichtliche Forschungen*. The leading authors of the nineteenth and twentieth centuries are here in the standard original editions. A large number of the contemporary writers are available also in English translations.

A great gap in the collection is in the literature of the sixteenth and seventeenth centuries. Only the more important reprints of the above-mentioned *Neudrucke, Deutsche Literatur*, and *Kürschner* are in the collection, which, however, does include the voluminous Weimar edition of Luther's works.

The Middle High German period is represented by a large number of standard editions of authors, but there are also many gaps. Von der Hagen's *Minnesinger* and *Heldenbuch, Deutsche Texte des Mittelalters,* and the more popular collections are in the Library. The standard dictionaries of Lexer,

Benecke-Müller-Zarncke are here, as well as individual volumes of the *Bibliothek des Literarischen Vereins in Stuttgart*. The complete set of this valuable work is available in the Library of Duke University, together with considerable other materials.

The collection of dialect dictionaries has been growing; among other acquisitions are the following: Fischer, Tobler, Schmeller, Schiller-Lübben, Martin-Lienhart, Unger-Khull, and Lexer.

Dutch and the modern Scandinavian literatures are represented by only a few books and sets. There are several histories of literature and a scattering of original editions, for instance, Ibsen, but most of the authors here are only in English translations. In the Dutch language, the Library owns Verwijs en Verdam, *Middelnederlandsch Woordenboek*.

The Library is, for the most part, well equipped with the handbooks, periodicals, and essential monographs in general Germanic linguistics, Gothic, and Old High German. For Gothic, there are not only the more modern editions and apparatus but also the older works, such as von der Gabelentz-Loebe, Bernhardt, and others. In Old High German, text editions, special dialect grammars, and essential monographs are here. Items now rather difficult to procure like the Steinmeyer-Sievers collection of glosses, Schade's *Altdeutsches Wörterbuch*, and Graff's *Sprachschatz* are available. The holdings in Old Saxon and Old Frisian are limited but adequate, insofar as their purpose is to support the other branches of Germanic languages, on which greater emphasis has always been laid. However, in Scandinavian, library resources in both older and later periods are quite inadequate for anything but introductory graduate instruction. They are practically limited to historical grammars and dictionaries of Old Icelandic (Vigfusson and Fritzner) and descriptive grammars and the ordinary hand dictionaries of the modern languages. Recently a partial set of the *Altnordische Saga-Bibliothek* and the special periodical *Acta philologica Scandinavica* were acquired.

For the periodicals essential to Germanic linguistics see above. Other periodicals and handbooks indispensable in this field are included under Comparative Linguistics.

Chapter 21

LANGUAGES AND LITERATURES

ROMANCE

William M. Dey

In 1901 the Department of Modern Languages was divided into two departments: the Department of Germanic Languages and Literatures and the Department of Romance Languages and Literatures. As the meager library appropriation had to be shared by German and French up to that time, it is easy to understand that, at the time of the above-mentioned division, the Library lacked many of the necessary working tools in both fields.

The Department of Romance Languages has two special funds for the purchase of French books: (1) The May Fund, established in memory of Samuel May, Instructor in Modern Languages at the University of North Carolina, 1896–1900, for the purchase of French and German books (the income being divided equally between the departments of Germanic languages and Romance languages): (2) The Shipley Fund, established in memory of Miss Katherine Morris Shipley and devoted to French language and literature.

The Library has the fundamental works in Romance philology and literary history, such as the following journals: *Romania*, *Revue des langues romanes*, *Zeitschrift für romanische Philologie*, *Romanische Forschungen*, *Revue de linguistique romane*, *Literaturblatt für germanische und romanische Philologie*, etc.; such works as Gröber's *Grundriss der romanischen Philologie*, Du Cange's *Glossarium*, Raynouard's *Lexique roman*, etc.; and the works of Gaston Paris, Paul Meyer, Meyer-Lübke, and other noted scholars.

The reference collection of the main Library is unusually good for Romance bibliography. It contains the *Catalogue* of the Bibliothèque Nationale, Brunet's *Manuel du libraire et de l'amateur de livres,* Lorenz's *Catalogue général de la librairie française,* Lanson's *Manuel bibliographique de la littérature française,* Talvert and Place's *Bibliographie des auteurs modernes de langue française,* and the *Bibliographie de la France.*

The Library has available for the use of the faculty and students photographic equipment for producing microfilm and photoprint reproductions. The Library also has the equipment for using film reproductions of manuscripts and rare books, which furnish materials for investigation at very low cost. The Hanes and Hunter Collections of incunabula and other rare books are made readily accessible for students in the department.

FRENCH

Old French.—Materials for research are especially rich in Old French language and literature. There is a good collection of the important journals (see above, to which should be added the *Revue de philologie française et de littérature*) and the dictionaries of Godefroy, Tobler, and von Wartburg. The publications of the Société des Anciens Textes Français are practically complete, as are also such collections as the *Classiques français du moyen âge,* the *Classiques de l'histoire de France au moyen âge,* and the *Anciens poètes de la France.*

Critical material on various Old French works is well represented in the Library, though some of the more recent studies are lacking. There are, of course, the works of Bédier on the epic and the *fabliaux,* of Petit de Julleville on the drama, of Gautier and Gaston Paris on the epic, and others.

Modern French.—Materials for research in the modern periods are also very good, especially in the sixteenth, seventeenth, and nineteenth centuries. The Library possesses the most important journals, such as *Humanisme et Renaissance;* the *Revue des études rabelaisiennes,* 1903–12, continued as the *Revue du seizième siècle* to 1933; the *Bulletin des amis de Montaigne;* the *Annales de la Société Jean-Jacques Rousseau;* the *Revue d'histoire littéraire de la France;* and such collections as the publications of the Société des Textes Français Modernes, the *Bibliothèque romantique*, and the *Études romantiques.*

Sixteenth century.—The material on the principal poetic movement of the century—*la Pléiade*—is quite complete. It includes *La Pléiade française* of Marty-Laveaux, the editions published by the Société des Textes Français Modernes, and a good deal of critical material on the movement. The memoirs and *contes* of the period are well represented, but many items on Calvin and the Reformation are lacking. The edition of Rabelais by Abel Lefranc and his collaborators, and some of the critical works of Plattard and Sainéan on Rabelais are here. With regard to Montaigne, there are several editions of the *Essais* in the Library, but none of the rare ones, and only a few of the studies on Montaigne, such as those of Strowski and Plattard.

Seventeenth century.—Besides a great deal of critical material on all the genres, the Library owns the following volumes of the *Grands écrivains de la France:* Corneille, Molière, Racine, Pascal, La Bruyère, Mme de Sévigné, Cardinal de Retz, and Saint-Simon. Material on Descartes is ample. Perhaps the greatest gap is in editions of the novels of the century, but the Library possesses the *Astrée* complete and all the recent works published on it.

Eighteenth century.—The Moland edition of Voltaire is available, and complete editions of Rousseau, Montesquieu, and Diderot, but there are not as many books on the works of these authors as should be available. Several years ago a complete edition of the *Encyclopédie* was presented to the Library. The dramatists are well represented, but here again essential critical works are lacking.

Nineteenth century.—Besides the complete works of all the major poets, the collection contains the critical studies of such scholars as Baldensperger, Estève, etc., the *Lundis*, the *Nouveaux Lundis,* and the *Portraits littéraires* of Sainte-Beuve, the *Études littéraires* of Faguet, etc. Souriau's *Histoire du romantisme* is to be found in the Library, besides the other less important histories of the movement.

The later poetic movements—*le Parnasse* and *le Symbolisme*—

are also well represented. A copy of the original edition of *Le Parnasse contemporain* and many of the critical studies on the Parnassian poets are here. Critical material on the symbolists is not so abundant.

The other genres have not been neglected, particularly the drama and the novel. The collection includes the Conard edition of Balzac, the Champion editions of Stendhal, Mérimée, and Gérard de Nerval, and the Calmann-Lévy edition of Anatole France. The works of the principal philosophers and historians are in the Library, but critical studies of them are lacking.

Twentieth century.—The Library has tried to keep up with the work of the leading contemporary authors, but the output has been so vast that it has been possible to purchase only a small part of it. Some of the works of François Mauriac, André Maurois, Pierre Benoît, Henry Bordeaux, Paul Claudel, Paul Valéry, and André Gide are available. There is a complete set of Marcel Proust and a good many of the critical studies concerning his work.

ITALIAN

The study of Italian has not been emphasized in the University curriculum, and consequently the collection of books in that field is a somewhat restricted one. There are available only one or two journals, such as the *Giornale storico della letteratura italiana* and the *Archivum romanicum*. The Library possesses the *Collezione di opere inedite o rare* and also Benedetto Croce's *Scritti di storia letteraria e politica*.

Standard editions of Dante, Petrarch, Boccaccio, Tasso, and Ariosto, and some of the critical studies on their works are here, but texts and critical material for modern Italian literature are lacking, the only important authors represented being Leopardi, Pellico, Manzoni, Fogazzaro, and Carducci.

SPANISH

Sturgis E. Leavitt

The collection of Spanish books is not so extensive as might be desired, but it is a representative collection, with special emphasis upon bibliography and nineteenth-century drama. The Library has the standard texts and source materials for class instruction in Spanish language and literature, and for research in certain fields.

In language it has Aldrete, *Del origen y principio de la lengua castellana;* Barcia, *Diccionario etimológico;* Covarrubias, *Tesoro;* the *Diccionario de autoridades;* Oudin, *Diálogos;* Terreros y Pando, *Diccionario;* Viñaza, *Biblioteca histórica;* and numerous editions of the dictionary of the Spanish Academy.

The collection of bibliography includes La Barrera; Foulché-Delbosc, *Manual de l'hispanisant;* Nicolás Antonio; *Bibliografía española* (1901–42); and Ford and Lansing, Río y Rico, and Rius for Cervantes. Among other bibliographies and biobibliographies are *Bibliografía zaragozana del siglo XV;* Catalina García, *Biblioteca de escritores de... Guadalajara;* Escudero y Perosso, *Tipografía hispalense;* Díaz y Pérez, *Diccionario... de autores, artistas y extremeños;* Gallardo, *Ensayo de una biblioteca de libros raros y curiosos;* Ruiz y Sainz, *Escritores burgaleses;* Hidalgo, *Diccionario general de bibliografía española;* Latassa, *Biblioteca... de escritores aragoneses;* Martínez Añíbarro, *Diccionario... de autores de la provincia de Córdoba;* Martí Grajales, *Diccionario... de los poetas en el reino de Valencia;* Méndez Bejarano, *Diccionario de escritores... de Sevilla;* Ossario y Bernard, *Periodistas españoles del siglo XIX;* Pérez, *Bibliografía y tipografía gaditanas;* Pérez Pastor, *Bibliografía madrileña, La imprenta en Toledo, La imprenta en Medina del Campo;* Ramírez de Arellano, *Catálogo biográfico de escritores... de Córdoba;* Salvá, *Catálogo;* Sánchez, *Bibliografía aragonesa;* Serrano y Morales, *Imprenta... en Valencia;* Serrano y Sanz, *Escritoras españolas;* Tejera, *Biblioteca del murciano;* Valdenebro y Cisneros, *La imprenta en Córdoba;* Ximeno, *Escritores... de Valencia.* Supplementary material includes Aguiló y Fuster, *Catálogo de obras en lengua catalana;* Anselmo, *Bibliografía das obras impressas em Portugal no século XVI;* Bover, *Biblioteca de escritores balearas;* Elías de Molins, *Escritores y artistas catalanes del siglo XIX;* Pastor Fuster, *Biblioteca valenciana;* Ribelles Comín, *Bibliografía de la lengua valenciana;* Silva, *Diccionario bibliographico portuguez.*

The most important general sets represented are the *Biblioteca de autores españoles,* the *Nueva biblioteca de autores españoles, Clásicos españoles, Libros raros o curiosos, Libros de antaño,* the *Theatro hespañol,* and most of the publications of the Hispanic Society of America. With regard to particular authors, the Library has the *Obras sueltas* of Lope de Vega (Antonio de Sancha), the two Academy editions of Lope de Vega, and standard sets of the most important authors.

In the magazine field, the list includes the *Boletín de la Academia,* the *Bulletin hispanique* (vol. 22 to date); *Cultura española; Hispania; Hispanic Review; Revista de archivos; Bibliotecas y museos; Revista de filología española;* and the *Revue hispanique.* Lesser known magazines held by the Library are the *Correo literario y político de Londres,* 1826; *Español constitucional,* London, 1818–25; *El Instructor,* London, 1834–41; *Semanario pintoresco;* and *Variedades,* London, 1823–25.

In addition to sets and individual plays of the best known Spanish dramatists, the Library has over thirteen thousand Spanish plays, mainly of the nineteenth century. These plays have not yet been catalogued, but they are bound in alphabetical order and can be located easily. A non-official catalogue by author, titles, and types has been made by members of the Spanish faculty.

In 1940 the University of North Carolina, Duke University, and Tulane University agreed upon a program of co-operation in Latin American studies and in the acquisition of library materials in this field. The division of interest was based largely upon holdings at the time of the agreement. Tulane was to be responsible for Mexico and the Caribbean region, and Duke and the University of North Carolina for South America. The special field of specialization for North Carolina was to be

Argentina, Chile, Paraguay, Uruguay, and Venezuela. Each university was free to buy general studies and books needed for class instruction, and the University of North Carolina was unrestricted in bibliography and folklore.

In dictionaries, the University of North Carolina has García Icazbalceta, Garzón, Malaret, Ramos y Duarte, Sandoval, Segovia, Santamaría, and numerous special vocabularies of more limited scope. The bibliographies held by the Library include all the Harvard series, practically all the works of Medina, Beristain and Ramírez, and Jones. For Costa Rica it has Dobles Segreda, *Indice bibliográfico;* for Chile, Anrique, *Ensayo de una bibliografía dramática;* Briceño, *Estadística bibliográfica;* Laval, *Bibliografía de bibliografías;* Leavitt, *Chilean literature;* Montt, *Bibliografía chilena;* Silva Castro, *Fuentes bibliográficas;* and Vaïsse, *Bibliografía general.* Colombia is represented by Laverde Amaya, *Apuntes,* and Posada, *Bibliografía bogotana;* Cuba by Bachiller y Morales, *Apuntes para la historia de las letras y de la instrucción,* and Trelles y Govín, *Bibliografía cubana del siglo XIX;* Mexico by Iguíniz, *Biblioteca de novelistas,* Nicolás León, *Bibliografía . . . del siglo XVIII,* Monterde, *Bibliografía del teatro;* and Uruguay by Scarone, *Bibliografía de Rodó.* Practically all the important histories of Spanish American literature are in the Library.

In the periodical field, the University has the following either complete or almost complete: for Argentina, the *Anales de la universidad de Buenos Aires, Atlántida, Biblioteca,* the *Boletín bibliográfico, Humanidades, Revista de Buenos Aires, Revista de la universidad de Buenos Aires,* and *Sur;* for Chile, the *Anales de la universidad de Chile, Atenea, Revista chilena* (1875–80), *Revista chilena* (1917–30), *Revista de artes y letras, Revista de Chile* (1898–1901), *Revista de ciencias y letras, Revista de Santiago, Revista del progreso, Revista de bibliografía chilena y extranjera,* and *Revista del Pacífico.* Outside the special field of the University, there are *Contemporáneos* for Mexico; the *Papel periódico ilustrado, Revista de las Indias,* and *Santafé y Bogotá* for Colombia.

The Library has a representative collection of the most important writers of Spanish America and is rapidly building up an extensive collection of writers in its special field of interest. It has the *Biblioteca aldeana* of Colombia, the *Grandes escritores argentinos,* and the complete works of Bello, Darío, Echeverría, Ingenieros, Martí, Sarmiento, and Zorrilla de San Martín.

VII

PHYSICAL SCIENCES

Chapter 22

CHEMISTRY

Ralph W. Bost

THE reputation which the Kenan Chemistry Library enjoys on this campus and in the South is largely due to the prudent foresight of Francis P. Venable, Charles H. Herty, and James M. Bell. This is particularly true with reference to the periodical sets. In more recent years, the generous contributions of William Rand Kenan and John Sprunt Hill have made it possible to add important reference books, additional sets of periodicals, and a fine collection of books on the history of chemistry. The Chemistry Library is located in Venable Hall.

The files of chemical periodicals are by no means complete, yet the Library contains those which would be used regularly in teaching and in research. Twenty-eight of the thirty-three common periodicals listed in Soule's *Library Guide for the Chemist*, 1938 (p. 37), are in the Chemistry Library. Twenty-two sets of these are complete, to the beginning of the World War, 1939. The remaining six sets lack only a few volumes. Among the complete sets are *Annalen der Chemie; Berichte der deutschen chemischen Gesellschaft; Bulletin de la Société Chimique de France; Comptes rendus de l'Academie des Sciences; La gazzetta chimica italiana; Journal of the American Chemical Society, Journal of Physical Chemistry; Journal für praktische Chemie; Recueil des travaux des Pays-Bas; Zeitschrift für analytische Chemie; Zeitschrift für anorganische und allgemeine Chemie; Zeitschrift für physikalische Chemie*.

In addition, many other important sets of periodicals are available in the collection. One weakness is the absence of the Russian journals. Fortunately, the Library possesses the chief abstract journals; *Chemical Abstracts* and *British Chemical Abstracts* are complete, but the *Chemisches Zentralblatt* is not complete. In a recent national survey of library holdings of 102 important chemical journal files, this library rated 724 points out of a possible 1,020, showing a surprisingly good record of strength in periodical literature.

The Chemistry Library has most of the important treatises, encyclopedias and comprehensive compilations of data, such as Beilstein, Beilstein-Prager-Jacobsen, Mellor, Gmelin, Thorpe, Watts, Ure, Ullman, Abegg, Richter, Stelzner, Houben, Heilbron, Roscoe, and Schorlemmer, Landolt-Börnstein, *International Critical Tables* and *Annual Tables*. Also the leading monographs and important reviews are on file. Among these are the series of *A. C. S. Monographs, Annual Reports*, and *Annual Review of Biochemistry*.

In the field of textbooks and reference books, the Library's holdings are strong. There are approximately three thousand volumes in this category, distributed as follows: inorganic textbooks, 173; analytical, 472; organic, 487; physical, 468; industrial, 652; physics, 315; miscellaneous, 303. Some of these are both old and valuable, but most of them have been added in recent years. New titles are added as they become available.

The Library possesses a valuable collection of reprints which deal with mineralogical, geological, chemical, and analytical methods, apparatus and related topics. This collection consists of approximately eight thousand items. Graduate students find them to be of unusual value in seminar work as well as in research. Other groups have been gathered on such chemical topics as antimalarials, anesthetics, plastics, hormones, and vitamins. In addition, a modest collection has been started on complete reprint sets of the publications of outstanding American chemists.

The Library owns several scores of alchemical prints which are framed for permanent display. In addition, there is an even greater number of engravings and photographic portraits of Nobel Prize winners in chemistry and of other famous chemists, which are mounted for exhibition on the walls of the Library, class rooms and halls.

Good use is made of a small but valuable collection on the history of chemistry, now numbering more than a thousand volumes. Two of the earliest volumes in the collection are the work of Giorgio Agricola, *De generatione delle cose*, 1550, and *De subtilitate* by Hieronymus Cardanus, the Physician of Milan, 1554. Many of these early volumes are in French, German, Latin, Chinese, and Italian, and frequently deal with physics, philosophy, medicine, and religion, as well as chemistry.

Chapter 23

GEOLOGY AND GEOGRAPHY

W. F. Prouty

THE GEOLOGY COLLECTION of the University of North Carolina Library consists of fourteen thousand volumes, and in addition is supported by unbound pamphlets, maps, charts, slides, and aerial photographs. The main features of the Collection are suggested in the following lists.

Principal bibliographies, indexes, and reference sets, include *Bibliographie des sciences geologiques; International Catalogue of Scientific Literature; Mineralogical Abstracts; Geophysical Abstracts; Ceramic Abstracts; Annotated Bibliography of Economic Geology; Geological Literature* of the Geological Society of London; Margerie's *Catalogue of Published Bibliographies;* Nickle's *Bibliography of North American Geology; Bibliography and Index of Geology Exclusive of North America* of the Geological Society of America; *Geologisches Zentralblatt*, Ellis' *Catalogue of Paleontology* (29 vols.); Dunstan's *The Science of Petroleum* (4 vols.); and the *Encyclopaedia Britannica.*

The Collection has all of the publications of the United States Geological Survey, including those of the Hayden, King, Powell, and Wheeler surveys, and in addition 3,657 State Geological Survey publications. There is some foreign geological material, that for Canada being more adequate than for any other country. The coverage is also good for Mexico, various parts of the British Empire, New Zealand, Queensland, and South Australia.

Periodical literature runs to 3,428 bound volumes. Important files include *American Journal of Science; Transactions* and *Journal* of the Illinois State Academy of Science; *American Mineralogist; Mineralogist; Mineralogical Magazine; Bulletins, Memoirs, Proceedings* and *Special Papers* of the Geological Society of America; *Geological Magazine; Journal of Geology;*

Pan American Geologist; Quarterly Journal of the Geological Society of London; *Bulletins, Memoirs,* and *Paleontologia Sinica* of the Geological Society of China; *Anales, Boletines,* and *Parergones* of the Instituto Geológico of Mexico; *Transactions* of the American Geophysical Union; *Geophysics; Bulletins* of the Seismological Society of America; *Monthly Weather Review,* a file of United States Weather Bureau maps since 1928; *Journal of Sedimentary Petrology; Bulletin* of the American Association of Petroleum Geologists; *Oil and Gas Journal; Rock Products; Southern Power and Industry; Bulletins of American Paleontology; Journal of Paleontology; Coal Age; Quarterly* of the Colorado School of Mines; *Engineering and Mining Journal; Transactions* of the Institute of Mining Engineers; *Transactions* and *Technical Papers* of the American Institute of Mining and Metallurgical Engineers; *Mineral Industry; Mines Magazine; Mining and Metallurgy; Mining Congress Journal; Bulletins, Economic Papers, Information Circulars, Reports of Investigation,* and *Technical Papers* of the United States Bureau of Mines; *Publications* of the United States Soil Conservation Service; *Bulletins* of the American Ceramic Society; and the *Journal of Photogrammetic Engineering.*

University geological publications are also available, including those from California, Glasgow, Princeton, Leland Stanford, Texas, and Toronto.

In addition to technical treatises, the Collection includes books about geology written for the layman, some biographies, thousands of reprints, guidebooks, accounts of early exploration and travel. There are also three thousand lantern slides, as well as some films exhibiting both geographical and geological topics.

The Library possesses a complete set of United States Geological Survey topographic maps and geologic atlases. In many instances several duplicates are available. Geological maps of the states and some foreign geological maps also are on hand, as well as aerial photographs of several counties and drainage basins in the southeastern United States.

Fields of emphasis include paleontology, economic and structural geology, mineralogy and petrology, geophysics, meteorology, cartography and photogrammetry, soils, and geography.

Special attention has been given to economic and human geography, and to the study and teaching of geography. There are included among the reference works 250 atlases and seventy-five gazetteers. Important complete files of journals are *Economic Geography; Geographical Review; Geographical Journal; Scottish Geographical Magazine; Annals of Association of American Geographers; Journal of Geography; National Geographic Magazine; Petermanns Mitteilungen;* also available in the collection are *Bibliographie géographique internationale;* Vidal de la Blanche's *Geographie universelle;* Madoz's *Diccionario geográfico estadístico-histórico de España;* Ameghino's *Obras completas; Bibliotheca geographica;* Vivien de Saint Martin's *Nouveau dictionnaire de geographie universelle;* and *The Great Soviet World Atlas.*

In addition there are several thousand volumes in the main Library and in the several departmental libraries which supplement the offerings in the Library of the Department of Geology and Geography.

Chapter 24

MATHEMATICS

Alfred Brauer

THE LIBRARY OF THE DEPARTMENT OF MATHEMATICS is housed in Phillips Hall along with the Library of the Department of Physics, with which it is closely integrated. The Library of the Department of Physics contains many periodicals and books which are of importance to the mathematician. There are also materials necessary for research work in mathematics in the main Library and in the libraries of other departments. For instance, there are the *Proceedings* of the National Academy of Sciences and the *Comptes rendus des séances de l'Académie des Sciences* (Paris), in the Library of the Department of Chemistry and the *Bulletin de l'Académie Royale des Sciences, des Lettres et des Beaux-Arts de Belgique* in the Library of the Department of Zoology.

The Library of the Department of Mathematics contains approximately 3,500 volumes. There are few so-called textbooks in elementary mathematics and calculus, since most of them do not correspond with modern standards of precision. The collection of American and English books in higher mathematics is quite complete compared with corresponding collections in other libraries. The situation regarding French, German, Italian, and other foreign books is different. It has been possible to purchase only a comparatively small part of the necessary volumes. It is impossible to mention all those volumes which are available. The listing of some of them, arbitrarily chosen, would give a completely wrong picture. Therefore, in order to describe this part of the Library correctly, all those available books are listed which were published outside the United States, England, and Canada during the last fifteen years. If this list should be extended to a list of the last twenty-five, or the last fifty years, it would give approximately the same picture to everyone who knows at least a little about books of modern mathematics.

The following books are available: *Enzyklopädie der mathematischen Wissenschaften* (vol. I, 2nd ed. as far as published; the complete first edition and the French edition are available); Kommerell, *Das Grenzgebiet der elementaren und höheren Mathematik;* Rademacher und Toeplitz, *Von Zahlen und Figuren;* Waismann, *Einführung in das mathematische Denken, die Begriffsbildung der modernen Mathematik;* Dubislav, *Die Philosophie der Mathematik in der Gegenwart;* Frege, *Die Grundlagen der Arithmetik;* Kaufmann, *Das Unendliche in der Mathematik und seine Ausschaltung;* Gauss, *Werke* (vols. I-IX, X, pt. 1, XI, and XII are available); Kronecker, *Werke* (vols. I-IV are available); Neugebauer, *Vorgriechische Mathematik;* Tropfke, *Geschichte der Elementarmathematik in systematischer Darstellung;* Perron, *Algebra;* van der Waerden, *Moderne Algebra;* Hausdorff, *Mengenlehre;* Krull, *Idealtheorie;* van der Waerden, *Gruppen von linearen Transformationen;* Zassenhaus, *Lehrbuch der Gruppentheorie;* Deuring, *Algebren;* Hasse, *Höhere Algebra;* MacDuffee, *The Theory of Metrices;* Ore, *L'algèbre abstraite;* Hadamard, *Leçons de géométrie élémentaire;* Hessenberg, *Grundlagen der Geometrie;* Hilbert and Cohn-Vossen, *Anschauliche Geometrie;* Cartan, *Leçons sur la géométrie projective complexe;* Reidemeister, *Vorlesungen über Grundlagen der Geometrie;* Julia, *Eléments de géométrie infinitésmale;* Heffter, *Grundlagen und analytischer Aufbau der Geometrie;* Schilling, *Die Pseudosphäre und die nichteuklidische Geometrie;* Alexandroff, *Einfachste Grundbegriffe der Topologie;* Alexandroff and Hopf, *Topologie;* Cartan, *La théorie des groupes finis et continus et l'analysis situs;* König, *Theorie der endlichen und unendlichen Graphen;* Kuratowski, *Topologie;* Reidemeister, *Einführung in die kombinatorische Topologie;* Seifert and Threlfall, *Lehrbuch der Topologie;* Chisini, *Lezioni di geometria analitica e proiettiva;* Schrier and Sperner, *Einführung in die analytische Geometrie und Algebra;* Blaschke, *Vorlesungen über Differentialgeometrie;* Duschek and Mayer, *Lehrbuch der Differentialgeometrie;* Tzitzéica, *Introduction à la géométrie différentielle projective des courbes;* Zariski, *Algebraic Surfaces;* van der Waerden, *Einführung in die algebraische Geometrie;* Tisserand, *Recueil complémentaire d'exercices sur le calcul infinitésimal;* Bieberbach, *Theorie der Differentialgleichungen;* Einstein, *Les fondements de la théorie de la relativité générale;* Seifert and Threlfall, *Variationsrechnung im Grossen;* Behnke and Thullen, *Theorie der Funktionen mehrerer komplexer Veränderliche;* Bieberbach, *Lehrbuch der Funktionentheorie;* Knopp, *Funktionentheorie;* Hahn, *Reelle Funktionen;* Appell and Goursat, *Théorie des functions algébriques et de leurs intégrales;* Klein, *Vorlesungen über die hypergeometrische Funktion;* Banach, *Opérations linéaires;* Kolmogoroff, *Grundbegriffe der Wahrscheinlichkeitsrechnung.*

There are approximately thirty-five periodicals in the Mathematics Library. All the essential American periodicals are available, hence it is not necessary to list them. But the number of foreign periodicals available is not very large. The following journals are available in complete sets: *Proceedings* of the Royal Academy of Sciences, Amsterdam; *Journal für die reine und angewandte Mathematik; Acta mathematica; Fundamenta mathematicae; Jahrbuch über die Fortschritte der Mathematik; Japanese Journal of mathematics; Journal de mathématiques pures et appliquées; Mathematica; Mathematische Annalen; Nouvelles annales de mathématiques; Revue semestrielle des publications mathématiques; Rendiconti del circolo matematico di Palermo; Proceedings* of the London Mathematical Society. Moreover, there are a number of volumes of the following periodicals: *Proceedings* of the Cambridge Philosophical Society; *Ergebnisse eines mathematischen Kolloquiums; Compositio mathematica; Mathematische Zeitschrifte; Mathesis; Quarterly Journal of Mathematics.*

Some of the foreign journals which are not available now and which should be added as soon as possible are *Journal* of the London Mathematical Society; *Abhandlungen aus dem Mathematischen Seminar der Hamburgischen Universität; Jahresbericht der Deutschen Mathematiker Vereinigung; Nachrichten der Göttinger Gelehrten Gesellschaft; Zeitschrift für angewandte Mathematik und Mechanik; Bulletin des sciences mathématiques; Bulletin de la Société Mathématique de France; Annales de l'Ecole Normale Supérieure; Annali di matematica; Commentarii mathematici.*

Chapter 25

PHYSICS

Nathan Rosen

THE PHYSICS LIBRARY shares quarters with the Mathematics Library in Phillips Hall. It provides facilities to satisfy the needs of all who work in physics, from the elementary student to the advanced research worker.

The periodical collection is exceptionally good in both American and foreign publications. The Library receives over fifty journals in physics and related fields, as well as a number in engineering. Among the journals are the following: *Physical Review; Proceedings of the Royal Society of London; Zeitschrift für Physik; Physikalische Zeitschrifte; Annalen der Physik; Helvetica physica acta; Journal of the Optical Society of America; Journal of the Acoustical Society of America; Annales de physique; Journal de physique; Physikalische Zeitschrifte der Sowjetunion; Physica; Journal of Chemical Physics; Physikalische Berichte;* and *Science Abstracts*. Most of the important journals are in complete sets, some of them consisting of large numbers of volumes, as *Annalen der Physik*, which runs to well over three hundred volumes. The Library has practically all the journals needed by the research physicist with the exception of *Comptes rendus*, which is available in the Chemistry Library, and some of the recent numbers of various foreign journals which have failed to come because of the war.

The Library possesses a considerable number of reference books, including general encyclopedias and dictionaries. The reference books of greatest importance to those working in physics are the various handbooks and collections of tables and data. Numerous sets of handbooks are available, including the *Handbuch der Physik, Handbuch der Experimentalphysik, International Critical Tables, Handbuch der Astrophysik, Dictionary of Applied Physics, Handbuch der Radiologie, Tables annuelles internationales de constantes et données numériques,*

Handbuch der Spectroscopie, Landolt Börnstein physikalisch-chemische Tabellen and others.

Classical physics is well represented by textbooks and treatises on mechanics, sound, heat, light, and electricity, as well as by the collected works of the older physicists, such as Gibbs, Lorentz, Abbe, Lord Rayleigh, and others. The collection includes books on astronomy and celestial mechanics, many of which are recent, and others date back to the eighteenth century.

Modern physics, both experimental and theoretical, is adequately covered by books in English and foreign languages on spectroscopy, atomic structure, quantum theory, wave mechanics, crystal structure, theory of metals, and nuclear physics. Most of the significant books on modern physics have been acquired. Among these are books by Einstein, Rutherford, Heisenberg, Dirac, Born, Schrödinger, Sommerfeld, de Broglie, Bragg, Brillouin, Heitler, Landé, Frenkel, Debye, and others who have played important roles in the development of modern physics.

There are also books on the applications of physics, including various kinds of engineering; on borderline fields, such as geophysics, meteorology, and biophysics; and on such related fields as chemistry and mathematics.

In addition to the technical treatises and manuals, the Library possesses the more elementary books for the younger student, both in general physics and in special branches. Also, there are books on popular physics, requiring little training for their appreciation, and a small but growing number of historical and biographical books providing background material.

VIII

SOCIAL SCIENCES

Chapter 26

ANCIENT HISTORY

W. E. Caldwell

As A RESULT OF a long-standing tradition of classical education in the University, the Library is well equipped for study and research in Greek and Roman history. In recent years fair collections for the study of preliterary and of Near Eastern history have been added.

Among general works can be listed the *Cambridge Ancient History;* Pauly-Wissowa, *Realencyclopädie;* Daremberg-Saglio, *Dictionnaire des antiquités;* Müller, *Handbuch der klassischen Altertumswissenschaft,* complete; Gercke-Norden, *Einleitung in die Altertumswissenschaft;* the *Legacy* series; and the works of such historians as Meyer and Rostovtseff.

Bibliographies are found in the volumes of the *Cambridge Ancient History;* Pratt, *Ancient Egypt: Books in the New York Public Library; The Year's Work in Classical Studies;* Bursian, *Jahresbericht;* the *Bibliotheca philologica classica;* Marouzeau, *Dix années de bibliographie classique* with its continuation, *L'Année philologique.*

In the field of preliterary history the Library has Ebert, *Reallexikon der Vorgeschichte,* the standard works of Macalister, MacCurdy, Osborn, Peake and Fleure, *The Corridors of Time,* and others; a good collection of monographs; three volumes of the publications of the caverns including the important Capitan, Breuil, Peyrony, *La Caverne de Font du Gaume,* and the important anthropological reviews.

In the field of Near Eastern history the Library, though lacking in the field of Semitic languages, has the works of Albright, Breasted, Budge, Capart, Erman, Gardiner, Jastrow, Maspero, Olmstead, Petrie, Rogers, Woolley, the publications of the Oriental Society at Yale, the Oriental Institute at Chicago, the University of Pennsylvania Museum, the bulletins and several volumes published by the Metropolitan Museum in New York, the bulletins of the American Schools of Oriental Research (some numbers lacking), twenty-five volumes of the *Archaeological Survey of Egypt,* thirty-four volumes of the *Memoirs of the Egypt Exploration Society,* the *Annual of the American School of Oriental Research in Jerusalem.* The Library is deficient in periodicals in this field.

For Greek and Roman history there are available the works of Beloch, Botsford, Bury, Busolt, Cavaignac, Croiset, Dessau, Dill, Evans, Frank (including the important *Economic Survey of Rome*), Glotz, Grote, Heitland, Holm, Mommsen (including the large work of Mommsen and Marquardt on Roman antiquities in the French translation), Pais, Schiller, and Seeck.

The Library contains complete sets of the Teubner, Oxford, and Loeb edition of classical texts, the monumental *Corpus inscriptionum Latinarum, Inscriptiones Graecae* with the attendant collections of Dessau, Dittenberger, Tod, and others, and the large collections of published papyri including *Oxyrhynchus* and *Tebtunis.* For further details with regard to these fields the reader is referred to the statement of the Department of Classical Languages and Literatures.

The Hanes Collection contains a few museum specimens from Egypt and Babylonia. The Art Department possesses a good collection of pictures.

Chapter 27

MEDIEVAL HISTORY AND CIVILIZATION, INCLUDING THE RENAISSANCE

Loren C. MacKinney

RESEARCH RESOURCES for Medieval and Renaissance civilization were not adequately built up in the University's earlier days, and since the comparatively recent establishment (1930) of a chair of Medieval and Renaissance history, the Library has had lean years. Consequently, there are serious gaps in scholarly holdings. However, most of the standard histories for general reading are available, including such secondary works as Gibbon, Hodgkin, Milman, Gregorovius, Thorndike, Burckhardt, Symonds, and the Cambridge histories; also such primary source books as Ayer, Coulton, Henderson, Robinson, *Translations and Reprints,* the Nicene Fathers, the Records of Civilization series, and the Loeb Library.

As far as graduate research is concerned, certain fields are well represented by monographs and scholarly journals; for instance, the French, English, Italian, and Spanish Renaissance periods; the history of literature and language, philosophy, folklore, the fine arts (especially music), and the sciences (especially chemistry and medicine). There are, however, conspicuous lacks in other fields, such as German, Medieval Italian and Spanish, Norse, Eastern European, and economic history, and in periodicals and bulletins for specific localities. On the other hand, the Hanes Collection of incunabula and the Smith and Roselle Johnson Collections of photo-reproductions of medieval manuscripts provide first-hand materials of unusual value in their respective fields, viz., the history of writing and printing and of alchemy and medicine. Resources in paleography and related subjects are supplemented by the holdings of the Classics Department.[1]

1. For details concerning holdings usable for Medieval research in classics and other supplementary fields (languages, literature, etc.), see the reports of these departments elsewhere in this volume.

In the great research collections there are many gaps; for instance, in the field of church history, the *Patrologia, Acta sanctorum* and *Concilia* are lacking. The Library does not possess the collections for Germany (*Monumenta*), and for northern and eastern Europe. Fortunately, some of these are available at Duke University. The way in which our holdings are thus supplemented can best be indicated by citing a recent survey concerned with "the relative strength of [64] institutional libraries in America in the 45 more important representative sets of interest to Medieval and Renaissance scholars." [2] Among the sixty-four institutional libraries, University of North Carolina holdings ranked thirty-second in the nation and fourth in the South; Duke University ranked second in the South. The survey calls attention to the fact that a co-operative arrangement, including regular loan service, between the Carolina and Duke libraries, "to avoid duplication in the purchase of the more expensive sets ... makes the total available holdings much higher than the score of either [institution] would show separately." Thus the *joint* ranking is twelfth in the nation, and first in the South. Of the forty-five standard sets, all but thirteen are available at one or the other Library. For instance, Duke's holdings on Germany and the Church, as has been pointed out above, supplement the University of North Carolina's collection in those fields, as Carolina's Spanish collections (*España sagrada, Documentos inéditos*) supplement the holdings at Duke.

Of the thirty-two combined holdings, Carolina possesses only eighteen, whereas Duke has twenty-nine and is acquiring additional sets. Among the sets available at Carolina not mentioned elsewhere in this volume are *Archiv für Literatur- und Kirchengeschichte des Mittelalters;* Hefele-Leclerq, *Histoire des conciles;* Muratori, *Rerum Italicarum scriptores; Recueil des historiens des Gaules et de la France;* Rymer, *Foedera, conventiones....* Few expensive collections were added at Carolina in the lean decade, notable exceptions being those in Spanish history, one by gift, another by funds from a foundation. The Duke-Carolina collaboration is sound, for it is obviously un-

2. *Progress of Medieval and Renaissance Studies,* Bulletin 16, p. 50; Bulletin 17, p. 49.

economical to build two strong duplicating research libraries for Medieval and Renaissance history in the same locality. But it should be made more effective, first by the avoidance of duplication in expensive collections, and second by Carolina's purchase of important sets in certain fields. With effective co-operation, materials now lacking could be acquired without straining the financial resources of either institution, and in time the Duke-Carolina area might match the leading institutions of the nation in Medieval and Renaissance holdings.

Chaper 28

MODERN EUROPEAN HISTORY

Mitchell B. Garrett and James L. Godfrey

THE LIBRARY has the essential secondary works, periodicals, encyclopedias, and guides for undergraduate instruction in Modern European history, but it is not so well provided with the materials essential for graduate instruction. Only in the field of the French Revolution and Napoleon, and to a lesser extent in the field of the First World War, has there been a modest effort to build up a collection of primary source material. Partially counterbalancing this weakness, however, is the excellent equipment in printed catalogues and other bibliographical guides (the best in the southern area). Candidates for the doctorate may therefore begin their research here, but to complete it they are usually obliged to migrate to other libraries or research centers.

SIXTEENTH AND SEVENTEEN CENTURIES

For this period the Library has most of the standard works in English and a few in French, German, and Spanish. The works of Ranke, Lamprecht, Sismondi, the *Histoire générale* by Lavisse and Rambaud, and the *Cambridge Modern History* are all here. Certain basic collections of source material are also here: for Germany, the Weimar edition of Luther's *Werke;* for France, the great *Collection de documents inédits,* the *Mémoires* of Saint-Simon and Michaud's *Nouvelle collection des mémoires;* and for Spain, the *Colección de documentos inéditos.* Erasmus is represented by the Allen edition of the *Opus epistolarum* and Calvin by the *Institutes.*

FRENCH REVOLUTION AND NAPOLEON

In this field the Library is fairly well equipped for both undergraduate and graduate instruction. Not only the standard works but also many volumes containing the latest results of research and interpretation are available. Besides, the Library has the largest and most valuable collection of source material in this field to be found in the southern area. The following is a partial list: The *Procès-verbal* of the Constituent Assembly; the *Journal des débats et des décrets* by Baudouin; the *Journal de Paris;* the *Révolutions de Paris;* the *Réimpression de l'ancien moniteur;* the *Collection des mémoires* by Berville and Barrière; the *Collection générale des décrets* by Baudouin; the fourth series of the *Collection de documents inédits;* the *Collection de documents relatifs à l'histoire de Paris;* the *Histoire parlementaire* by Buchez and Roux; and the *Correspondence de Napoléon premier.* In addition, there are almost complete files of all the important periodicals, such as: *La Révolution française; Revue historique; Revue d'histoire moderne et contemporaine; Revue des questions historiques; Revue des études napoléoniennes.* Serious gaps remain to be filled. The Library does not have, for example, the *Collection de documents inédits sur l'histoire économique de la révolution française,* or the *Archives parlementaires.*

NATIONAL HISTORY IN THE NINETEENTH CENTURY

In this field the Library has the materials essential for undergraduate instruction and for the lower levels of graduate instruction, but it is deficient in materials essential for research. For example, the parliamentary papers, journals, and debates of the continental governments are lacking; there are no collections of laws, no files of contemporary European newspapers, and only a scattering of memoirs (usually in translation) of prominent Europeans. A few secondary works by such European historians as Weill, Croce, Debidour, Sybel, Treitschke, and Sombart are here, but absent are the works of Stern, Onken, Flathe, De La Gorce, and many others. There is no historical material in the Russian language.

WORLD WAR (1914–18) AND AFTER

The Library's resources for the study of contemporary European history are good for titles published in English. There are few books of foreign origin and the important public documents of the European governments are lacking. The publications of the League of Nations constitute the single important collection of official or semiofficial materials.

For the World War of 1914–18 there are two important scrap-book collections and a large miscellaneous collection. The first and most important of these is a nine-hundred volume scrap-book collection of English newspaper clippings made for the Conservative Party of England. It covers a wide range of subjects from the middle of the nineteenth century through the First World War with the greatest concentration in the war period. Unfortunately, its value is limited by the absence of a working index. The second scrap-book collection consists of 109 volumes made up almost entirely of pictorial material. The third, the Bowman Gray Collection, includes a very large selection of newspapers, pamphlets, books, posters, and other propaganda material relating to the First World War. This collection can not be used effectively until it is catalogued and suitable quarters are secured for its housing.

On the Paris Peace Conference (1919–20) the Library has the privately published Miller's *Diary* but no other materials of special significance. The post-war period is covered by a large collection of assorted titles especially suitable for undergraduate instruction. It is in this period that the resources suffer especially from the lack of foreign books and government publications.

INTERNATIONAL RELATIONS

The Library has the League of Nations Treaty Series, the official publications of the United States government, and the volumes published under the auspices of the Carnegie Endowment and the Royal Institute of International Affairs, and is reasonably well supplied with the secondary works necessary for undergraduate instruction. The Library does not have the great collections essential to research and graduate instruction. The first ninety-three volumes of the *Archives diplomatiques* are boxed up and can be used only with difficulty; the *Livres Jaunes, Documents diplomatiques, Staats Archiv,* and the *British and Foreign State Papers* are lacking. The presence of the *Grosse Politik der europäischen Kabinette* and the *British Documents on the Origins of the War* is offset by the absence of the *Documents diplomatiques français* and the *Oesterreich-Ungarns Aussenpolitik.* The Library has a part of the series of treaties begun by George F. von Martens, but never has acquired such important national treaty series as the collection by the Hertslets for Great Britain and Jules de Clerq for France. Files of most of the English and American periodicals on international affairs are present, though frequently incomplete.

A beginning is being made in important collections on South American aspects of international relations with the recent acquisition of *Colección completa de los tratados* (Calvo); *Colección de tratados celebrados por la república Argentina con las naciones extrangeras; Tratados, convenciones, protocoles y demas actos inter-nacionales vigentes... republica Argentina; Los tratados de Chile; Tratados y convenios de Colombia; Tratados publicos y acuerdos internacionales de Venezuela.*

EUROPEAN JOURNALS AND NEWSPAPERS

The Library's holdings in foreign journals are good for France but almost non-existent for other continental countries. Even in the French section several files are incomplete. The *Revue des deux mondes* lacks only a few issues, but serious gaps exist in the *Revue de Paris,* the *Mercure de France,* the *Revue politique et litteraire,* the *Revue historique,* and the *Revue des questions historiques.* The Library has files of two German journals of historical value: the *Historische Zeitschrifte,* which is complete, and the *Deutsche Rundschau,* with wide gaps. Other important historical journals of France and Germany are not represented, and there are no files of journals in this field from any other continental country.

For all practical purposes, there is no collection of European newspapers. The Library has the *Frankfurter Zeitung* (August 1914 to April 1916), *Vorwaerts* (April–September, 1915), and the *Nationalzeitung* (1877). A few scattered volumes of *Le Moniteur* represent French journalism from Napoleon I to Napoleon III. No other countries are represented.

Chapter 29

ENGLISH HISTORY

J. C. Russell

THE LIBRARY possesses a substantial collection of books in the field of English history, which includes most of the monographs and sets of national scope. A good beginning has been made in local history. The chronological distribution is fairly even, the thirteenth and eighteenth centuries being especially well represented. This collection is supplemented by the holdings of departments with related interests, such as law, political science, economics, English, and social work, and by the large collection of books in the near-by Duke University Library. Most of the recent works in the field are available.

The bibliographical resources include the usual encyclopedias (*Britannica, Italiana*, etc.) and standard works, such as those by Gross, Davies, Hall, Humphries, Milne, and Morgan, as well as the *Bulletin of the Institute of Historical Research*, Le Neve's *Fasti* and such less common books as Tanner's *Bibliotheca Anglo-Hibernica*. Although the Library has acquired most of the better known catalogues of manuscript collections, such as the British Museum, Bodleian, Cambridge colleges, John Rylands, and Lincoln Cathedral, it does not have the *Catalogue of the Manuscripts Preserved in the Library of the University of Cambridge*, 1856–67. Coxe's catalogue of the Oxford colleges is at Duke. There are also catalogues of printed books of libraries in Edinburgh, Manchester, and London (London Library and the new catalogue of the British Museum). It also has the *English Catalogue, The Stationers' Register*, and *Publishers' Circular*.

In government publications the Library is well equipped. The publications of the Public Record Office (the Rolls Series, Calendars of State Papers, Patent Rolls, etc.) are practically complete, even to the old series which included *Domesday*

Book and the Statute Rolls. Many recent publications of certain boards, such as Education and Trade, and those of some of the ministries are also available, but the list is not complete. It includes Hansard's *Debates*, the *Parliamentary Papers*, the Naval Operations section of the official history of the War (1914–18), and the reports of the Historical Manuscripts Commission. The Library, however, does not have the *Rotuli parliamentorum*, and the lists and indexes of the Public Record Office.

The Library possesses many of the general periodical sets, including the *English Historical Review, History, Archaeologia*, and *Antiquity*. The *Victoria County History* (in large part), the *Acta sanctorum*, and the *Monumenta Germaniae historica* are in the Duke Library. The Library has the publications of the British Academy, the Early English Text Society, English Place-Names Society, Royal Historical Society, Camden Society, and the Selden Society. Holdings in local society publications are limited but include the works of the Surtees Society, Oxford Historical Society, Royal Institution of Cornwall, and the Cumberland and Westmorland Antiquarian and Archaeological Society. Among the publications of the scientific academies those of the British Association for the Advancement of Science, the Manchester Literary and Philosophical Society, and the Royal Irish Academy are represented. The files of the *Annual Register* are practically complete. There are also files of such modern periodicals as the *Fortnightly Review, London Quarterly and Holborn Review*, the *New Statesman and Nation, Spectator*, and *Punch*. The Library receives no English daily papers except the overseas edition of the *Daily Mail*, but has the weekly issues of the London *Times* and the *Manchester Guardian*.

In the field of intellectual history, the Hanes Collection of manuscripts and incunabula is valuable for the late medieval and early modern period, while the volumes more particularly related to the English, Romance Language, and Classics departments are helpful. The collection of materials relating to schools and universities is extensive. In religious history the collection contains the publications of the Canterbury and York Society, British Society of Franciscan Studies, the Henry Bradshaw Society, and the Parker Society. In addition there are Hefele-Leclerq, *Histoire des conciles*, Dugdale's *Monasticon Anglicanum*, Foxe's *Acts* and *Martyrs*, and many collections of sermons, besides the standard histories of the church.

Englishmen figure largely in the Library's extensive biographical collection. Some are in such sets as the *Dictionary of National Biography*, Lee's *Great Englishmen of the Sixteenth Century*, and various *Lives*, such as those of the archbishops of Canterbury and the lord chancellors, not to mention those of notorious highwaymen. By far the greater number are monographs like Workman's *Wyclif*. Except for the relatively complete memoirs and letters of literary men, this type of biographical information needs much strengthening.

This lack is perhaps the greatest weakness in political history, although the collection includes some larger sets, such as Greville's *Memoirs* and the correspondence of George III. With history, political science, and law contributing to it, the political phase may be studied in such books as those of Pollock and Maitland, Stenton, and Pollard. Some of the older items (Madox, etc.) have not yet been acquired. The history of law and governmental institutions is better represented than foreign policies and war.

Many items on description and travel in England, ranging from the *Beauties of England and Wales* to Traill and modern books upon English social work, make it possible to study English culture (used sociologically) historically. The pictorial side could be strengthened to advantage. In economic history the collection has been supplemented by purchases by the School of Commerce, which subscribes to most of the general economics and economic history periodicals, but receives few of the English trade journals.

Except for resources dealing with United States colonial history, the British Empire is not well represented. More items are available for Canada than for other parts of the empire. Even the Celtic areas of the British Isles are not covered satisfactorily; the works are largely general (such as Kenney) or included in such collections as the Rolls Series.

Chapter 30

UNITED STATES HISTORY

A. R. Newsome

THE LIBRARY'S RESOURCES in history are richest in the field of United States history. The advantages of age, the generosity of friends, and the sustained interest of professors for fifty years have produced an American history section which ranks among the best in the South, but not in the nation. Except in the fields of Southern and North Carolina history, it must be supplemented heavily for advanced studies. The areas of greatest strength are North Carolina, the South, the colonial period, and the periods of the Civil War and Reconstruction.

BIBLIOGRAPHY

The Library is relatively strong in bibliographical materials and reference works. It is nearly complete in bibliographies in American history, in periodical and newspaper indexes, and in printed calendars, guides, and catalogues of manuscript collections. The Library's holdings as a depository and its bibliographical resources of files of catalogue cards from the Library of Congress and other university libraries are described elsewhere in this volume.[1]

PRIMARY SOURCES

The Southern Historical Collection of approximately 1,800 collections, five thousand volumes and two million manuscripts, well distributed geographically, topically, and chronologically, is the richest existing concentration of manuscript materials relating to virtually every phase of the history of the South.

The Library has a fair representation of published diaries and memoirs (John Quincy Adams, U. S. Grant, Philip Hone,

1. *Supra*, pp. 12-15; 61; 75-77.

James K. Polk, W. T. Sherman, George Washington, Gideon Wells, etc.), travel accounts (Thwaites, *Early Western Travels, 1748–1846,* and many individual accounts), and writings and correspondence of prominent men (John Adams, John Quincy Adams, James Buchanan, John C. Calhoun, Henry Clay, Jefferson Davis, Albert Gallatin, Alexander Hamilton, Sam Houston, John Jay, Thomas Jefferson, Abraham Lincoln, James Madison, James Monroe, W. H. Seward, Charles Sumner, George Washington, Daniel Webster, etc.). But its chief printed primary sources consist of government publications. As a depository library since 1884 for publications of the federal government, it has an extensive but not complete file of the publications of the executive, legislative, and judicial branches of the government. Of colonial and state documents, the collection for North Carolina is relatively complete; there are seventy-six thousand volumes with varying representations from all the other states, particularly full for the Southern states; and the collection of state legislative journals and collected documents (many in microfilm) of the eastern half of the United States is perhaps the most complete in existence outside the library of Congress. The published series of colonial and early state records are available for New Hampshire, Massachusetts, New York, Pennsylvania, New Jersey, Delaware, Maryland, Virginia, North Carolina, and Georgia. The collection of approximately five thousand volumes of local documents deals chiefly with North Carolina towns.

The newspaper collection of over three thousand volumes is particularly strong for North Carolina, with 1,700 volumes of 388 titles extending from the late eighteenth century. There are files of the *New York Times* (1851–92, 1914 to date); the *National Intelligencer* (1819–63); and many scattered newspapers in the North and South.

Useful for social, economic, and cultural as well as political history are more or less complete files of *Niles' Weekly Register, The Southern Literary Messenger, The Southern Quarterly Review, De Bow's Review, The American Register, The American Museum, The American Quarterly Review, The American*

Whig Review, Harper's Weekly, The North American Review, and many other periodicals.

The Library has an extensive collection of the publications of national, regional, and state historical associations and societies including, among others, the American Historical Association, American Antiquarian Society, Southern History Association, Southern Historical Society, Mississippi Valley Historical Society, Filson Club, Essex Institute, Huguenot Society of South Carolina, South Carolina Historical Association, and the historical societies of New Hampshire, Vermont, Massachusetts, Rhode Island, Connecticut, New York, Pennsylvania, New Jersey, Mississippi, Louisiana, Indiana, Illinois, Michigan, Wisconsin, Missouri, Kansas, South Dakota, North Dakota, and Wyoming. These publications contain secondary as well as primary materials.

SECONDARY SOURCES

The general histories of the United States, as well as the series of university studies, are virtually complete; monographic works are numerous and well distributed but incomplete, especially for those published since 1930; publications of historical associations and societies are extensive; state and local histories are weak; and the collection of twelve thousand volumes of biography is particularly strong for the South and North Carolina.

Of special importance is the collection of over three thousand volumes on the South, due in large part to the aid of the Kenan Fund established in 1907. More than half of these deal with the Civil War and Reconstruction.

The North Carolina Collection of 1,700 bound volumes of North Carolina newspapers, over 17,000 books, 49,000 pamphlets, 750 maps, 500 pictures, and 25,000 mounted clippings is the largest and most important collection of North Caroliniana in existence.

There are long runs of about forty American historical periodicals and numerous shorter files. National and regional periodicals (*The American Historical Review, The Historical Magazine, Magazine of American History, The Mississippi Val-*

ley Historical Review, The Journal of Southern History, The Pacific Historical Review, The New England Historical and Genealogical Register, etc.) are virtually complete; state periodicals, such as The Pennsylvania Magazine of History and Biography, The Virginia Magazine of History and Biography, The Georgia Historical Quarterly, The Louisiana Historical Quarterly, Chronicles of Oklahoma, The Ohio State Archaeological and Historical Quarterly, The Wisconsin Magazine of History, Minnesota History, and The Oregon Historical Quarterly, are well represented; and local periodicals, such as The Medford Historical Register and The Filson Club History Quarterly, are few.

The American history resources of the Library are reinforced by those of the Law Library and of economics and commerce, sociology, rural social economics, education, and political science, as well as those of the departments in the divisions of the humanities and the natural sciences.

Chapter 31

LATIN AMERICAN HISTORY

W. W. Pierson, Jr.

THIS DIVISION of the Library was started, so far as the effort to assemble special collections was concerned, about thirty years ago; and, in consequence, it has been handicapped by this late beginning. The institutional history of the eighteenth century, the colonial *Cabildo* and the *Intendencia*, Alberdi and a few of the other political thinkers of republican Latin America were the subjects of this early effort. The many gaps in the works of reference were filled by purchases of a general variety when opportunity occurred and fiscal resources permitted. The travels in Latin American countries of certain professors were made the occasions of special appropriations, and limited purchases were made on the ground. No consistent plan has been followed over the years because of lack of funds, and book acquisitions in this field all along have had to be made as opportunity and a modest budget permitted. Further, the claims of other fields of history and government to larger budgetary support in the acquirement of library materials, locally justifiable, made an even, consistent policy impractical. None the less, an effort has been made to assemble for introductory and undergraduate teaching and study a collection that is general, covering all periods and countries and embracing such conventional phases of history as might be designated political, institutional, ecclesiastical, cultural, diplomatic, and economic. Secondly, attempts were made to obtain library materials that would justify and facilitate some graduate work and research. Collections were sought and slowly built up in subjects and areas in the field in which students and faculty manifested interest. This led to an emphasis upon the eighteenth century, the struggles for independence, and the area of South America—and within that continent upon Chile, Argentina, and Venezuela. Thirdly, a fairly successful attempt has been made to acquire bibliographical guides to historical literature for both the Hispanic-European and American countries.

Grants from the General Education Board enabled the Library to acquire a collection of printed bibliographies and of book lists from leading libraries of the country. The University has an excellent working bibliography for this field. These grants further enabled it to obtain some of the sets of printed documents and some public documents concerning laws and reports, boundary disputes and arbitrations, and works of notable writers of history and literature.

An agreement between Duke University, Tulane, and North Carolina called for a definite delimitation of fields for the acquisition of research materials. Argentina, Chile, Uruguay, Paraguay, Venezuela, and the island republics became the area of North Carolina's effort. Under grant from the General Education Board and with supplements of library funds, several thousand volumes have been added with this concentration in mind. North Carolina had indicated a special interest in the colonial *Cabildo* and the *Intendencia*, in the eighteenth century reforms in imperial control, and purchases in these fields are made without geographic limitation.

Although gaps in the book, archival, and periodical collections exist with respect to all the fields of Latin American history, the Library here warrants the graduate instruction of those whose investigations are concerned with the later periods of the colonies, the struggles for independence, the development of political thought, diplomatic relations, and the "national" periods of Venezuela, Chile, Argentina, and Uruguay. Some progress has been made in assembling materials relative to the local history of Venezuela.

The considerable collection of photostat and typewritten copies of manuscripts and documents secured by the North Carolina Historical Commission is accessible to students. The interlibrary loan system and exchanges between Duke University and North Carolina are effectively administered, and they make it possible to designate North Carolina as a "center" for Hispanic studies.

BIBLIOGRAPHICAL AIDS AND GUIDES

The bibliographies of bibliographies include the volumes by Binayán (Argentina), Trelles (Cuba), Laval (Chile), and Jones (general). The Library has the bibliographical publications of the Hispanic Society of America, including, of course, the *List of Works for the Study of Hispanic-American History* by H. Keniston. For Spain, there are such works as those of Ballester (*Bibliografía de la historia de España*), Sánchez y Alonso (*Fuentes de la historia española*), Serrano y Sanz (*Apuntes para una biblioteca de escritores españolas, 1401-1833*), the Hidalgo (*Diccionario general de bibliografía española*), the *Bibliografía española* (22 vols.), and the many *guías* in such treatises as those of Lafuente *Historia general de España,* Vol. XXX, Altamira *Historia de España,* Vol. IV, and Ballesteros *Historia de España,* Vol. V. For Portugal and Brazil, there are such items as Da Silva, *Diccionario bibliographico portuguez* (23 vols.), the *Catalogo da exposição de historia do Brazil,* and the Rodrigues, *Catalogo annotado dos livros sobre o Brasil.* The Library has a special interest in Henry Harrisse's *Bibliotheca Americana vetustissima.* The general bibliographies on Latin America include the Medina, *Biblioteca hispano-americana* (1493-1810), Palau y Dulcet, *Manual del librero hispano-americano* (7 vols.), Maggs Bros., *Bibliografía americana,* and many handbooks and topical guides. The Library has a considerable group of regional and national bibliographies, some of which are the Laval, *Bibliografía general de Chile,* and the volumes on Chilean bibliography by Montt, Vaïsse, and Anrique and Silva Cruz. There are periodicals devoted strictly to bibliography, as the *Revista de bibliografía chilena,* the *Boletín bibliográfico argentino,* and the *Boletín bibliográfico* (Peru). Many periodicals are available which give bibliographical information.

PRINTED SOURCES

There are available such items as the *Documentos inéditos,* the *Documentos para la historia de España,* the collection of

Fueros of municipalities, and the *Libros* or *Actas* of the Cabildos of such cities as Lima, Quito, Havana, and Santiago de Chile. There are the *Documentos para la vida pública del Libertador* and the *Cartas de Bolívar*. Likewise, there is the *Archivo de Miranda*. The collection of printed laws and legislative journals is decidedly incomplete, but of the complete sets is that of the *Recopilación de leyes y decretos de Venezuela*. The Library has an unusually good collection of printed materials dealing with the period of Guzmán Blanco in Venezuela. Although the collection of *memorias* is fragmentary, a beginning has been made. The literature of this subject is rich in the *diccionario* type of writing, and the Library has examples such as the Martínez Alcubilla (*Diccionario de la administración española*), the Escriche (*Diccionario razonado de legislación*), Castillo, (*Teatro de legislación*), and Zamora y Coronado, (*Biblioteca de la legislación ultramarina*).

The Library has secured the printed works of many eminent writers of the "national" period, such as those of Alberdi, Bello, Sarmiento, and Martí.

PAMPHLETS AND PERIODICALS

Of the vast number of *folletos*, *efemérides*, and *discursos*, the Library has some examples. A conscious effort has been made to collect those of Venezuela.

The acquisition and maintenance of complete files of Latin-American journals are by no means easy. Files of the *Boletín de la Academia Nacional de la Historia* of Venezuela and of the *Boletín del Archivo Nacional* are almost complete. The Library receives some thirty-four *revistas* which offer matter of interest to students of history.

Chapter 32

COMMERCE AND ECONOMICS

Guelda E. von Beckerath

THE COMMERCE AND ECONOMICS collection consists of both government and non-government materials. The United States government documents set constitutes a primary source of information, and students in this field have ready access to the publications of the Bank for International Settlements; Bureau of the Budget; Department of Agriculture; Department of Commerce (Bureau of Foreign and Domestic Commerce, Reconstruction Finance Corporation, Export and Import Bank of Washington, Civil Aeronautics Administration); Department of the Interior; Department of Labor (Bureau of Labor Statistics); Federal Security Agency; U. S. Office of Education and Social Security Board; Federal Deposit Insurance Corporation; Federal Power Commission; Federal Reserve System; Federal Trade Commission; Interstate Commerce Commission; U. S. Maritime Commission; Securities and Exchange Commission; Tariff Commission; Department of the Treasury (Bureau of the Comptroller of the Currency, Bureau of Internal Revenue, Bureau of the Mint, Bureau of the Customs); and congressional hearings, reports, and Senate documents.

The non-governmental material consists of a representative collection of the works of the leading economists (American, German, French, Austrian, and Italian); a set of historical treatises, reports, and texts; a collection of reference materials (dictionaries, encyclopedias, atlases, directories, bibliographies, handbooks, and yearbooks); periodical sets of 450 American and foreign economic and business journals, letters, proceedings, exchanges, services, and newspapers; vertical files of corporate financial statements (near three thousand), miscellaneous pamphlets and press releases; and extensive files of the publications of independent, as well as university research organizations.

ECONOMIC THEORY

The collection is prepared for general research in the field of economic theory and the history of economic thought since 1776, as it contains substantially all of the materials listed in the *Encyclopedia of Social Sciences*.

There is a complete collection of the English mercantilist writers; the major works of the English eighteenth, nineteenth, and twentieth centuries are represented, as well as a selection of the works of the minor writers. The German, Austrian, and French eighteenth-, nineteenth-, and twentieth-century writers are substantially complete, whereas there are only a few of the French minor writers. The collection is extensive in the minor German writers, and the American section is complete since 1875, but the more important Italian writers are lacking.

Bibliography includes Henry Higgs's *Bibliography of Economics, 1751–1775*; Adolph Jurgens' *Ergebnisse deutscher Wissenschaft;* Magdalene Humpert's *Biblographie der Kameralwissenschaften;* the *Economic Literature of Latin America; Bibliography of Economic Science*, compiled by the Institute of Economic Research, Osaka University of Commerce, Tokyo; Massie's *Collection of Books and Tracts, 1557–1763;* H. E. Batson's *A Select Bibliography of Modern Economic Theory, 1870–1929;* and J. R. McCulloch's *The Literature of Political Economy*.

The Library is also well supplied with economic journals: *The Quarterly Journal of Economics* (vol. 1 to date), *American Economic Review* (vol. 1 to date), *Journal of Political Economy* (vol. 28 to date), *Economic Journal* (vol. 1 to date), *Economica* (vol. 1 to date), *Oxford Economic Paper* (1939–), *Revue economique internationale* (vols. 5-31), *Journal des economistes* (1876–99, 1902–1907), *Weltwirtschaftliches Archiv* (vols. 3-52), and *Jahrbücher für Nationalökonomie und Statistik* (vols. 1-149).

This section contains reprints of scarce tracts in economic

and political science published by the London School of Economics and Political Science and by the Johns Hopkins Press; Palgrave's *Dictionary of Political Economy,* the *Encyclopaedia of the Social Sciences,* and the publications of the National Bureau of Economic Research and the Harvard Economic Series.

TRANSPORTATION AND PUBLIC UTILITIES

The legal phases of transportation are cared for by the Law Library, with its reports of decisions of the state appellate courts, as well as the annotated laws (state and federal).

The regulatory phases of public utilities are covered by reports of various state commissions, *Public Utility Fortnightly* (vol. 3 to date), Law; *Public Utility Reports* (1915–44), Law; *United States Aviation Reports* (1928–43), Law; and also by the periodical sets which are both in Law and Commerce.

The collection includes considerable material of a historical nature, texts, treatises, monographs, regional and rate studies, and periodical sets: *Traffic World* (vol. 33 to date); *Railway Age* (vol. 69 to date); *Journal of Land and Public Utility Economics* (vol. 1 to date); *Nautical Gazette* (vol. 97 to date); and *Bell Telephone Magazine and Quarterly* (1940–).

The Library has files of the publications of the Association of Traffic Clubs (1940–); The Association of American Railroads; Bureau of Railway Economics (1942–); *Yearbooks* of the Eastern Railroad Presidents' Conference Committee on Public Relations (1932–); *Official Guides* of the National Railways Publishing Company and Automobile Manufacturers Association; *Facts and Figures in the Automobile Industry* (1924–).

The Library subscribes to the White and Kemble Atlas service and receives in addition the services listed under *Corporation Finance.* It also maintains a file of fifteen hundred annual reports of railroads and public utilities. Reference books include *Freight Traffic Yearbook* and *Official Guide to Railways,* as well as proceedings of the Chicago Transportation Conference (1933–35), Southern Transportation Conference (1914) and the League of Nations Committee and Conference reports on transportation.

INTERNATIONAL TRADE

History of the development of the theory of international trade may be traced in a complete set of the writings of the modern economists, as well as materials for the study of international trade policies.

International economy is represented by the files of the Foreign Policy Association: *Foreign Policy Bulletins* (vol. 5 to date), and *Foreign Policy Reports* (vol. 3 to date), *Foreign Affairs* (vol. 1 to date), *Pacific Affairs* (vol. 9 to date), *Far Eastern Quarterly* (vol. 1 to date), *Far Eastern Survey* (vol. 8 to date), as well as reports of congresses and conventions, i.e., National Foreign Trade Convention (1917–). The Library also has the publications of the League of Nations, particularly the *Payment of Balances* and *World Trade* surveys, as well as all other reports of the Economic and Financial sections of the League. There are files of the U. S. Chamber of Commerce, The International Chamber of Commerce bulletins and serials (Clearing and Payments Agreements), and other miscellaneous publications. In addition the Library subscribes to the journals of the leading industries: *Coal Age* (vol. 12 to date), *Steel* (vol. 87 to date), *U. S. Tobacco Journal* (vol. 99 to date), *Textile World* (vol. 57 to date), *Textile Bulletin* (vol. 57 to date), *Mining and Metallurgy* (1905–); the publications of the Stanford University Research Institute, known as *Grain Economic Series, Commodity Policies Studies*, and *War-Peace Pamphlets*. This collection is supplemented by such reference works as *Commodity Year Book*, Chisholm's *Handbook of Commercial Geography, International Yearbook of Agricultural Statistics*, and the publications of the American Iron and Steel Institute and *Metal Statistics*.

Technical and mechanical phases of the subject may be followed further through *Shipper's Guide, Lloyd's Register, Exporters' Encyclopedia*, Kelly's *Directory of Merchants, Manufacturers and Shippers of the World, International Trader's Handbook, Dictionary of Tariff Information;* and files of periodicals: *Nautical Gazette* (1919–), *Export Trade and Shipper* (1944–), *The Board of Trade Journal* (1927–), *The Economist* (vol. 94 to date), *The Protectionist* (v. 40-52), *The Royal Economic Society Memorandum* (No. 5 to date), *London and Cambridge Service* (vol. 4 to date), *Journal of Commerce* (1851–), *Commercial and Financial Chronicle* (vol. 1 to date) and *New York Times* (1851–).

Source material on the history of American Commerce may be found in the *Reports of the Secretary and Treasurer of Navigation, American State Papers,* as well as Seybert's *Statistical Annals,* Pitkin's *A Statistical View of the Commerce of the U. S.,* Johnson's *History of Domestic and Foreign Commerce of the U. S.,* and various other historical treatises, books, and monographs.

The periodical subscription list includes numerous other titles which are useful. These are essentially the same as those listed under Economic Theory, with the addition of *Dun's Review* (vol. 31 to date) and *The Economist* (vol. 1 to date), *Svenska Handelsbanken* (1928–38), and a recently acquired collection of Latin-American materials: bank letters, releases, and publications of private concerns.

The collection is weak in foreign documents, especially the Great Britain Department of Overseas Trade bulletins.

LABOR AND LABOR PROBLEMS

This collection contains historical and special studies of labor conditions in America and foreign countries, as well as treatises on labor legislation and arbitration.

The Library receives the leading American and English labor periodicals, including *Index to Labor Periodicals* (vol. 1 to date), official proceedings and serial publications of the American Federation of Labor and affiliates, the C. I. O., and those of individual labor unions.

A number of services are received: *The Labor Relations Reporter* (vol. 1 to date), *The Wage and Hour Reporter* (vol. 1 to date), *Institute of Labor Studies* (vol. 1 to date), publications of the International Labour Office (1919–), National Industrial Conference Board, American Management Association, and Commerce Clearing House Labor Law service.

In the collection are the proceedings of The International Labor Congress (1920-41); also the reports of other conventions. There are complete sets of Columbia University *Studies in History, Economics and Public Law;* Johns Hopkins University *Studies in Historical and Political Science; Annals* of the American Academy of Political and Social Science (vol. 1 to date); *American Labor Legislation Review* (vol. 1 to 32); *Labour* (vol. 1 to date); *Labor Cases* (vol. 1 to date); *Labor Relations Reference Manual* (vol. 1 to date); *Economic Almanac* (vol. 1 to date). Also there are handbooks of the Bureau of Labor, the American Council on Public Affairs, and other reference books such as *Labor Fact Book, American Federation of Labor History Encyclopedia Reference Book,* and *American Labor Press.*

The Library subscribes to a number of newspapers: *American Federation of Labor Weekly News Service* (vol. 17 to date), the *C.I.O. News* (vol. 1 to date), a dozen labor newspapers, and weekly and monthly publications of the leading individual labor unions.

PUBLIC FINANCE

Sources in public finance include files of *Proceedings of the National Tax Association* (vol. 1 to date), *Bulletin of the National Tax Association* (vol. 4 to date), various tax services: Alexander Tax Reports, Commerce Clearing House State and Local Tax Service, Commerce Clearing House *Tax Systems of the World,* Commerce Clearing House Federal Income Tax; also periodical files of *Taxes* (vol. 4 to date), the *Commercial and Financial Chronicle* (vol. 1 to date), *The Peoples Lobby* (vol. 1 to date), and publications of the Twentieth-Century Fund. The League of Nations studies on the subject are also available.

In the literature of public finance there are few gaps. The American and English sources are complete. There are special studies of the public finance of many foreign countries including Mohammedan and Greek. Foreign sources are available in the original in the following languages: German (with works of Wagner, Foldes, Eheberg, and Gerloff), Italian, French, Mexican, Brazilian, Uruguayan, and Argentinian. The sources on Latin and South American finance are especially good.

The Library has a few early American documents, such as letters of statesmen (Washington, Jefferson, Hamilton, and Madison), which deal with finance. It is especially strong in colonial documents, having copies of original statements beginning with 1663. Special attention should be directed to the set of original documents of the State of North Carolina and the reports made by its officials in their official and unofficial capacities.

The reports of city pressure groups, such as taxpayer associations and governmental research organizations, are fairly extensive, and there is also a complete file of state tax commission reports.

MONEY

The Library has representative works of most of the well-known classical economists from the time of Adam Smith, including the works of the leading monetary theorists, both American and European, as well as complete sets of texts, monographs, and treatises.

The set of historical treatises is well chosen, though by no means complete, although the part which deals with English monetary history is adequate. This set is supplemented by proceedings of monetary conferences: Great Britain Gold and Silver Conference (1887), reports of the U. S. Monetary Commission of (1911), International Monetary Conference at Paris (1878), and publications of the League of Nations dealing with the subject of money (1921–).

The collection contains files of the leading economic journals listed under the headings, "Economic Theory" and "Business Cycles," and in addition, files of the *Annalist* (vols. 1-56) and *Commercial and Financial Chronicle* (vol. 1 to date).

The collection includes reference books as follows: *Poor's Register of Directors and Executives, International Banking*

Directory, and Rand and McNally's *Bank Directory; Dictionary of Banking Terms* and Kettridge's *Dictionary of Commercial and Financial Terms;* Polk's *Banker's Encyclopedia,* Mun's *Banker's Encyclopedia,* and *Banker's Almanac and Yearbook.*

The periodical subscription list includes American financial journals: *Banking* (vol. 14 to date), *Banker's Magazine* now *Banking Law Journal* (vol. 1 to date), *Commercial and Financial Chronicle* (vol. 1 to date), *The Economist* (vol. 1 to date), *Survey of Current Business* (1922–), *Journal of the Institute of Bankers* (vol. 62 to date) and the financial newspapers and services listed under "Corporations and Investments."

There are files of bank letters from twelve Federal Reserve banks and thirty-four foreign and domestic banks, including several Latin American banks. These are supplemented by the reports of state banking commissions and proceedings of state bankers associations.

BUSINESS CYCLES

The subject of business cycles covers many fields, including finance, monetary theory, economics, and industry. Most of the representative primary and secondary sources are available, including the important theoretical works. In addition there is a complete file of the publications of research organizations listed under other heads: the National Bureau of Economic Research, National Industrial Conference Board, International Labour Office, League of Nations. There is an extensive periodical set: Journal of the *American Statistical Association* (vol. 1 to date), *Review of Economic Statistics* (vol. 1 to date), *Journal of the Royal Statistical Society* (vol. 80 to date), *London and Cambridge Service* (vol. 4 to date), *Harvard Business Review* (vol. 1 to date), *Vierteljahrhefte zur Konjunturforschung* (vols. 1-27), as well as the list included under "Economic Theory." In this field the collection is weak in foreign periodical sets and publications of business cycle institutes.

CORPORATIONS AND INVESTMENTS

The Library possesses all of the standard financial services, including Fitch, Standard and Poor, Brookmire, Babson, Moody's *Investment Service,* and Dodge's *Statistical Service,* as well as sets of Moody's *Manuals* (1909–), the supplement service, and sets of Poor's Manuals. The collection also includes Kimber's *Manual of Government Debts,* Keane's *Manual of Investment Trusts,* Sprague's *Bond Tables,* M. Scudder's *Manual of Extinct Securities,* and the Commerce Clearing House *Federal Tax Service* and *State and Local Tax Service.*

The Library subscribes to *The Commercial and Financial Chronicle* (vol. 1 to date), *Banker's Magazine* (vol. 1 to date), *The Annalist* (vols. 1-56), *Trusts and Estates* (vol. 18 to date), *Barron's* (vol. 7 to date), *Magazine of Wall St.* (vol. 25 to date), *Fortune Magazine* (vol. 1 to date), and the *Wall St. Journal* (1942–), *Journal of Commerce* (1851–) and the *New York Times* (1851–).

Vertical files of corporate financial statements have been maintained over the years; they now total nearly three thousand items, supplemented by a miscellaneous clipping file.

For study of the beginnings of the American corporation, there are *Hunt's Magazine* (43 vols.), *Niles' Register* (70 vols.), and *Merchant's Magazine* (44 vols.). The collection contains also the requisite secondary sources, including texts, treatises, and theses.

MARKETING

Only a few of the primary sources are lacking, and the secondary sources have been selected carefully from the vast amount of marketing data issued by private concerns, publishing companies, and economic research service concerns. The collection includes the publications of such agencies as the U. S. Chamber of Commerce, National Automobile Chamber of Commerce, National Retail Dry Goods Association, National Association of Manufacturers, National Association of Purchasing Agents; reporting services on marketing conditions; in addition to the five services previously listed under "Corporations

COMMERCE AND ECONOMICS 209

and Investment," the American Management Association, Marketing series, Taylor Society, Standard Rate and Data Service, American Institute of Food Distribution, American Railway Association, Bureau of Railway Economics, publications of the Chicago Board of Trade and of the Cotton Textile Institute.

The Library is well stocked with handbooks: *The Market Data Handbook,* issued by the U. S. Department of Commerce, and the market data handbooks of independent publishing companies, for instance, *Management Handbook, Merchant's Manual, Handbook of Sales Organization, Rand McNally Commercial Atlas and Market Guide.* The publications of research foundations such as the Twentieth Century Fund, Crowell Publishing Company, Curtis Publishing Company, National Markets, and National Advertiser are available. The Library also has files of the market research publications of the university bureaus of business research, such as Harvard, Illinois, and New York University; also such special reports as those of the 100,000 Group of American Cities, and *Media Records.*

The collection of periodicals includes *Journal of Marketing* (vol. 1 to date); *Chain Store Age* (vol. 6 to date); *Sales Management* (vol. 8 to date); *Bulletins* of the Taylor Society (1915–), now the Society for the Advancement of Management; *Harvard Business Review* (vol. 1 to date); *Business Week* (1929–); *Printers' Ink Monthly* (vols. 1-43); and *Printers' Ink Weekly* (vol. 91 to date); *Retail Management* (1943–); *Journal of Retailing* (vol. 1 to date); and *Proceedings* of the Boston Conferences on Distribution, (1931–).

ADVERTISING

Facilities for the study of advertising include histories, texts, research reports of national associations and the individual broadcasting companies, and type books, color books, advertising award books, and art books.

Most of the periodicals in this field are available, including *Advertising Age* (vol. 11 to date); *Advertising and Selling* (vol. 3 to date); *Sales Management* (vol. 8 to date); *Printers' Ink Weekly* (vol. 91 to date); *Printers' Ink Monthly* (vols. 1-43);

Standard Rate and Data Service (1942–); and *Media Records*. Many government publications are also valuable as source material, such as *Survey of Current Business* and *Commerce Yearbook*. These are supplemented by such reference books as *Advertisers' Handbook; Broadcasting and Broadcast Advertising; Standard Advertising Register;* Thomas' *Register* and McKittrick's *Directory of Advertisers;* publications of the Association of National Advertisers; Ayers' *Directory of Newspapers and Periodicals*. The collection on radio advertising has not been developed thoroughly; however, a good working set has been assembled.

STATISTICS

The Library's extensive holdings of non-governmental source materials include the five reporting services listed under "Corporations and Investments," the back files of the Harvard Economic Service; *Statesmen's Yearbook; World Almanac; Yearbook of Research and Statistical Methodology; Inter-American Financial and Economic Handbook; Inter-American Statistical Yearbook; International Yearbook of Agricultural Statistics; Spectator Insurance Yearbooks;* Mulhall's *Dictionary of Statistics;* Kurtz and Edgerton *Statistical Dictionary*. The statistical publications of the International Labour Office and the League of Nations also furnish valuable source material.

Among the periodicals devoted to studies utilizing the statistical method and the development of statistical theory are *Review of Economic Statistics* (vol. 1 to date); *Journal of the American Statistical Association* (vol. 3 to date); *Econometrica* (vol. 1 to date); *Journal of the Royal Statistical Society* (vol. 80 to date); and *Annals of Mathematical Statistics* (vol. 1 to date).

In addition to these sets, the publications of such research bureaus as the National Bureau of Economic Research, Cowles Commission, and those issued by several universities and trade associations, are also available.

Chapter 33

EDUCATION

W. C. Ryan

OVER THE YEARS the Library has acquired a collection of books on education that is characterized by good distribution over all fields rather than specialization. The nucleus of the present collection was the School of Education Library formerly housed in Peabody Hall, supplemented by regular acquisitions and a Curriculum Laboratory reasonably well supplied with syllabi and pamphlet material of special value to students of the curriculum.

GENERAL REFERENCE WORKS

Among general reference works on education the Library has the standard four-volume *Cyclopedia of Education,* edited by Paul Monroe; Foster Watson's *The Encyclopedia and Dictionary of Education;* and F. Buisson's *Nouveau dictionnaire de pédagogie* (Paris, Hachette, 1911) though it lacks Wilhelm Rein's corresponding work in German. It also has the newer *Encyclopedia of Educational Research,* edited by Walter S. Monroe and the *Encyclopedia of Modern Education,* edited by Harry N. Rivlin and Herbert Schueler. Of older works, chiefly of historical interest, the Library has Kiddle and Schem's *Cyclopaedia of Education* (1877), and Sonnenschein's *Cyclopaedia of Education* (1889). Two important bibliographies are Walter Scott Monroe's *A Bibliography of Bibliographies* and F. C. Touton's *Selected and Annotated Bibliography of Professional Literature in Education.*

For college and university lists the Library has issues of *Minerva: Jahrbuch der gelehrten Welt* (Berlin, Walter de Gruyter) through 1938; *World's Universities,* publication of the British Universities Encyclopedia, Ltd.; the 1938 edition of *Index Generalis: The Yearbook of the Universities* (Paris,

Masson, and New York, F. S. Crofts); also the 1939 *Universities Yearbook* (London, G. Bell and Sons); the current *Patterson's American Educational Directory* (1943) and the *Phi Beta Kappa Directory*, 1941.

HISTORY AND PHILOSOPHY OF EDUCATION; COMPARATIVE EDUCATION

The historical material is adequate, though not distinguished. A good balance has been maintained between older works and current publications in this field, with considerable emphasis on history of universities and schools in the United States and abroad. Older classics—Mulcaster, Comenius, John Locke, Charles Hoole—are well represented, as well as the latter-day educational historians—E. P. Cubberley, Paul Monroe, F. P. Graves, E. H. Reisner, and Edgar W. Knight.

In philosophy of education there are not only such works as that of Compayré (*Lectures on Pedagogy*) but of all the later nineteenth- and early twentieth-century figures from De Garmo, William James, the McMurrys, and G. Stanley Hall, to Sir John Adams, Whitehead, John Dewey, William H. Kilpatrick, B. H. Bode, John S. Brubacher, John L. Childs, and others, including Catholic writers in this field, notably Thomas E. Shields.

Works on foreign educational philosophies and systems are available in good numbers, though the distribution is scattering. There are interesting individual items, such as Nohl and Pallat's *Handbuch der Pädogogik*, Georg Kerschensteiner's work on citizenship education, and certain British Board of Education reports. There is reasonably good representation for China, India, and the Near East, with a few references from South Africa and a very few from Latin American countries, chiefly Mexico, Argentina, and Chile. International education conferences are represented, not too adequately, by reports of the World Federation of Education Associations and the New Education Fellowship, e.g., the fifth World Conference at Elsinore, Denmark, the regional conferences in South Africa, Australia, and New Zealand.

EDUCATION 213

FEDERAL AND STATE REPORTS AND ASSOCIATION PROCEEDINGS

Education is one field in which Federal publications are of special importance; for three quarters of a century the United States Bureau (now called Office) of Education has been a major source of help to students of education. The Library is fortunate in having a complete set of the Reports of the United States Commissioner of Education, of the Bulletin series, and almost all of the Circulars, all of which are rich in materials on educational systems, philosophies, and practices in the United States and foreign countries.

State reports on Education are important in certain types of educational research; for some eight or ten states the Library has complete issues of these.

Association proceedings and yearbooks are another valuable source of help to students of education. The Library has sets of proceedings for the National Education Association, including its research bulletins, the yearbooks of its departments; the materials from the special Educational Research Service; the National Society for the Study of Education, reaching back through the early period when it was the Herbart Society; the Conference for Education in the South; the National Society of College Teachers of Education; the John Dewey Society; and less complete sets of the proceedings of such organizations as the New York Society for the Experimental Study of Education, the Ohio State Education Conference, Schoolmen's Week of the University of Pennsylvania, and the Eastern States Association of Professional Schools for Teachers. A rather curious lack is in the proceedings of the American Institute of Instruction, of which the Library appears to have only an occasional copy. The Library has a complete set of the annual reports of the Carnegie Foundation for the Advancement of Teaching (1906–), as well as reports of other educational foundations.

Also available are the reports of the recent research commissions—the Commission on Teacher Education of the American Council on Education; the Educational Policies Commission; the Progressive Education Association's Commissions on School and College, Reorganization of the Secondary School Curricula, and on Human Relations. Among yearbooks worthy of special mention are *El año pédagogico hispanoamericano,* the *Educational Yearbook* of the International Institute of Teachers Colleges (1924–), and the yearbook of the Educational Press Association of America.

EDUCATIONAL PSYCHOLOGY, CHILD DEVELOPMENT, GUIDANCE

The Library is well equipped in the modern materials on human growth and development with special reference to education, as well as in the more conventional educational psychology and educational measurement. Child study, study of personality, and mental hygiene are fairly strong, with representation from such writers as Gesell, Zachry, Blos, Blatz, Ruth Andrus, Prescott, in North America, and Ferrière, Decroly, Piaget, Rank, Anna Freud, from Europe. Publications in this field are available from the Child Study Association of America, the University of Chicago, the University of Iowa, and other research centers.

Material is abundant in educational testing of the various types, as represented by the work of Binet, Thorndike, Terman, Trabue, Gray, Freeman, Tidyman, Thurstone, Stoddard, and many others. The social psychology and sociology relationships to education are exemplified in books by Raup, Anspach, Hart (*A Social Interpretation of Education*), Groves (*Social Problems in Education*), Bolton, Finney, Peters, Kulp, Schorling and McClusky (*Education and Social Trends*), Roucek, and Smith, Cressman, and Speer (*Education and Society*).

Educational practice dependent upon the newer psychology of human growth and development is covered by representative books on the nursery school, kindergarten, and elementary schools of the experimental type by such writers, investigators, and practitioners as Harold Rugg and Ann Shumaker (*The Child-Centered School*), Evelyn Dewey, Gertrude Hartman, Caroline Pratt, Lucy Sprague Mitchell, Winifred Bain, James S. Tippett, Hollis Caswell, the Lees (*The Child and His Curriculum*), Agnes de Lima, Lois Mossman, F. G. Macomber,

EDUCATION 215

Inga Olla Helseth, Robert Hill Lane, Carleton Washburne, J. W. Wrightstone.

The Library is fairly well equipped with "guidance" material of the various types—child guidance and youth counselling as well as vocational guidance.

OTHER FIELDS

Secondary education is represented by all the important standard books and many of the special research reports in this field made under the direction of Briggs, Aikin, and others. There is excellent historical and current material on experimental secondary schools, both public and private.

In health and physical education the Library has recently been strengthening its resources, especially in school health. It has, for example, a full set of the reports of the Joint Committee on Health Problems in Education of the National Education Association and the American Medical Association. There is a better than average collection in physical education and athletics; fairly good materials in safety education; and decided lacks in "special education," particularly the education of the physically handicapped, though there has been some recent increase in the books available on the education of the deaf and hard-of-hearing as a result of the introduction of a university course in this field.

Teacher education is well covered, both historically and contemporaneously, from *The Journal of Cyrus Peirce and May Swift* down to the recently issued reports of the Commission on Teacher Education of the American Council on Education.

Except for their historical aspects, industrial arts and vocational training have not been emphasized in recent additions to the library collections, presumably in accordance with the plan for allocation of work in this field to the State College unit. An attempt is made, however, to have available such general books in this field as will be important for students of educational administration, the curriculum, and guidance.

Negro education is well represented in books and reports by Horace Mann Bond (*Socio-economic Approach to Educational*

Problems), Ina Corinne Brown, Ambrose Caliver, Rossa B. Cooley (*School Acres*); in accounts of Hampton Institute; and in the reports of the various foundations, particularly the General Education Board, the John F. Slater Fund, and the Rosenwald Fund.

Reasonably good files of the important educational periodicals are available in the Library. Also valuable for educational research are the more than four hundred theses in education prepared by master's and doctor's degree candidates at the University during the past thirty years; special research materials such as those used by C. W. Dabney in writing his *Universal Education in the South*, and materials on education in the Southern Historical Collection.

Chapter 34

FOLKLORE

Ralph S. Boggs

ALTHOUGH FOLKLORE has numerous publication outlets under its own name, a majority of its materials appear in publications of related fields. The Library has over a thousand volumes directly in folklore, and many times this number of auxiliary works in related fields. The building up of the sections of interest to the English department for some time past, and of those sections pertinent to Hispanic-American studies more recently, has made the Library especially strong in Anglo-American and Hispanic-American folklore. Folklore interests of the departments of music and dramatic art have led to the development of those sections also.

In its files of the *Southern Folklore Quarterly, Publications of the Modern Language Association,* and *Handbooks of Latin American Studies,* the Library has the important current annual bibliographies of folklore, supplemented by the general bibliography section. It also has most of the important periodicals and series in English, such as the English *Folklore* journal and its series of publications; the *Journal of American Folklore* and its memoir series; the *California Folklore Quarterly;* the *Texas Folklore Society Publications;* the *Vassar Folklore Foundation Publications;* and the *Indiana University Publications' Folklore Series.* But those in foreign languages constitute one of the greatest needs of the Library, which has seven volumes of the *Revue de folklore français et de folklore colonial,* a few volumes of *Folklore Fellows Communications,* and the publications of the Folklore sections of the Institute of Argentine Literature of the University of Buenos Aires.

The collection of handbooks and general reference books includes Krappe's *Science of Folklore,* Thompson's *Motif-index,* Bolte and Polivka's *Anmerkungen zu den Kinder- u. Hausmärchen der Brüder Grimm,* Köhler's *Kleinere Schriften,* Dähnhardt's *Natursagen,* Frazer's *Golden Bough* and *Folklore in the Old Testament,* Pessler's *Handbuch der deutschen Volkskunde,* Spamer's *Deutsche Volkskunde,* Carrer y Candi's *Folklore y costumbres de España,* Ginzberg's *Legends of the Jews,* and the *Handwörterbuch des deutschen Aberglaubens.* However, a number of important works of this type are still needed to round out the collection. The text collections of folklore materials in the Library cover a wide range, being fairly complete in some sectors and fragmentary in others. Richest are the sections on folk music, song and ballad, and the proverb collections.

There are also in the Library manuscript copies of twenty-two doctoral and masters' theses on folklore by University of North Carolina students; they include such titles as H. A. Stevenson's "Herbal Lore as Reflected in the Works of the Major Elizabethans," F. C. Hayes' "Use of Proverbs in *Siglo de oro* Drama," A. C. Morris' "Folksongs of Florida and Their Cultural Background," and A. P. Hudson's *Folksongs of Mississippi* (University of North Carolina Press, 1936).

Two important private libraries on the campus accessible to students are the Pan-American folklore library of R. S. Boggs, professor of Spanish, and the international proverb library of Richard Jente, head of the German department. The Pan-American library, of over two thousand volumes, is one of the richest in Latin American folklore. It contains the *Archivos del folklore cubano, Mexican Folkways, Anuario de la Sociedad Folklórica de México, Boletín de la Asociación Folklórica Argentina,* and numerous other periodicals which regularly contain folklore sections, such as *Cultura política* of Rio de Janeiro and the *Revista do Arquivo Municipal* of Sao Paulo, as well as a few European periodicals, such as *Folklore Fellows Communications* (complete), *Commentationes archivi traditionum popularium Estoniae* and *El folklore andaluz.* It has the *Volkskundliche Bibliographie* complete. It is especially strong in its section on folktales of Spain, and somewhat strong in its section on Latin American folkspeech vocabularies. As a secondary interest, it has developed a section on folklore in world literature, in which appear large sets like Burton's English translation of the *1001 Nights* (17 vols.), the Tawney-Penzer *Ocean of Story* (10 vols.), and the *Jataka* (6 vols.) by Cowell and others. Irving A. Leonard, in "A Survey of Personnel and Activities in Latin American Aspects of the Humanities and Social Sciences at 20 Universities of the United States" (*Notes on Latin American Studies*, April 1943, no. 1, p. 22), makes the following statement relating to the Library at Chapel Hill: "The general collection of the University Library is strong... and probably outstanding in Latin American folklore, if the personal library of Professor Boggs is included."

The proverb library of Richard Jente is one of the most comprehensive ever assembled. Of the 3,500 items, over five hundred are rare collections from the sixteenth and seventeenth centuries. There is practically a complete series of the English, German, and Latin works of this period, besides many in other languages. Some of these volumes are of the utmost rarity and many are unique in America. All the important bibliographies are represented, as well as the standard collections in more than thirty languages. All modern handbooks and proverb studies, besides several hundred dissertations and pamphlets on various aspects of proverb investigation, make this one of the most complete libraries for the student of proverb lore.

Chapter 35

LAW

Lucile M. Elliott

THE LAW LIBRARY is primarily a working collection of Anglo-American law, but there is present also a nucleus of historical materials. The depression and the present war made it necessary to discontinue collecting the historical materials and to emphasize only current publications. This will be apparent in the following description.

OFFICIAL LEGAL DOCUMENTS, COLLATERALS, INDEXES AND SEARCH BOOKS

The most used section of the Library is that of public documents, not only those of the federal government, the state of North Carolina and other states in the Union, but also those of England and Canada, together with their collaterals, indexes, and search books. These fall under almost identical categories which can be most succinctly outlined by means of the accompanying chart.

TEXTS, TREATISES, AND HISTORIES

The text section shows the continuous development of Anglo-American law from the early English historical material, which holds the roots of American law, to the latest legal texts published in the United States.

English.—The Library has the five books of high authority which reflect the state of English law from the twelfth to the eighteenth century. They are by Glanville, Bracton (two volumes of the set on order), Littleton, Coke, and Blackstone. There is a long line also of early texts of secondary importance by such authors as Britton, Fleta, Horne, and others. The principal general histories of law are in the collection. The leading historians represented are Maitland, Holdsworth, and Pollock.

Worthy of special mention are works on the English Constitution by Adams, Amos, Bagehot, Dicey, and others.

American.—This division carries the thread of law to the present day. All late brief student texts and scholarly definitive treatises, such as Wigmore's *Evidence,* Williston's *Contracts,* Tiffany's *Property,* and others, are in the Library. Exhaustive treatises for both students and practitioners are included. Typical are Schneider's *Workmen's Compensation,* Appleman's *Insurance,* and Fletcher's *Corporations.* Since a course in legal philosophy is given, every school of jurisprudence (according to some of the leading authorities) is represented in the text section.

North Carolina.—The section of early texts is incomplete, but the collection of late publications of a legal nature is practically complete.

The Library offers special studies by federal and state governments. A few are the report of the Attorney General's Committee on Administrative Procedure, the report of the New York Constitutional Convention, various reports of the National Commission on Law Observance and Enforcement, and others.

PERIODICALS

Judged from the standpoint of scholarly content, the periodical collection ranks third in importance. It includes every current legal periodical indexed in the *Index to Legal Periodicals* and many more. Two hundred are received currently, the major portion of which come in exchange for the *North Carolina Law Review.* In the Library's holdings are fifty-three law school publications from thirty-six states, and thirty periodicals on various legal and allied subjects. In addition, thirty-five bar organs are received regularly. In all there are 3,315 bound volumes of serials.

There is a collection of periodicals from the British Isles, and there are a few from British regions outside the Isles. A number of foreign countries are represented also, but they are not in full sets, as many of them have been discontinued by their publishers for the period of the war.

The Library's files of North Carolina periodicals are complete. In the order of their appearance they are: *Carolina Law Repository*, 1813; *Man of Business*, 1833; *North Carolina Law Journal*, 1900; *North Carolina Journal of Law*, 1904; *North Carolina Law Review*, 1922; *Popular Government*, 1931; *Law and Contemporary Problems*, 1933; and *Duke Bar Association Journal*, 1933.

Two sets of the indexes to periodicals are complete also: the *Index to Legal Periodicals* (A. A. L. L.) and *Current Legal Thought*. The publications of the Jones-Chipman and the Commerce Clearing House are in broken sets.

REFERENCE BOOKS

The term reference is used here to distinguish the following types of secondary publications from those described above.

Encyclopedias.—The Library is provided with all the general encyclopedias of law published in America since 1887. The two current sets are *Ruling Case Law—American Jurisprudence* and *Corpus Juris—Corpus Juris Secundum*. Of the five general English encyclopedias, the Library has only one, Halsbury's *Laws of England* (1907–17).

Legal dictionaries.—The only old dictionary in the collection is by John Rastel, *Les Termes de la Ley*. The later ones are the leading American legal dictionaries by Ballantine, Black, Bouvier, and Cochran. The Library has the only judicial dictionary in its new edition, *Words and Phrases*. There is a small number of publications of dictionary character, such as *Latin for Lawyers, Abbreviations Used in Law Books, Uniform System of Citations*, and *Legal Maxims*.

Miscellaneous.—There is a general selection of helpful reference materials such as almanacs and atlases.

BIBLIOGRAPHIES

The Library's collection of bibliographies is adequate for research. There are both form bibliographies (all inclusive) and critical bibliographies (restricted and limited in scope), as well as manuals and indexes.

Form bibliographies.—(1) *Check Lists:* these cover state documents, bar reports, administrative tribunals' publications, and serials. (2) *Catalogues* (in bound form): (a) published by dealers, presses, and government printing offices; (b) published by fifteen schools, court and bar libraries; (c) depository card catalogues of the Duke Law Library and the Law Library of Congress. (3) *General bibliographies.* The collection of English and American bibliographies offers all the standard volumes of general bibliography, except a few items. Those available are (a) *English,* by Dugdale, 1665; Walthoe, 1714; Bridgman, 1817; Worrell, 1877; Ram, Jelf, Fox, Holdsworth, Jenks, Read, Crawford, and Stubbs; (b) *American,* by Bishop, Hoffman, Kent, Marvin, Wallace, Warren, and Soule.

Critical bibliographies.—(1) *Card catalogue.* In the Library's card catalogue there are approximately six hundred cards calling attention to short bibliographies to be found in legal textbooks. (2) *Pamphlets.* The Library has collected a considerable group of bibliographies published in pamphlet form by libraries, government departments, and national organizations. (3) *Bound volumes.* These deal with twenty separate subjects, such as year book studies, crime, and early North Carolina laws and reports.

Manuals.—The Library's collection of manuals for the course in legal bibliography is complete.

Indexes.—See Official Documents chart.

REPORTS AND PUBLICATIONS OF LEGAL ASSOCIATIONS AND ORGANIZATIONS

The Library keeps an up-to-date file of the proceedings and publications of associations organized for the improvement of the law. Among those most used are the reports of state and national bar associations, associations of American law schools, American Law Institute (and their Restatements), judicial councils, and attorneys general.

SPECIAL COLLECTIONS

The Library's two most noteworthy special collections are the following:

Loose leaf services.—In the fields of law which are new or are subject to constant change, and in those which require quick service, the Library carries a collection of loose leaf services kept up to date by weekly insert pages. These cover the subjects of taxation, both federal and state, administrative law, war law, and United States law.

Braille books.—The Library of Congress has deposited in the Law Library a set of Braille books of over two thousand volumes on the basic subjects of law—pleading, criminal law, torts, contracts, equity, property, agency, constitutional law. In addition, there are texts on the following subjects: insurance, wills, domestic relations, partnership, mortgages, conflict of laws. At intervals the Library of Congress adds new titles to this collection.

Within the last twenty years the Library has grown from a school library to a university law collection, despite its limited holdings in historical materials. Significant research work has been done in its reading rooms, resulting in the regular editing of two periodicals, *North Carolina Law Review* and *Popular Government*, both published in the University, the writing of many books and more dissertations, the preparation of independent studies and scholarly articles, as well as much case and court work. The Library is, furthermore, one of the co-operating law libraries in an interlibrary loan arrangement which serves the state. What the future of the collection will be depends on what the state will support. A plan now in preparation outlines the Library's needs in the development of new fields of law, which have become significant during the war, and calls for the completion of the basic public documents section, and the strengthening of resources in fundamental secondary material.

Official Documents, Collaterals, Indexes and Search Books

I. CONSTITUTIONS

	TEXT OF CONSTITUTION	CONVENTIONS, JOURNALS, AND RECORDS	COLLATERALS
ENGLISH	None	None	None
CANADIAN	None	None	None
UNITED STATES (Federal)	In the following: 1. *United States Code*, 1940 2. *Constitution of United States of America* (annotated) 1923 3. *United States Code, Annotated* 4. Old United States codes (See III, this chart).	Elliott, *Debates of the Federal Constitution* Farrand, *Records of the Federal Convention* *Documentary History of the Constitution of the United States of America, 1786-1870*	See list below for "other states" for text of United States Constitution
NORTH CAROLINA	In N. C. Session Acts and in N. C. codes and compilations. (See III, this chart)	Broken collection	Connor and Cheshire, *Annotated Constitution of North Carolina*, 1911 See "N. C." in the books listed below
ALL OTHER STATES	In old and current state codes (See III, this chart)	See under "Political Science" in this volume.	Kettleborough, *The State Constitutions* Columbia University, *Index-Digest of State Constitutions* N. Y. Constitutional Convention, *Constitutions of States and the United States* Poore, *Federal and State Constitutions* Thorpe, *American Charters, Constitutions and Organic Laws*

II. COURTS

	LOWER COURT REPORTS	INTERMEDIATE APPELLATE COURT REPORTS	HIGHEST COURT REPORTS	BRIEFS AND RECORDS
ENGLISH	*Law Reports* *Law Reports* *Law Reports*	*Chancery Division* *Probate Division* *King's Bench Division*	English reports by old reporters— broken set *Law Reports—Appeal Cases*	None
CANADIAN			*Dominion Law Reports*	
UNITED STATES (Federal)	*Federal Cases* *Federal Reporter* *Federal Supplement* *Federal Rules Decisions* *Court of Claims Reports* (separate volumes)	*Federal Reporter*	*United States Supreme Court Reports*	Broken set for Circuit Court of Appeals
NORTH CAROLINA	None	None	Complete set of early reports, original editions *Supreme Court Reports,* complete sets in reprints and late editions	All since 1927, Fall Term

ALL OTHER STATES	1. N. Y. complete except for city court reports.
	2. Ohio
	   Ohio Law Reporter
	   Ohio Law Abstract
	3. Pennsylvania
	   District
	   County
	   Distr. & County
	4. Pa. (Side Repts.)
	   Dauphin
	   Delaware
	   Lackawanna
	   Luzerne
	   Montgomery
	   York
		Separate sets for:
		Illinois
		Mass.
		Missouri
		New York
		New York Supplement
		Ohio
		Pa. (Superior)
		Tenn.
		Texas (Civil Appeals)
		Texas (Criminal Appeals)
			All states with preliminary volumes complete except for o.p. volumes (on order)
			
			Alaska and Hawaii
				None

LAW

II. COURTS

COLLATERAL REPORTS	ANNOTATED AND SPECIAL SUBJECT REPORTS (Covers all courts)	CITATORS	DIGESTS
Placita Anglo-normannica *Yearbooks* (in Selden Society publications) *Yearbooks* (pub. by Harvard Press) *English Reports* (reprint) *Times Law Reports* *Law Times Reports* *Law Journal Reports*	*English Ruling Cases* *British Ruling Cases* *Cox's Criminal Law Cases*	In *English and Empire Digest* (See Annotations) Vol. 23 of *Mews' Digest*	Abridgments by: (1) Brooke 1576, (2) Fitzherbert 1577, (3) Rolle 1668, (4) Shepard 1675, (5) Bacon 1795. *Comyn's Digest* Current Digests: (1) *English and Empire Digest*, (2) *Mews' Digest*
United States Reports, Lawyers' edition *Supreme Court Reporter*	*United States Aviation Reports* *American Bankruptcy Reports* *American Maritime Cases* *Insurance Law Journal* *American Negligence Reports* *Negligence and Compensation Cases* *Public Utilities Reports* *American Decisions* *American Reports* *American State Reports* *Annotated Cases* *Lawyers' Reports Annotated* *American Law Reports*	*Shepard's Federal Citations* *Shepard's United States Citations*	(new) *Federal Digest* (West) (new) *United States Supreme Court Digest* (West) *American Digest*
In *South Eastern Reporter*		*Allen's Reported Cases* Shepard's *N. C. Citations*	Complete sets of old N. C. Digests Current Digests: 1. *N. C. Digest* (West) 2. *N. C. and South Eastern Digest* (West) 3. *American Digest*
In National Reporter System, both highest and intermediate Appellate Court Reports		*Shepard's Citations* for every unit of the National Reporter System *Shepard's New York Supplement Citations* *Shepard's New York Court of Appeals Citations*	*American Digest*

III. LEGISLATURES

	SESSION LAWS	CODES AND COMPILATIONS	LEGISLATIVE JOURNALS	SPECIAL INDEXES	COLLATERAL STATUTES
ENGLISH	Statutes at Large from Magna Charta to 39 Victoria The Law Reports, Statutes 1876 to date	Chitty's Statutes	None	None	
CANADIAN	Canadian 1857-1926; Prince Edward Island 1929-43; Quebec 1930-43				
UNITED STATES (Federal)	United States Statutes at Large	All old United States compilations and supplements from 1873 to current Codes United States Code, 1940 and 1943 Supplement United States Code Annotated	Current volumes of the Congressional Record Current volumes of United States Code Annotated, Congressional Service. See under "Political Science" in this volume	Scott and Beaman v. 1. 1789-1873 v. 2. Index to Federal Statutes 1874-1931 for United States Statutes at Large	United States Compiled Statutes United States Compiled Statutes (compact edition) Federal Statutes Annotated
NORTH CAROLINA	*All except 1791-93, 1795-96, 1798-1800, 1809, 1817	*All except Swann's Revisal 1751 and Davis' Collection of Acts, and 2nd edition of each	*House and Senate Journals from 1834 to date except a few volumes	No special index but in State Law Index with other states (See below)	None
ALL OTHER STATES	All current session acts Group 1: Southern states from early 1800. Ala. and Fla. about 1855. Group 2: States whose Legislation is significant to Law Library, U.N.C.: Calif. Mich. N. Y. Wisc. Conn. Minn. Ohio Ill. Mo. Pa. Ind. N. H. R. I. Me. N. J. Texas start about 1850 except Calif., N. H. and Texas which start around 1900 Group 3: Other states start around 1895	All current codes and compilations Group 1: Southern States. Va., starts 1619; S. C., 1682; Fla., Tenn. & Ky. start early 1800. Ga. & La. weak. Group 2: Codes start about 1919. Group 3: Around 1915	See under "Political Science" in this volume	State Law Indexes complete from 1925 to date	None
	*These are in main Library	*These are in main Library	*Early ones in main Library		

LAW

IV. ADMINISTRATIVE TRIBUNALS, DEPARTMENTS AND AGENCIES

REPORTS, CASES, RELEASES, ETC.	NUMBER OF VOLUMES	LAWS, RULINGS, PROCLAMATIONS
None	None	None
1. *Attorneys' General Opinions* 2. *Attorneys' General Reports* (Annual) 3. *Federal Power Comm. Reports* 4. *Federal Reserve Reports* 5. *I.C.C. Reports* (Opinions) 6. *I.C.C. Reports* (Annual) 7. *Nat'l Labor Relations Board Decisions and Orders* 8. *Nat'l Labor Relations Board Reports* (Annual) 9. *Nat'l War Labor Board, Releases* 10. *Tax Court of the United States, Reports* 11. *Treasury Decisions* (Internal Revenue) 12. *United States Board of Tax Appeals, Reports* 13. *United States Official Patent Gazette* 14. *United States Customs Court, Reports* 15. *War Department, Judge Advocate General Opinions* 16. *War Labor Reports* °	Vols. 29-39 1913 to date Vols. 1-2 1923-40 1887-1934 1887-1928 complete complete 1943-44 Vol. 1 to date 1914-42 complete Last 5 years Vol. 1 to date complete Vols. 1-12	*Federal Register,* practically complete *Code Federal Regulations,* complete ° *Commerce Clearing House Guide to Administrative Procedure,* service ° *United States Law Week*
1. N.C. Attorneys' General reports 2. Clerks of Superior Court yearbooks 3. Corporation Commission reports 4. Industrial Commission cases 5. Insurance Commissioner's reports 6. N.C. Board Railroad Commission reports 7. N.C. Utilities Commission reports 8. Probation Commission reports 9. Unemployment Compensation Commission decisions	1897 to date 1938 to date 1899 to 1934 Vols. 1 to 3 complete 1930-41 1891-98 1935-42 1937-42 complete	
See under "Political Science" in this volume. Law Library has ° *State Attorneys' General Digest of Opinions*	See under "Political Science" in this volume.	
° Not official		° Not official

Chapter 36

LIBRARY SCIENCE

Lucile Kelling

THE SCHOOL OF LIBRARY SCIENCE has a library consisting primarily of the books, pamphlets, periodicals, reprints, and clippings which are illustrative materials for the teaching and study of the various courses in the curriculum of the professional student in librarianship. While the immediate aim has been the collection of necessary materials for a one-year curriculum, careful thought has been given to the needs of an enlarged program which will some day, it is hoped, include advanced professional study.

GENERAL PROFESSIONAL LITERATURE

Periodicals and society journals form the nucleus of this collection, which includes also essays and books on librarianship, the biographies of librarians, and the whole body of literature in the field of library science. Among the periodicals and journals are such titles as *Bulletin of the American Library Association, Library Journal, Library Quarterly, Library Association Record, Special Libraries, College and Research Libraries, Journal of Documentary Reproduction,* and *Zentralblatt für Bibliothekswesen.* Munthe's *Librarianship from a European Angle,* Johnson's *The Public Library—a People's University,* and Branscomb's *Teaching with Books* are examples of background professional literature. The School's collection of biographical material includes, among many others, the publications in the series *American Library Pioneers.* Books on library science, which comprise surveys, reports, staff manuals, material on the many types of libraries as well as the various specific phases of library work, are drawn upon for a study of the broad aspects of librarianship and a better vision of its objectives, its organization, and its place in the social order.

ADMINISTRATION

The collection of professional literature forms the background for the four courses now given in the field of library administration. There is a large file of reports, publications, and bulletins of libraries of all types and sizes, such as those of the Library of Congress, New York Public and State Libraries, St. Louis Public Library, and such specific titles as *News Notes of California Libraries; Revista de la biblioteca, archivo y museo,* Madrid; *Bodleian Quarterly Record,* and the *Bulletin of the John Rylands Library,* Manchester, England. In addition to these files, a small miscellaneous group of reports is used as examples of effective and ineffective publicity, printing, compilation of data, etc. There has been gathered together working material devoted entirely to library literature, consisting of small pamphlets, newspaper and periodical clippings, and reprints. Staff manuals and library handbooks (printed, mimeographed, and typed) are available from such libraries as the Woman's College, University of North Carolina, Oklahoma Agricultural and Mechanical College, and the Enoch Pratt Free Library. Typical surveys are Downs's *Resources of Southern Libraries* and Wilson's *Report of a Survey of the University of Florida Library for the University of Florida.* The large collection of books and pamphlets on library technology is used for the study of specific library problems: ordering of books; processing of books; personal problems; work with special groups, as the blind, the technician, and the businessman; buildings, equipment, supplies; and many others. This collection, which is the largest shelved in the School of Library Science, includes Flexner's *Making Books Work,* Wheeler and Githens' *The American Public Library Building,* Special Libraries Association's *Special Library Resources,* Randall and Goodrich's *Principles of College Library Administration,* McDiarmid's *The Administration of the American Public Library,* and Herbert's *Personnel Administration in Public Libraries.*

BOOK SELECTION

For the courses in book selection for adults, the entire Library of the University of North Carolina is available in addition to the relatively small collection in the School of Library Science of minimum essentials and of illustrative editions of standards and classics. Very recent books are rented from the Bull's Head Bookshop. The school has strong working collections of books for young people and books for children. It has a group of children's books in foreign languages and books showing the development of children's literature from the chap book to the present time. The Libraries of the Chapel Hill Elementary School and the Chapel Hill High School are also open to student use. Occasionally the North Carolina Library Commission and the State Department of Public Instruction give or lend books to the School. The School's files include publishers' catalogues and reading lists from the Library of Congress, Los Angeles Public Library, Enoch Pratt Free Library, and other libraries of all types. The School subscribes to book-reviewing periodicals such as *The Times* (London) *Literary Supplement, The Saturday Review of Literature,* and *Subscription Books Bulletin.* In addition, the periodical files of the University are available for reviews referred to in the *Book Review Digest, Technical Book Review,* and the *Bibliographie der Rezensionen,* and for reviews of books in subject fields, such as the *American Historical Review.*

CATALOGUING AND CLASSIFICATION

There is in the School of Library Science a laboratory collection of books, including duplicates, which present various problems in cataloguing, and the University Library is used for additional subject material and for specialization such as maps, music, etc. Special problems are arranged with the University departmental libraries and with the Chapel Hill Public Schools for advanced students or those interested in particular types of cataloguing. Materials are at hand for the study of such classification systems as the Dewey Decimal, Library of Con-

LIBRARY SCIENCE

gress, Brown's Subject Classification, and the *Classification décimale universelle*. The availability of the Depository Catalogue of the Library of Congress (with added cards from the John Crerar Library, Harvard College Library, Folger Shakespeare Library, and Princeton University Library) and the Union Catalogue of Libraries in the State of North Carolina (Duke University, Duke Hospital Library, State College Library, and for special materials, Wake Forest Library, Guilford College Library, Charlotte Public Library, etc.) is an asset for both present use and future development of cataloguing courses.

HISTORY OF BOOKS AND LIBRARIES

The University Library's large general collection of books on bookmaking, the history of printing, book decoration, private and university presses, as well as those on famous book collections, collectors, and libraries from ancient to present times, is available to students in Library Science. The Hanes Collection of materials for the study of the origin and development of the book, particularly the incunabula collection, is of inestimable assistance to students in the School. A small collection of lantern slides, which belongs to the School, is used for illustrative purposes.

LIBRARY MOVEMENT IN THE SOUTHEAST

Surveys, reports, periodicals, and the collection of technical literature are available for the study of library development in the southeastern region, as well as the large body of social science literature in the University Library.

REFERENCE AND BIBLIOGRAPHY

The collection of books in library science includes such books as Hutchins' *Introduction to Reference Work*, Wyer's *Reference Work*, and Butler's *The Reference Function of the Library;* and the periodicals, journals, and technical books cover the organization and administration of reference departments and libraries. The School has a collection of minimum standard reference books working towards a model collection for a small library. Latest editions of the *World Book Encyclopedia, Compton's Pictured Encyclopedia,* and *Britannica Junior* are at hand. The University Library's collection, however, forms the bulwark of the work in reference and bibliography. Dictionaries in English and foreign languages, including special dictionaries and books for the study of the development of language; such encyclopedias as the *Encyclopaedia Britannica, Encyclopedia italiana, Brockhaus' Konversations-Lexikon, Encyclopédie française,* and the *Enciclopedia universal ilustrada europeo-americana;* periodical indexes including the U. S. general indexes, the *Subject Index to Periodicals,* and the *Internationale Bibliographie der Zeitschriftenliteratur;* the subject indexes such as the *Agricultural Index, Art Index,* and the *Education Index* are available. Reference works in subject fields are to be found in the University Library or in the Departmental Libraries, as well as the popular and standard works of reference suited to smaller libraries. The Library is a depository of U. S. Government Publications and has in addition many British documents and some from other foreign countries. It has practically all of the documents of the Southern states. The strong bibliography collections of the Libraries of the University of North Carolina and Duke University, which include many of the national and trade bibliographies, universal and general bibliographies from incunabula and early printed books to the present time, the chief subject bibliographies, and many author bibliographies, together with the holdings of some of the principal libraries of the world in printed or card form, fulfill the School's present needs and should make an advanced curriculum possible in the future.

Chapter 37

POLITICAL SCIENCE

C. B. Robson

FOR RESEARCH in political science, the University Library is supplemented by the Law Library, the School of Commerce Library, and the Institute of Government. With the exception of the material in the Institute of Government and certain types of material in the Law Library all items are covered by the card catalogue in the University Library. In the following account of these collections, the arrangement is by type of material rather than by subject matter.

PUBLIC DOCUMENTS

The federal government.—Since July 1, 1884, the University has been a designated depository for documents published by the United States. Congressional documents and the official orders and reports of the executive departments and independent establishments are kept in the University Library; the court reports are in the Law Library. For the period before 1884, the file of federal government publications is substantially complete. The policy of filling in existing gaps whenever the material becomes available is systematically followed.

State governments.—The University Library has one of the most extensive collections of the public documents of the colonies and territories to be found anywhere outside the Library of Congress. Designated in 1933 as the Documents Division of the North Carolina State Library, the University Library received the State Library's holding of legislative journals, collected documents and departmental reports of other states accumulated throughout its history, with the exception of the sessions laws and court reports, which were placed in the Supreme Court Library in Raleigh. Under this provision the University Library receives on exchange basis most of the documents of other states, with the exception of session laws and court reports. By legislative act the University Library is allotted a quantity of North Carolina official publications for use on an exchange basis. The Law Library's files of session laws and court reports have been substantially completed in this manner. This Library also has all recently published state codes and a number of the earlier ones.

Since 1933, the University Library has made the systematic extension of its holdings in state documents a matter of primary concern. In this undertaking, the head of the Documents Department has had the special co-operation of Professor William Sumner Jenkins of the Department of Political Science. By means of exchange of duplicates, purchase, and gifts, the files of documents for all states and in all categories, legislative journals and reports, the records and reports of executive departments, bureaus, and commissions, have been steadily expanded. There is also a definite program of co-operation in state documents with the Duke University Library. Responsibility for the entire field has been divided between the two institutions, with deliberate duplication in certain chosen fields. Filling in the gaps in the earlier periods is a special objective of the co-operative plan. Through these efforts a collection of state documents has been built up which, when taken in connection with that in the Duke Library, is as complete as is to be found anywhere. Through collaboration with the Library of Congress in a legislative journals microfilm project, directed by Professor Jenkins, the series of legislative journals of the American colonies, territories, and states has been rendered practically complete, either in original or in microfilm. The extensiveness of the holdings may be illustrated by the statement that the University Library has a complete file of the official collected documents of the State of New York for the past thirty years, running to about twenty volumes for each year, and most of the material published since 1830.

Smaller civil divisions.—In the publications of local units there are few sustained files. However, there are two particularly valuable collections of material on local government in North Carolina. One of these is the accumulation of a thirty-year clipping and filing service of the Rural Social Economics Library. The other consists of records, forms, reports, ordinances, and other working material of North Carolina cities and counties assembled by the Institute of Government. In the general collection of North Caroliniana and in the Southern Historical Collection, there is much material, both published and in manuscript, that is of value in the study of the development of local government in this region.

Foreign governments.—The University Library has a complete file of British parliamentary debates from Cobbett's *Parliamentary History*, through Hansard, to the current official records. Otherwise, its holdings in foreign government publications are scattered. For Germany, there are principally the publications of the foreign office, including a set of *Die grosse Politik der europäischen Kabinette 1871–1914;* for France, an extensive collection of documents and monumental publications for the Revolutionary and Napoleonic periods, and comparable material for earlier times, but few documents from the Third Republic; for the other European countries, only scattered reports are available.

The Latin American republics are well represented by such foreign office or other official publications as have been issued relative to the wars of independence, boundary disputes, wars, and other aspects of foreign relations. The Library also has the principal monumental publications, including those published under the auspices of universities or learned societies. Recently issued statistical reports are on hand.

Documents relating to international relations, organization, and law.—In addition to the official publications of the United States and the scattered publications of the foreign offices of other nations, the University Library has complete sets of the League of Nations and International Labor Office publications. It also has the material issued by the Pan-American Union and all of the publications of the Carnegie Endowment for International Peace, as well as the material published serially or occasionally by learned societies and other institutions or organizations, such as the American Institute of International Law, the American Society of International Law, the Royal

Institute of International Affairs, the Academie de Droit International de la Haye, the World Peace Foundation, and others. Standard compilations, such as the De Martens treaty collections, are available, as are also such rarer items as David Hunter Miller's *My Diary at the Conference of Paris, with Documents.*

Bibliographical aids in the use of public documents.—In addition to the official catalogues, bibliographies, and indexes, the University Library has such non-official guides as Hasse's *Index to United States Documents Relating to Foreign Affairs, 1828–1861;* the Hasse series of indexes of economic material in documents of the United States pertaining to the several states; and the various mimeographed guides compiled by Jerome K. Wilcox. The separately published guides to state publications include Bowker's *State Publications* and the National Association of State Libraries' check lists of state statutes, session laws and legislative journals, compiled by Grace E. Macdonald, together with the supplement compiled by William S. Jenkins. A check list of collected documents prepared by Professor Jenkins with the collaboration of the Documents Librarian is available to research students. This check list is to be issued as a publication of the National Association of State Libraries and at present is in loose-leaf manuscript form. For the microfilm collection of journals made by Professor Jenkins there is a photo-print check list. Hodgson's *The Official Publications of American Counties, a Union List* and the non-official listing in Petersen's *Bibliography of County Histories of the 3050 Counties in the 48 States* represent the guides for the smaller civil divisions.

The collection of bibliographical aids for Great Britain contains *A General Index to the Reports from Committees of the House of Commons, 1715–1801,* a complete set of the *General Indexes to the Accounts, Papers ... of the House of Commons* (1801–1929), the companion volume for the reports, etc., of the House of Lords from 1801 to 1885, and a file of the *Consolidated List of Government Publications* (1922–). These official indexes are supplemented by the *Catalogue of Parliamentary Papers, 1801–1900* with its supplements published by P. S. King, the Royal Colonial Institute's series of *Overseas Official Publications* (1927–32), and Cole's *A Finding List of*

Royal Commission Reports in the British Dominions. The Library also has the *List of the Serial Publications of Foreign Governments, 1815-1931;* the Library of Congress' *Official Publications of Present-day Germany* compiled by Otto Neuburger in 1942; the *Key to League of Nations Documents;* Ker's *Mexican Government Publications;* and Child's *The Memorias of the Republics of Central America and of the Antilles.*

REFERENCE MATERIAL

Encyclopedias and dictionaries.—Along with the general reference material, described elsewhere in this volume, there are items of special usefulness for research in political science. Besides the American encyclopedias and dictionaries in the fields of law, government, and the social sciences, the University Library has the *Handwörterbuch der Staatswissenschaften,* Palgrave's *Dictionary of Political Economy,* the *Dictionnaire diplomatique,* and the *Grand dictionnaire socialiste.*

Biographical dictionaries and directories.—In addition to the official registers and directories of the United States and the states, there are the standard American and foreign biographical references sets, such as the *Dictionary of American Biography,* the *Dictionary of National Biography,* the *Allgemeine deutsche Biographie,* the *Diccionario histórico y biográfico de Chile* and the *Biografías Argentinas y Sud-Americanas.*

Who's Who in America, the corresponding compendiums for foreign countries, such as *Who's Who, Wer Ist's?, Who's Who in Latin America,* etc., and specialized professional directories, such as *Who's Who in Government,* are also on the shelves.

Statistical abstracts and yearbooks.—Besides the statistical materials and official yearbooks published by the United States, the states, the League of Nations, and the International Labor Office, the University Library is supplied with recent and contemporary material of this type issued for the United Kingdom, India, and the Dominions, and that of the Latin-American republics. The file of the *Statistisches Jahrbuch für das deutsche Reich* is complete since 1912. Other nations or political units are represented for the most part only by yearbooks published in the English language, such as the *China Year Book*, the *Japan Year Book*, or the *Soviet Union Year Book*. Files of such standard issues as the *Statesman's Year Book*, *Europa*, *The International Year Book*, the *South American Yearbook*, and the *Political Handbook of the World* are complete.

PERIODICALS, SERIALS, NEWSPAPERS

Scientific and professional journals.—Complete files of nearly all scientific and professional journals published in the United States in the various branches of political science and related fields are in the University Library. Files of British journals of this character include the *Political Quarterly*, the *Political Science Quarterly*, and *Public Administration*, together with several in related disciplines. In the international field, in addition to the *American Journal of International Law*, there are the *Revue de droit international et législation comparée*, the *Revue général du droit international public*, and the *Nordisk Tidsskrift for International Ret*.

Law Reviews.—In the Law Library are files of the various law reviews published in the United States, together with the principal publications of this type throughout the world. These files are maintained through exchanges of the *North Carolina Law Review*.

Publications of associations of government officials, civic organizations and governmental research institutions.—The University Library regularly obtains the publications of those organizations affiliated with the Public Administrative Service and of national institutions, such as the National Municipal League and the Institute for Government Research of the Brookings Institution. In exchange for its *Popular Government*, the Institute of Government receives a great variety of material in this category.

Serial publications.—Serial publications of learned societies, such as the *Proceedings of the Academy of Political Science* and the *Annals of the American Academy of Political Social Science*, are available in complete files. The same is true of series issued by universities, many of which are maintained by exchange for *The James Sprunt Studies in History and Political Science* published under the direction of the Departments of History and Political Science. Foreign material of this type is represented by such items as the *British Yearbook of International Law*, the annual and occasional publications of the Royal Institute of International Affairs, and the substantial files of the publications of the Academie de Droit International de la Haye and the Academie für Deutsches Recht, the latter in the Law Library.

GENERAL LITERATURE

Classical works in political theory, philosophy and science are found in the University Library in good editions. Memoirs, correspondence and other published papers of statesmen are available, especially for Great Britain and the United States. Recent and contemporary secondary material, whether of general or monographic character, is fully represented so far as that published in the United States is concerned. The more specialized books published abroad are chiefly in the fields of international or foreign affairs, theory, and constitutional history. The principal British works in the fields of public law and public administration, as well as those discussing current political economic and social problems, are also available.

Chapter 38

SOCIOLOGY

Rupert B. Vance

WE SHOULD expect to find that the materials required for research in sociology are as many and as varied as the facets of man's social life and institutions. Sociology has both its historical and its contemporary interests. In its historical phase, sociology depends largely on research materials that have been evaluated in the sections of this survey on the classics, philosophy, and the historical studies, especially social history. But, whatever the divergent interests in the field, it must be agreed that general sociology and social theory are basic. Here the University Library is modestly adequate rather than exhaustive in its resources.

Most of the basic materials for general sociology are available to the student. The Library is well provided with those reference handbooks that delimit the general field, such as Reuter, *Handbook of Sociology;* R. E. Park, ed., *An Outline of the Principles of Sociology;* Henry P. Fairchild, *A Dictionary of Sociology;* E. E. Eubanks, *The Concepts of Sociology;* L. L. Bernard, ed., *The Fields and Methods of Sociology;* and the *Encyclopaedia of the Social Sciences.* Most of the general and special bibliographical aids are found, including *Social Science Abstracts; The London Bibliography of the Social Sciences;* Monroe Work, *Bibliography of the Negro in Africa and America;* A. F. Kuhlman, *Guide to Material on Crime and Criminal Justice.* In addition to general sociological journals published in the United States, such as *American Journal of Sociology, Social Forces, Sociology and Social Research, Journal of Social Philosophy, Annals of the American Academy, Southwestern Political Science Quarterly, American Sociological Review,* etc., the Library has files of those published in Great Britain, France, and Germany, including *The Sociological Review* (Manchester), *Revue internationale de sociologie* (Paris), and *Jahrbuch für Soziologie* (Berlin). Strangely enough, it lacks a file of *L'Année Sociologique,* founded by Emile Durkheim in 1898.

In materials for research in social theory the Library has most of the standard secondary works in English and the major European languages except Russian. For sustained research in theory there are gaps in several fields. Main figures in European philosophy are represented, and adequate work can be done in the major social theorists of England, France, and America. A check against the Bernards' *Origins of Sociology in America* shows that while the works of Henry Hughes and George Fitzhugh are here, approximately half the lesser works discussed therein are not available. German theorists are not well represented. Few Russians are represented, and no one would select the University as a place to study classical Chinese thought, Hindu theorists, or in fact, the sociology of either the Near or the Far East. The Library is adequate only as long as social theory is confined to Western Europe and North America. Work in Latin-American sociology is less limited because of the Library's holdings in Latin American history (*q.v.*). In addition, the Library has files of many of the journals sporadically issued from those countries, including the *Revista argentina de ciencias politicas* (Buenos Aires), *Revista mexicana de sociología* (Mexico City), and *Sociologia* (Sao Paulo).

While the University has not developed the fields of physical anthropology and ethnology, it has the collection of North Carolina Indian material that resulted from the North Carolina surveys of 1937–39, jointly sponsored by the Archeological Society of North Carolina, the State Museum, and the University. The collection of several thousand pieces is housed on the fourth floor of Alumni Building, but it lacks a custodian. The Library, however, provides many of the basic materials necessary for work in the related sciences of man and culture. In addition to files of the standard journals, such as the *American Anthropologist, Journal of Physical Anthropology, Anthropos, Transactions* of the American Ethnological Society, the Library has complete files of the monographs of the Bureau of American Ethnology, the Smithsonian Institute, the American Museum of Natural History, etc., as well as the series of several university departments dealing with the American Indian, notably those of California and Nebraska.

The University has paid much more attention to the social and cultural aspects of anthropological science. While no especial efforts have been made to establish collections on African materials, the Library has funds for maintaining its resources in race relations and Negro life and culture. Apart from the exclusively historical works, the Negro collection now numbers some fifteen hundred volumes. Here are found important early studies, such as the Atlanta University surveys, as well as W. E. B. Du Bois' survey of Philadelphia. In addition to files of the *Negro Yearbook*, basic journals dealing with the Negro, such as *Journal of Negro Education, Journal of Race Development, Journal of Negro History,* and *Phylon,* are complete.

For the study of social institutions and social problems, the Library resources are no more than fair, showing in places the effects of recent budgetary limitations. For research on the developing institutions related to public welfare and social planning at the state and regional level, attention should be called to the Library's excellent collection of state documents. With few gaps, the collected legislative documents and reports of various state departments dating from the early nineteenth century are available for research into functions that range from public safety, public health, state housing, metropolitan and town planning, to more usual departments such as boards of probation, public works, mental health, loan agencies, etc. The materials are supplemented by the published reports of various private charitable and philanthropic agencies. Reports of North Carolina institutions, public and private, are practically complete. For sociological analysis of educational, political, and economic institutions, materials placed in the Library by other departments are available. The Library is relatively weak in materials for research in religious institutions. For study of the family institution, the Library has most of the standard works. Here, as elsewhere, Library resources are supplemented by specialized collections which faculty members make available to advanced students.

The Law Library offers facilities for research in legal institutions as well as in problems of crime and delinquency. Standard writings on sociological jurisprudence such as those of Dean Roscoe Pound and others are re-enforced by complete files of the *Journal of Criminology and Criminal Law*, *Journal of Political and Legal Sociology*, etc. The Library owns no bound sets of *Archives de philosophie du droit et de sociologie juridique*, *Archiv für Kriminologie* (Leipzig), *Archiv für Rechts und Sozial-Philosophie*. In addition to standard surveys and reports, such as the *Missouri Crime Survey*, 1926; the *Illinois Crime Survey*, 1929; the *Report of the Montana State Crime Commission*, 1930; the 1931 reports of the Wickersham Commission on *Crime and the Foreign Born*, *Causes of Crime*, etc., the Library has the standard treatises on criminology, penology, criminal sociology, and juvenile delinquency. Many monographic studies of foreign countries, however, are lacking in both the main and the Law Library. Resources in domestic law and domestic relations, including such allied fields as those of adoption, are adequately covered for sociological study. The Library has Chester G. Vernier's *American Family Law: A Comprehensive Study of the 48 States and Territories*, with its supplementary volume. For research in social legislation, there are the indices of state legislative acts and the various state codes.

In the study of population, the community, and regional and rural sociology, the University has undertaken definite specialization. The standard treatises on population are available, together with the basic statistical series of the League of Nations, and the series of reports on vital statistics published by the United States Bureau of the Census. Related publications and journals covering the field of social statistics are currently received and a complete file of the *Population Index* has been added. There has been no attempt to collect for foreign countries, and the Library has no census holdings exclusive of the United States.

In its special fields, the Sociology Department has, in addition to treatises, attempted to collect the outstanding examples of regional and community surveys. In its exhibit room the Department has a display of world and regional maps and charts. Also on display is a complete set of the early Social Study Series of the University of North Carolina Press, the Press's later regional monographs, the surveys of the National Resources Planning Board, together with federal and state publications bearing on national and regional planning.

While the collection of housing and related surveys is far from complete, the Library has the basic materials in urban sociology including Charles Booth's monumental survey, *Life and Labor of the People of London* (16 vols., London, 1892) and the 1935 resurvey by the London School of Economics in eight volumes; the *Pittsburgh Survey*, edited by Paul U. Kellogg (6 vols.); the *Springfield Survey; Social Conditions in an American City*, edited by Selby M. Harrison; George F. Kengott's *The Record of a City; a Social Survey of Lowell, Massachusetts;* and the Middletown studies of Robert S. Lynd. It lacks the great fifty-volume series *Groszstadt Dokumente* (Berlin, 1905), edited by Hans O. A. Ostwald. While the Library has complete files of the *National Municipal Review, The American City*, etc., its holdings in the field of city planning are not large.

Some of this material is located in the Rural Social Economics Library. This is the Library's largest collection of exclusively social science materials and is devoted largely to rural life in the nation and the South. In addition to complete files of journals in the rural field, such as *Rural Sociology, Journal of Farm Economics, Journal of Agricultural History, Journal of Land and Public Utility Economics*, etc., this Library has the general reference aids such as Sorokin, Zimmerman, and Galpin, *Systematic Source Book in Rural Sociology*, and all standard treatises on rural sociology and agricultural economics. A unique feature of the Library is a collection of the best novels dealing with rural life in this and other countries.

In addition to some 3,600 bound volumes, the collection contains approximately 43,000 pamphlets, 105,000 clippings and 25,000 press releases. Some of this material is fugitive in character, and, although it is not catalogued and classified in permanent library form, it is so organized and assembled as to be readily accessible for research with a minimum of expenditure of time and effort. The research student can find here much of the material he needs for an elaborate study, and he will also find therewith bibliographical references indicating where additional material on the subject may be obtained.

The Rural Social Economics Library includes files dealing with recent developments in social legislation, regional planning, rural resettlement, land utilization, reconstruction in all its phases, county government, transportation, family relations, crime, and rural electrification. The county government files are remarkably rich, and rural community surveys and regional planning are featured. This special collection, however, is not kept open at night, and its value is greatly diminished by the failure of the Library to provide an attendant.

IX

LIBRARY EXTENSION

Chapter 39

LIBRARY EXTENSION SERVICES TO THE STATE

Agatha Boyd Adams

THE EXTENSION LIBRARY opens the door of the University Library to the whole State; through its services books may go to the most remote mail boxes high up in the Smokies or out on the dunes of Manteo. One of the first sections of the Extension Division to be established in 1912, the Extension Library has been built up and developed since that time as an active agency in adult education. From the beginning its concern has been to supply books and other library materials to teachers, debaters, correspondence students, off-campus classes, school dramatics organizations, women's clubs, forums, and individual readers. To serve this purpose it maintains a collection of approximately twelve thousand volumes. Some three hundred volumes are withdrawn each year and the same number added, so that, while the number of books remains more or less static, the collection is constantly revised. By this means it is kept responsive to current needs.

The collection in the Extension Library is made up in the main of the novels, poetry, biography, books of travel, and books on current affairs which supply the club programs published each year by the Library, and of the books which are currently in demand by the groups of readers mentioned above. There is a small reference collection at hand of such ready reference works as *Current Biography* and the *Reference Shelf*. Books which are in active use in correspondence courses are kept on the shelves. There is a drama collection of about five thousand plays. All current Broadway plays are purchased as soon as they are published in book form. One large group of plays has been especially chosen for use in the school room.

Co-operation with the Carolina Playmakers helps to keep this collection alive.

The Extension Library subscribes to fifty-four periodicals of the popular type, such as *Time, Life, Theater Arts Monthly, Current History,* the *Atlantic Monthly,* and *Asia and the Americas.* These are not bound but are kept in readily accessible files, so that they may be sent out when a special article is requested, or information not available elsewhere is sought.

The resources of the Extension Library include a vertical file of pamphlets and clippings classified under approximately one thousand different subjects. A large section of the file contains material on North Carolina people, places, history, gardens, old homes, and other topics of local interest.

The Bull's Head Bookshop is an integral part of the organization of the Extension Library and an important supplement to its resources. The Bookshop maintains, in one end of the same room in which the Extension Library is located, an active collection of current fiction, biography, and travel of the better sort, new mystery stories, art books, recent poetry, and new plays, all of which may be either rented or purchased. The publications of the University Press are available there, as well as other recent books relating to North Carolina. Through the Extension Library Bookshop books may be sent out to borrowers in the state, or may be purchased by mail.

Another auxiliary of the Extension Library at the present time is the War Information Center. This current collection of books, pamphlets, and periodicals has been designed to bring together as much information as possible about the different phases, geographical, political, and sociological, of the Second World War. New books about the war are made available to readers as rapidly as possible. Pamphlets from the various organizations interested in international affairs, such as the Commission to Study the Organization of Peace, the Carnegie Endowment, the Foreign Policy Association, the International Labour Office, the Royal Institute of International Affairs, and others, and also pamphlets from such sources as the British Information Services, the Inter-Allied Information Center, the Embassy of the U.S.S.R., and other such national groups, are classified and filed and may be borrowed. An extensive file is also kept on hand of the periodical publications of such agencies as those mentioned above. All material in the War Information Center may be used by residents of the state as well as by members of the University.

In addition to the materials in the above-mentioned special collections, the Extension Library is free to draw upon the resources of the Main Library in answering requests. Any book in the Library except those in the reference room or on reserve for student or faculty use may be sent out if called for. This fact, of long standing but perhaps not fully comprehended everywhere in the state, puts the University Library at the service of everyone in North Carolina. The departmental libraries on the campus, with their special collections on pharmacy, botany, medicine, law, music, geology, mathematics, and physics are available to borrowers through the Extension Library; theses from the Library of the School of Commerce are frequently sent to persons interested in technical economics. This service is not restricted to residents of the state; it is open to and often used by readers from other states, especially in the Southeast.

The staff of the Extension Library is organized to take care of requests from different groups of readers. A careful effort is made to find the precise information or book or list of books which has been asked for, and in case it is not available, to make intelligent substitutions. A reference librarian takes care of requests that need searching to supply specific information or titles; she also gives especial attention to keeping the books on education up to date to meet the needs of teachers and to filling requests from teachers. Debate material is handled in co-operation with the Extension Division. Constant co-operation is maintained with the Bureau of Correspondence Instruction in order to be able to send out books needed in the preparation of these courses. Material for club programs is in charge of another member of the staff, who keeps a schedule of meetings of all clubs who subscribe to this service and mails the books in advance of their programs. Not only the six club programs published each year are used, but programs of earlier years, with the books which they refer to, are kept on file and are frequently called for.

The publication of these programs has been one of the most interesting and productive activities of the Extension Library over the entire period of its existence. Most of the outlines have been written by members of the University faculty or of the Library staff; some of them have had such distinguished authors as Addison Hibbard, James F. Royster, Howard Mumford Jones, and Paul Green. The editorial policy of selecting subjects of vital interest and authors with a knowledge of books and a talent for this type of outline presentation has maintained a high standard of quality in the series. Among earlier bulletins which are still used are: *Studies in American Literature*, by Addison Hibbard; *Our Heritage, a Study through Literature of the American Tradition*, by James Holly Hanford; *The Negro in Contemporary Literature*, by E. L. Green; *Contemporary Southern Literature*, by Howard Mumford Jones; *Below the Potomac*, by Marjorie Bond; *American Humor*, by E. C. and R. B. Downs. Two series of outlines have been so consistently popular that a new one is published each year; they are *Adventures in Reading*, which has survived through various authorships, and *Other Peoples' Lives*, which was originated and is still written by Cornelia Spencer Love of the Library staff. Among recent titles have been these: *Some Leaders of the World at War*, by E. S. and J. L. Godfrey; *Places and Peoples of the Mediterranean*, by Dale and Walter Spearman; *The New Frontier*, by W. W. Drake (based on H. W. Odum's *American Regions*), and *Music in America*, by Adeline McCall. The Extension Bulletins are popular and widely used, not only in North Carolina, but all over the country. The service which they embody is recognized as unique by those interested in adult education. Over two hundred libraries, both public and in colleges and universities, subscribe to the series.

The requests which come in from individual readers carry an interest beyond the more definitely patterned work with club programs. These requests are as varied as the personalities and localities from which they come. Often there is a story behind each letter. Sometimes from an initial request a correspondence will develop between the librarian and the borrower, until the former comes to know well the reader's preferences and requirements. Several readers in different parts of the state leave a standing order to keep them supplied with reading matter on some given subject, or just to have the new books sent to them as they come out.

The development of the Extension Library over the more than thirty years of its existence has been consistently toward the promotion of an intelligent fruitful program of adult education. Its organization is flexible enough to be adaptable to new needs and trends, yet it is based on thorough-going experience with the reading problems of individuals and groups in rural communities, or those inadequately supplied with libraries. Even in localities with public libraries there are apt to arise demands which can only be satisfied by the wider resources of a university library. As reading interests are stimulated by increased educational opportunities, the service which the Extension Library offers to the state should continue to expand and develop to meet these widening interests.

INDEX

Aaron Burtis Hunter Collection. *See* Hunter Collection
Acoustics, 120
Acting, 113
Administrative tribunals, 229
Adult education, 251, 254-55
Advertising, 209-10
Aesthetics, 110, 120
Agriculture, 32, 34, 42, 44, 246
Alabama, 40
Alchemy, 181
Alderman, E. A., 15, 28
Alexander Boyd Andrews Collection. *See* Andrews Collection
Alexander, Eben, 16
Alumni Building, 243
Alumni Loyalty Fund, 41
American Library Association. Committee on Resources of Southern Libraries, 22
American history. *See* United States history
American literature, 146-49
Anatomy, 90
Ancient history, 52, 129, 179-80
Andrews, A. B., 41
Andrews, William J., 29
Andrews Collection, 32
Anthropology, 243
Archaeology, 52, 129-30, 134
Archibald Henderson Collection of American Drama. *See* Henderson Collection
Architecture, 9, 35, 105-11
Argentina, 19, 161, 196, 197, 206, 212
Arkansas, 40
Armfield, Eugene, 16
Art, 9, 34, 52, 105-11, 252; history, 106
Art Reference Library, 106
Atlases, 169, 170, 200

Bacteriology, 89
Bahnson, H. T., 88
Ballet, 113
Baptists, 56
Battle Collection, 32
Battle, President K. P., 728
Bell, James M., 165
Bennehan, Richard, 3
Bernard, W. S., 9
Bibles, 50, 51
Bibliography, 12, 13, 16, 20, 37, 51, 55-67, 87, 89, 90, 106, 114, 116, 122, 130-31, 136, 139, 141, 143, 146, 152, 155-56, 159-60, 161, 168, 189, 192, 197, 198, 200, 201, 217, 219, 223, 233, 234, 238
Biochemistry, 89
Biography, 36, 91, 146, 191, 193, 230, 239, 251, 252
Biological and related sciences, 85-101; botany, 85-87; medicine, 88-90; pharmacy, 91-96; psychology, 97; zoology, 99-101
Biophysics, 175
Blount, Thomas, 3
Boggs, R. S., 218
Book Selection, 232
Bookmark, 52
Books, history of, 233. *See also* Hanes Foundation
Botany, 34, 85-87, 93, 253
Braille books, 224
Brazil, 206
Brewer, Fisk P., 28
Briefs, 226
British Empire, 191
Browsing Room, 52
Bull's Head Bookshop, 232, 252
Business. *See* Commerce
Business cycles, 207
Byrd, William, 42

257

INDEX

Cabildo, 196, 197
Caldwell, President Joseph, 3, 5
California, 244
Canada, 191
Carmichael, W. D. Sr., 41
Carnegie, Andrew, 47
Carnegie Corporation, grants from, 14, 20, 41, 105
Carnegie Library Building, 4, 5, 9, 16, 30
Carolina Playmakers, 114, 115, 116
Carr, Claiborn McD., 41
Cartography, 170
Cataloguing, 232-33
Chapel Hill Elementary School, 232; High School, 232
Charlotte Public Library, co-operation with, 21, 56, 233
Chatham, Thurmond, 41
Chatham, Mrs. Thurmond, 47
Check lists, 59
Chemistry, 9, 11, 165-67, 175, 181
Chemistry Library, 165
Chicago, University of, cards from, 12, 21, 56
Child development, 214
Chile, 19, 161, 196, 197, 212
Chinese language and literature, 113, 167, 212, 243
Church history, 33, 36, 182
Civil War, 39, 192, 194. *See also* Confederate materials
Classics, 9, 129-35, 242
Classification, 232-33
Clippings, 36, 115, 230, 231, 237, 246, 252
Club programs, 251, 253-54
Codes and compilations, 228
Collaterals, 220, 225-29
Collections and foundations, 27-52; North Caroliniana, 27-38; Southern Historical, 39-46; Hanes, 47-52. *See also* Special Collections
Colonial history, 42
Commerce, 42, 195, 200-10; Library, 191, 235, 253
Comparative linguistics, 136-37; Breton, 137; Church Slavic, 137; Hittite, 137; Indo-European, 136; Indo-Iranian, 137; Irish, 137; Lettic, 137; Lithuanian, 137; Old Prussian, 137; Sanskrit, 137; Tocharian, 137; Welsh, 137
Confederate materials, 31, 32, 34, 42, 45. *See also* Kenan Collection, Kidder Collection; Kurz and Allison Civil War lithographs
Connor, Robert D. W., 29, 31
Constitutions, 225
Cook, Olan V., 14
Co-operative relationships, 12, 13, 17-23
Corporations, 208
Costuming, 113-14
County government, 247
Court reports, 226, 236
Courts, 226
Craige, Burton, 41
Crime, 246, 247
Cuneiform writing, 49
Curriculum Laboratory, 211
Curry Collection, 45, 46

Dakota Playmakers, 716
Dashiell Collection of fashion plates, 46
Davidson College Library, co-operation with, 21
Davie Collection of Early American Travel, 12, 32
Davie, Preston, 32
Davie, William Richardson, 3. *See also* Davie Collection of Early American Travel
Debate material, 253
Delaware, 193
Delinquency, 245
Departmental libraries, 5, 6, 253. *See also names of departments*
Dialect dictionaries, 154
Dialect studies, 139
Dialectic Literary Society, 3, 4
Diaries, 44, 186, 192, 238
Dictionaries, 66, 69, 93, 106, 118, 137, 139, 154, 161, 174, 200, 222, 239
Dispensatories, 92
Dissertations, 56, 66, 121, 150-51, 216, 218, 219
Documents, 14, 75, 235-38; Federal, 75, 100, 193, 200, 220, 234, 235; State, 21, 33, 38, 75, 76, 193, 206, 235-36, 244; Foreign, 76, 77, 186, 189-90, 197, 198-99, 210, 212, 225-29, 234
Downs, R. B., 13, 14, 16, 22
Drama, 112-16, 148, 158, 160, 251-52; American, 112; British, 112; French, 113; Greek, 113; German, 112; Hungarian, 113; Japanese, 113; Latin-American, 113; Spanish, 113, 160

INDEX

Dramatic Art Department, 114
Duke Hospital Library, 233
Duke University Divinity School, 125
Duke University Library, co-operation with, 12, 13, 14, 18, 19, 56, 90, 129, 137, 160, 182, 183, 189, 197, 233, 234, 236
Dunbar, Sir William, 43

Ecology, 99
Economics, 42, 189, 195, 200-10: history, 191; theory, 201
Edenton, 42
Education, 32, 43, 120, 195, 211-16; History of, 212; Philosophy of, 212; Health, 215; Physical, 215; Safety, 215; Secondary, 215; Special, 215; Teacher, 215
Education Library, 211
Educational psychology, 214
Educational testing, 214
Elisha Mitchell Scientific Society, establishment of, 7; exchanges, 9; *Journal*, 7, 34
Embryology, 99
Emmons Survey, 34
Encyclopedias, 65, 69, 93, 106, 118, 166, 174, 184, 200, 211, 222, 234, 239
Engineering, 174, 175; electrical, 9
English history, 189-91
English language and literature, 9, 18, 52, 58, 62, 113, 138-51, 181, 189, 201, 219, 237, 243; Old English, 139-41; Middle English, 139-41; Renaissance English, 141-43; after 1660, 143-46
Epigraphy, 133
Ethnology, 243
European history, 52, 179-91
Executive Committee of the Board of Trustees, 30
Extension Library, 38, 116, 251-55

Facsimiles, 141, 148
Family, 244, 247
Fashion plates. See Dashiell Collection
Fayetteville, 37
Federal depository library, 75, 235
Fiction, 147, 158, 246, 251, 252
Finance, public, 205-6
Fine Arts and Philosophy, 105-25: Art and Architecture, 105-11; Drama, 112-16; Music, 117-21; Philosophy, 122-25

Florida, 40
Folger Shakespeare Library, 56, 233
Folklore, 20, 161, 181, 217-19
Folklore Council of the University of North Carolina, 120
Folk music, 120, 218
Folk songs, 35, 120, 218
Formularies, 92
French language and literature, 9, 62, 113, 167, 181, 187, 201, 206, 237, 243; Old French, 156; 16th century, 157; 17th century, 157; 18th century, 157; 19th century, 157; 20th century, 158
Friends of the Library of the University of North Carolina, 16, 52

Gazetteers, 170
Garden Club of North Carolina, 35
Gautier, Joseph, 3
Genealogy, 21, 36, 44, 45, 46. See also Southern Historical Collection
General Education Board, grants from, 12, 13, 18, 55, 197
Genetics, 99
Geography, 168-70; economic, 170; human, 170
Geological surveys. See Emmons; Kerr; Olmstead-Mitchell
Geology, 34, 168-70, 253; economic, 169; structural, 169
Geophysics, 169, 175
Georgia, 40
German language and literature, 9, 52, 62, 113, 152-53, 167, 187, 201, 206, 219, 237, 243; Middle High German, 153-54; Old High German, 154; German linguistics, 154
Glossaries, 139
Government. See Political Science
Government publications. See Documents
Graduate School, 9, 38
Graham, E. K., 15, 31
Grammars, 139
Graphic arts, 109-10
Gray, Gordon, 41
Gray, James A., 41
Greek history, 179-80. See also Ancient history
Greek language and literature, 52, 113, 129-35, 206
Guidance, 214-15
Guilford College Library, co-operation with, 21, 56, 233

Hamilton, J. G. deRoulhac, 29, 31, 33
Handbooks, 70, 71, 72, 94, 137, 200, 209, 217-18, 219, 231, 242
Handicrafts, 35
Hanes, Alexander S., 47
Hanes, Anna Hodgin, 47
Hanes Foundation for the Study of the Origin and Development of the Book, 12, 47-52, 60, 156, 180, 181, 233
Hanes, Dr. Frederic M., 51
Hanes, James G., 47
Hanes, John W., 47
Hanes, Ralph P., 47
Hanes, Robert M., 47
Harvard University, cards from, 12, 56, 233
Henderson, Archibald, 29, 114
Henderson Collection of American drama, 12, 114, 148
Herbals, 85, 93
Herty, Charles H., 165
Hill Collection of North Caroliniana. *See* North Carolina Collection
Hill, John Sprunt, 29, 31, 41, 165
Hines, Peter Evans, 88
Historical guides, 73
Historical Society of North Carolina, organization of, 7, 28
Historical Society of the University of North Carolina, 7, 28, 39
History, 9, 35, 179-99, 242
Hogg, James, 43
Hogg, John, 43
Hogg, Robert, 43
Holt Collection, 114-15
Holt, Mrs. Constance D'Arcy, 115
Holt, Roland, 115
Housing, 244, 246
Hume, Dr. Thomas, 8
Hunter Collection, 12, 48, 51, 156
Hunter, Dr. Aaron Burtis, 48
Hydrobiology, 99

Incunabula, 48, 49, 50, 51, 52, 60, 139, 156, 181, 190, 233. *See also* Hanes Foundation; Hunter Collection
Indexes, 220, 221, 223, 225-29, 245
India, 212
Indians, American, 35, 44, 243
Industry, 42
Institute for Research in Social Science, 38, 40, 41
Institute of Folk Music, 120

Institute of Government, 235, 237
Intendencia, 196, 197
Interlibrary loans, 38, 129, 197, 224
International conciliation, 9
International education, 212
International relations, 186-87, 237
International trade, 203
Investments, 208
Italian language and literature, 113, 158, 167, 181, 201, 206

Jacocks Collection, 12, 51
Jacocks, Dr. W. P., 51
James Sprunt Collection. *See* Sprunt Collection
James Sprunt Historical Monographs, beginning of, 7
James Sprunt Studies in History and Political Science, 38
Japanese language and literature, 113
Jenkins, William Sumner, 76, 236
Jente, Richard, 218
John Crerar Library, cards from, 12, 56, 233
John McDowell Collection. *See* McDowell Collection
Johnson Collection of Photo-reproductions of Medieval Manuscripts, 181
Joint Committee on Intellectual Cooperation, 18, 20

Kemp Plummer Battle Collection. *See* Battle Collection
Kenan, Mrs. Graham, 41
Kenan, William Rand, 165
Kenan Chemistry Library, 165
Kenan Collection of Confederate States Publications, 31, 194
Kentucky, 40
Kerr Survey, 34
Kidder Collection of Southern Newspapers, 31
Kistler, A. M., 41
Koch, Frederick H., 114
Kommission für den Gesamtkatalog, 49
Kurz and Allison Civil War Lithographs, 46

Labor, 204-5
Land utilization, 247
Languages and literatures, 129-62: classical languages and literatures, 129-35; comparative linguistics, 136-37; English language and literature, 138-51; Germanic language and lit-

INDEX

erature, 152-53; Romance language and literature, 155-62. See also *individual names,* e.g., Spanish
Lantern slides, 169, 233
Lassiter, Mrs. Robert, 47
Latin-American history, 196-99
Latin-American materials, 12, 13, 14, 19, 63, 64, 113, 120, 160-61, 187, 206, 207, 212, 217, 218, 237, 243
Latin language and literature, 52, 113, 129-35, 167, 219
Law, 9, 11, 189, 220-29, 253
Law Library, 38, 195, 202, 220, 235, 236, 240, 244
Learned societies. See Society publications
Legal associations, report of, 233; publications of, 223
Legislative journals, 228. See also Documents
Legislatures, 228
Lenoir Collection, 32
Leonard, Irving A., 219
Lewis, Kemp P., 41
Library administration, 231
Library Extension Publications. See Club programs
Library movement in the Southeast, 233
Library of Congress, depository cards, 12, 21, 56, 193, 224, 233, 235, 236; Legislative journal microfilm project, 76, 236
Library of University of North Carolina, development of resources for graduate study and research, 8-11; early concentrations of materials, 6-8; financial support, 5, 9, 10; historical background, 3-6; librarians, 5, 15; manuscript division, 39; quarters, 5
Library Science, 230-34; School of, 16, 52, 230
Librettos, 115
Lighting, stage, 113
Linguistics. See Comparative linguistics
Literature. See Languages and literatures
Lithographs. See Kurz and Allison Civil War Lithographs
Loose leaf services, 224
Loan agencies, 244
Louisiana, 40
Lurcy, Georges, 105

McDowell Collection, 32
Make-up, 113
Mangum, Charles S., 88
Manuscripts, 58, 60, 141, 190, 192, 197, 237. See also Southern Historical Collection; Hanes Foundation
Maps, 37, 46, 66, 67, 168, 169, 245-46
Margaret Dashiell Collection. See Dashiell Collection
Marketing, 208-9
Maryland, 40, 193
Massachusetts, 193
Mathematics, 171-73, 175, 253; Department Library, 171
May Fund, 155
May, Samuel, 155
Medical School Library, 88, 101
Medicine, 34, 88-90, 167, 181, 253
Medieval history, 181-83
Memoirs, 185, 191, 192, 241
Mental health, 244
Meteorology, 170, 175
Mexico, 206, 212
Microfilm abstract cards, 56
Microfilms, 14, 76, 120, 145-46, 156, 193
Milburn Fund, 105
Mineralogy, 169
Mississippi, 40
Missouri, 40
Mitchell, Professor Elisha, 4, 5, 6
Modern European history, 184-88: 16th and 17th centuries, 184; French Revolution and Napoleon, 184-85; 19th century, 185; contemporary, 186
Money, 206
Monographs, 94, 159, 181, 193, 202, 241, 243, 245, 246
Morehead, J. M., 41
Morphology, 99
Murphey Hall, 114
Music, 34, 117-21, 181, 217, 253; in notation, 119-20
Musicology, 117
Mycology, 85
Mythology, 129, 134

Nathan Wilson Walker Collection. See Walker Collection
Naval history, 45
Near Eastern studies, 169, 179, 212, 243
Nebraska, 244
Negro education, 215-16

Negroes, 19, 56, 244
New Bern, 37
Newby, G. E., 88
New Hampshire, 193
New Jersey, 193
New York, 193, 236
Newspapers, American, 19, 74, 75, 200, 205, 240; Foreign, 19, 74, 75, 185, 187, 188; State, 21, 32, 37, 193, 194
North Carolina, Historical Commission, 7; State Department of Archives and History, 21; State Library, 21, 235; State Library Commission, 21, 232; Department of Agriculture, 34; Department of Conservation and Development, 34; Geological and Economic Survey, 34, 165; Supreme Court Library, 235
North Carolina Archaeological Society, 243
North Carolina Collection, 12, 27-38, 194
North Carolina Division of Cooperation in Education and Race Relations, 19
North Carolina Historical Society. See Historical Society of North Carolina
North Carolina History, 27-38, 76, 192, 193, 221, 235. See also Southern Historical Collection
North Carolina legislative journals. See Legislative journals
North Carolina Room, 33
North Carolina Society, 41
North Caroliniana, 9, 12, 39, 237. See also North Carolina Collection
Numismatics, 129, 135

Old East Building, 5
Olmsted-Mitchell Survey, 34
Order books of the Revolution, 46
Oriental literature, 12
Oriental studies, 137

Painting: 18th century, 106-7; 19th and 20th centuries, 108
Paleography, 132, 141, 181-82
Paleontology, 169
Pamphlets, 199, 200, 211, 219, 230, 231, 246, 252
Papyrology, 129, 133
Paraguay, 19, 161, 197

Parker, Junius, 41
Pathology, 89
Patterson, Rufus, 41
Peabody Hall, 211
Pennsylvania, 193
Periodicals, 35, 36, 74, 77, 78, 79, 86, 88, 89, 90, 95, 96, 97, 98, 99-101, 106, 114, 118, 122, 129, 130, 136, 140, 145, 146, 148, 149-50, 152, 153, 155, 160, 161, 165-66, 168-69, 173, 174, 184, 190, 193-95, 197, 199, 200, 201, 205, 206, 207, 208, 209, 216, 221, 222, 230, 232, 240, 243, 252, 253
Person Hall, 106
Petrology, 169
Pettigrew Collection, 32
Pharmacology, 89
Pharmacopoeias, 92
Pharmacy, 91-96, 253
Philanthropic Literary Society, 3, 4
Phillips Hall, 171, 174
Philological Club, founding of, 8
Philosophy, 70, 71, 122-25, 149, 167, 181, 242; ancient, 123; medieval, 123-24; modern, 124
Photogrammetry, 170
Photographs, 115, 116, 166, 168
Physical science, 165-75; chemistry, 165-67; geology and geography, 168-70; mathematics, 171-73; physics, 174-75
Physics, 167, 174-75, 253; Department Library, 171, 174
Physiology, 99
Planning, town, 244
Plantation system, 42
Playbills, 116
Poetry, 251, 252; American, 9, 141; French, 157-158
Political science, 149, 189, 195, 202, 235-41
Population, 245
Portuguese language and literature, 62
Potter, F. W., 88
Preliterary history, 169
Princeton University, cards from, 21, 56, 233
Printing, history of, 50, 181
Probation, 244
Proverbs, 218, 219
Pruden, Dossey, 41
Psychology, 97, 98, 120
Public health, 90, 244
Public Health, School of, 90

INDEX

Public school journals, 32
Public utilities, 202
Public welfare, 244
Public works, 244

Quakers, 56

Radio advertising, 210
Railroads, 32. See also Transportation
Raleigh, 37
Raleigh Memorial Collection, 12, 36
Raleigh, Sir Walter, 36. See also Raleigh Memorial Collection
Rare books, 60-61. See also Hanes Foundation
Reconstruction in the Southern states, 192, 194, 247
Records, phonograph, 117, 120
Reference resources, 68-82, 130
Regional catalogue, 21
Regional planning, 247
Regional research, 32
Religion, 42, 70, 71, 125, 129, 134, 167
Religious history, 189
Renaissance, 105, 139, 141, 181-83
Reprints, collections of, 87, 101, 166, 169, 201-2, 230, 231
Reserved Book Room, 138
Rider, Fremont, 49
Roanoke Colony Memorial Association, 37
Roanoke Island, 37
Rockefeller Foundation, 12, 13, 19, 63
Roland Holt Collection. See Holt Collection
Roman history, 179-80. See also Ancient history
Romance languages and literature, 9, 52, 155-62
Roselle Johnson Collection of Photo-reproductions of Medieval Manuscripts. See Johnson Collection
Rowan Historical Society files, 32
Rural electrification, 247
Rural resettlement, 247
Rural Social Economics Library, 38, 40, 195, 237, 246-47
Rush, Charles E., 14, 16
Russian history, 185, 243
Ruth Faison Shaw Collection. See Shaw Collection

St. Augustine's College, 48
Salisbury, 32, 37
Scenery design, 113

Sciences, 71, 80-82, 86-101
Scores, musical, 117
Scrapbooks, 46, 114, 115, 116, 186
Sculpture, 109
Search books, 220, 225-29
Semitic languages, 169
Session laws, 228, 236
Shaffner, Henry F., 41
Shakespeare Club, founding of, 7, 8
Shannonhouse, Rev. R. G., 52
Shaw Collection of Kurz and Allison Civil War lithographs, 46
Shipley Fund, 155
Shipley, Katherine Morris, 155
Siewers, Nathaniel Shober, 88
Sinhalese language, 12
Skaggs, Mrs. M. L., 14, 22
Slavery, 42
Smith, C. Alphonso, 16
Smith Collection of Photo-reproductions of Medieval Manuscripts, 181
Smith Hall, 4, 5, 6
Smith, James S., 88
Social legislation, 245, 247
Social planning, 244
Social Sciences, 18, 71, 179-247; history, 179-99; ancient, 179-80; medieval, 181-83; modern European, 184-88; English, 189-91; United States, 192-95; Latin-American, 196-99; commerce and economics, 200-10; education, 211-16; folklore, 217-19; law, 220-29; library science, 230-34; political science, 235-44; sociology, 242-47
Social system of the old South, 42
Social theory, 43, 242
Social work, 189
Society libraries, 4, 5
Society publications, 79, 80-82, 118, 123, 140-41, 142, 193, 212, 230, 240
Sociology, 33, 195, 242-47
Soils, 170
Sondley, Dr. Foster A., 41
Sondley Memorial Library, co-operation with, 21, 56
Sound effects, 113
South Building, 5
Southern Historical Association Publications, 31
Southern Historical Collection, 12, 13, 16, 32, 33, 39-46, 192, 237
Southern literature, 148-49
Spanish language and literature, 58, 59, 62, 113, 159-62, 181, 182, 218

INDEX

Special collections, 11-12, 114, 224. *See also* under names of collections:
  Andrews, 32
  Battle, 32
  Curry, 45, 46
  Dashiell, 46
  Davie, 12, 32
  Hanes, 12, 47-52, 60, 156, 180, 181, 233
  Henderson, 12, 114, 148
  Hill Collection of North Caroliniana, 12, 27-38, 194
  Holt, 114, 115
  Hunter, 12, 48, 51, 156
  Jacocks, 12, 51
  Johnson, 181
  Kenan, 31, 194
  Kidder, 31
  Lenoir, 32
  McDowell, 32
  North Carolina, 12, 27-38, 194
  Pettigrew, 32
  Raleigh, 12, 36
  Smith, 181
  Southern Historical, 12, 13, 16, 32, 35, 39-46, 192, 237
  Sprunt, 32
  Walker, 32
  Winge, 114
Sprunt Collection, 32
Stage settings, 113
State College of Agriculture and Enginnering, 21, 35, 56, 233
State regional catalogue, 56
Statistics, 210, 239; vital, 245
Stearns, A. L., 52
Stephens, George, 16, 41
Studies in Philology, establishment of, 8, 9; exchanges, 9
Swain, David Lowry, President, 6, 27, 29, 39

Tarboro, 37
Tennessee, 40
Texas, 40
Textbooks, 34, 166
Theatre Museum, 114
Thompson, Holland M., 29
Thornton, Mary L., 30, 38
Toxicology, 94
Transportation, 202, 247. *See also* Railroads
Travel, 34, 169, 193, 251, 252. *See also* Weeks Collection; Davie Collection

Tulane University Library, co-operation with, 12, 13, 19, 160, 197
Union catalogue, 56, 233
Union lists, 56, 57
United States history, 42, 148, 192-95
University Library Building, present, 5
Universtiy Magazine, 7
University of North Carolina, Press, 15, 16, 52, 246, 252; Extension Division, 16, 251; Consolidated University, 21; State College of Agriculture and Engineering, 21, 35, 56, 233; Woman's College, 21, 51; classes of 1910 and 1932, 21; Bureau of Correspondence Instruction, 253
Uruguay, 19, 161, 197, 206

Venable Hall, 165
Venable, President F. P., 16, 165
Venezuela, 19, 161, 196, 197
Virginia, 40, 193

Wachovia Historical Society, co-operation with, 21
Wagstaff, Henry M., 29
Wake Forest College Library, 56, 233
Walker Collection, 32
War Information Center, 252-53
Weeks Collection, 31, 32, 39
Weeks, Stephen B., 29, 38
Weil, Herman, 105
Weil, Leslie, 52
Weil, Lionel, 135
Wesleyan University, cards from, 22, 56
Whitaker, W. A., 41
White, Carl M., 13, 16
Wiggins, A. L. M., 41
William Lenoir Collection. *See* Lenoir Collection
William Richardson Davie Collection. *See* Davie Collection
Wilmington, 32, 37
Wilson, H. V., 101
Wilson, L. R., 9, 16, 29, 31, 46
Winge Collection, 114
Winge, John H., 114
Winston, George T., 15
Woman's College of the University of North Carolina, 21, 51
Wood, Thomas F., 88
World War I, 186
World War II, 252-53

Yearbooks, 200, 239

Zoology, 34, 90, 99-101

www.ingramcontent.com/pod-product-compliance
Lightning Source LLC
Chambersburg PA
CBHW021121300426
44113CB00006B/237